OUT OF THIN AIR

OUT OF THIN AIR

More Irregular Essays from Public Radio

David Bouchier

ISBN-13 : 9781974382156
ISBN-10 : 197438215X
Library of Congress Control Number: 2017913639
CreateSpace Independent Publishing Platform
North Charleston, South Carolina

Also by David Bouchier

Lucky Man - A Life in Essays
Not Quite a Stranger
Peripheral Vision
The Song of Suburbia
The Cats and the Water Bottles & Other Mysteries of French Village Life
Writer at Work
A Few Well-Chosen Words
The Accidental Immigrant
The Feminist Challenge
Radical Citizenship
Idealism and Revolution

Mid Atlantic Productions
New York, 2017

Contents

Preface

What a queer thing life is! So unlike anything else, don't you know; if you see what I mean.

P.G. WODEHOUSE

Public Radio imposes a modest discipline on its commentators. Every topic, no matter how complicated, must be wrapped up in five minutes or less. But I have heard it on good authority that brevity is the soul of wit, and the reader will be happy to discover that the vast majority of the essays in this book are delightfully short. I have grouped them together under seven themes, hoping to give the many and varied topics a certain coherence. But each essay stands by itself as the product of a particular thought or experience at a particular moment. The overall theme, if there is one, is summed up in the wise words of P.G. Wodehouse that appear at the top of this page.

Essays, as Michel de Montaigne demonstrated five hundred years ago, are about everything including the writer. "Whatever my subject," he wrote, "It is myself that I portray." An essay has no story, and no plot. It is the writer talking to you, one on one, about something that he or she finds interesting, annoying, bewildering, or funny. A lot of things seem funny to me, and I have sometimes been accused of committing humor in serious places. You may therefore assume that any traces of humor you may detect in these pages were placed here deliberately, and with malice aforethought.

Public Radio is one of the last places on the airwaves where you can hear personal essays read by their authors. These essays usually vanish as soon as they are broadcast, although they may have a tenuous afterlife on web pages and as podcasts. Here, in the interests of historical preservation and literary history, I have collected commentaries that were aired by stations of the WSHU Public Radio Group in New York and Connecticut between 2011 and 2017.

My constant companion and interlocutor in all the events, travels, and arguments recorded here has been my wife Diane, who is also my best editor, and severest critic. She can take full credit for all the good stuff. The errors of fact, taste, and punctuation are entirely my own.

David Bouchier, St. Quentin le Poterie, France, 2017

Theme I

TIME AND MEMORY

Time is everything.

KURT VONNEGUT

Nothing is more responsible for the good old days than a bad memory.

FRANKLIN PIERCE ADAMS

WAITING FOR THE END

The anticipation of the end of the world is one of my most treasured childhood memories. Twice a year my parents would take me into the city for a movie or a musical. The London theater district was a magnet for old men with a message carried on sandwich boards or placards or on smudgy little leaflets they would press into your hand. "The end of the world is nigh" or "Prepare Ye for the Terrible Day of Judgement." The old men looked so much like the prophets in my illustrated Bible that I had to believe them. I never expected to be around now, in the twenty-first century. I didn't think we'd make it to 1950.

I admired the old men for their persistence. Year after year as I grew up they stalked the city streets with the same message. Some died and were replaced by ready-trained squads of new old men. The end of the world was always nigh in the 1940s. The war damage reminded us of it, and the atomic bomb reminded us of it. In an uncertain universe, it was good to have something definite to look forward to, and I always cherished the hope that the world would end before the next math test at school.

But the old men never delivered on their promise. Time passed, I failed my math tests, the war ended, and the hope and fear of the apocalypse receded. But it has never quite gone away. As we tiptoe anxiously through the twenty-first century we are still surrounded by prophets of doom. They tend to use social media instead of placards paraded in the street, but they are no more dependable because of that.

Prophecy is tempting because it is so easy. All you need to do is look back a hundred or a thousand years, find something nasty that happened then (war, plague, flood, economic disaster) and predict that the same thing will happen again soon. Nobody will argue. We have been conditioned by a lifetime of gloomy predictions to believe every bad thing we hear. The future is virgin territory, and any pessimist can claim it.

We had a flurry of silly predictions about the end of the world before the year 2000, and in the unanticipated decade that followed. The Rev. Harold Camping of California promised the return of Christ and an apocalyptic earthquake for May 21, 2011. This failed to happen and we had to wait a whole year for the next apocalypse, based on an ancient Mayan Long Calendar, the last page of which ended abruptly on December 21st 2012. This failed too, but the Mayans weren't around to defend their eccentric calendar, as their own world had ended a thousand years before. The Mayans, for goodness sake! They knew some astronomy, and they accidentally built a major tourist attraction, but they certainly didn't know the future. It's yet another example of the mysterious reverence some people have for "the wisdom of the ancients," when the ancients in fact understood almost nothing about anything and would certainly have flunked an SAT test.

December 21st, 2012 was big business for a while, just as the year 2000 had been. There were doomsday specials on television, dozens of books, hundreds of web sites, and a Hollywood disaster movie called 2012 starring John Cusack. The movie was two hours and thirty-eight minutes long. The actual end of the world needs to be snappier than that, or we will lose interest (average adult attention span: twenty minutes). There are no doubt more doomsdays in the prophetic pipeline but credibility requires that they should be revealed one at a time at discrete intervals. It's not the sort of thing you can get right twice.

The advantage of knowing the exact date of the end of the world is that it simplifies life. The future is much more manageable if it stops at a definite point. You can mark it on your calendar, as I did in 1999 and again in 2012. Then there's much less to plan and worry about. That's why prophecy, and especially apocalyptic prophecy, is one of the oldest games in town. Unfortunately, our modern prophets often fail to observe the golden rule followed by seers and soothsayers down the ages: be vague about the dates and the details. The end of the world at the end of this week is just too precise. When it fails to happen, everybody will notice

It is hard to know how to plan for these events. It would be wasteful to buy cat food for the whole week if the world is due to end on Wednesday, and foolish to pay off the mortgage if next year would be the last year of payments anyway. But any preparations for the end of the world are pointless, because the end will be the end. There won't be any recriminations, or second thoughts, or even any cleaning up afterwards.

When such prophecies do not work out, which they never have yet, there is the potential for embarrassment and even humiliation for the prophet. But this reveals a fascinating aspect of human nature. If we want to believe something we can be extraordinarily stubborn about it. Back in 1956 a classic study of this phenomenon was published by social psychologist Leon Festinger. In this case the end of the world was scheduled for December 21, 1954. What is it, I wonder, about December 21st as an end date? Could it be the desire to avoid holiday shopping? Anyway, the researchers studied what would happen to the followers of this cult when nothing happened on December 21st. What they found was that the cult continued as before but with a new date. This fiasco was repeated several times until apocalypse fatigue set in. Belief in the end of the world is the same kind of stubborn conviction against all the evidence that leads people to support losing football teams or political parties. The belief itself is liberating. The movie "Doctor Strangelove" spelled it out in the subtitle in 1964: "How to stop worrying and love the bomb." Apocalypse is catharsis, and we have been inundated with disaster movie ever since.

The popularity of doomsday fantasies provokes a disturbing thought. What if most of the people around us find their lives so tedious and exasperating that they almost welcome the idea that the whole thing could be flipped off like a light switch at any time. They could care less, even if they have children, or money, or cats. Consider the scene on an early commuter train on a freezing January morning and compare it to a sudden, instant, painless end. It's no contest, really. In that situation we are all, in some sense, ready to go.

The history of futurology shows that the only way to achieve notoriety is to predict the worst. A happy prophet is a contradiction in terms. Nobody ever got onto the front page by forecasting that next week will be very much the same as this week, or that universal happiness and prosperity are just around the corner. We are, in short, a credulous and gloomy species, and we get the prophets and the prophecies that we deserve.

ESCAPING FROM HISTORY

When Abraham Lincoln addressed the United States Congress in 1863, he began with these words: "Fellow citizens, we cannot escape history." It was a noble sentiment, and perhaps it was true them. But it's not true now. Not only *can* we escape history, we *have* escaped history, by the simple process of forgetting most of it, especially the parts we don't like.

What we remember, what we choose to forget, and how our memories change with time and age are among the great psychological mysteries. Apart from those rare individuals who really can remember everything (and how annoying they are), most of us practice a kind of automatic selective forgetting. Any college student facing an exam asks, first: What do I *need* to remember? But long after we leave college we unconsciously use the same technique. For example, I saw a news item about an argument between someone called JZ and someone called Solange. Now I had not the faintest idea who JZ was, or Solange either, and I didn't need to know. Why should I clutter up my few remaining brain cells with such useless information? It's hard enough to remember where I left my car keys, or indeed my car. But this story was all over the news, so I asked my wife who told me that JZ and Solange were incredibly famous persons known and worshipped by just about everyone in the world except me. I took care to forget this information at once.

Ephemeral celebrities are easy and indeed essential to forget. But then there's the important stuff: the history of who, what and why we are. We live in the flow of time whether we like it or not, but history is scarcely taught in schools anymore, so we can expect that people in the future will have even fewer long-term memories of any kind. Yesterday's TV news will be more than enough.

Report after report confirms that our knowledge of our own past is pathetically thin. The Department of Education discovered that six out of ten high school seniors couldn't say how the United States came into existence. (Answer: through illegal rebellion against the authority of the British king). Fifty per cent of high school seniors couldn't say what the Cold War was. (Answer: the Cold War was a political mistake, but an economic stroke of genius). National history knowledge tests show that most fourth-graders can't identify the opening passage of the Declaration of Independence, and that most high school seniors can't explain the checks-and-balances theory that is or used to be the rationale behind the three branches of the United States government. These young people will be voting soon, and some are voting already.

If there is anything worse than not teaching history at all it is teaching fake history, a comforting, patriotic fairy tale with no social protests, no imperial adventures, no bitter race or class conflict, in short no inconvenient truths, and above all nothing that might encourage students to challenge authority. The idea of smiley face history may be attractive to some conservative school boards, but students are already overprotected, and feeding them lies about the nature of reality is an insult too far. It's an insult to the teachers too. Teaching itself is hard enough without being pressured to teach nonsense.

Anyone who tries to teach real history is up against movies, television, and video games, that offer cartoon versions of a past that consists entirely of Hollywood-style battles between good guys and bad guys in

7

which the good guys usually win. It is depressing enough to see some of the stuff that passes for history in the mass media, without asking schools to add to the confusion.

Professional historians have also helped us to forget the real past. We can understand how by looking at the journals in which academic historians talk to each other. They are talking about almost anything *but* history, as we used to understand it. "Rewriting Single Pregnancy." "Politics and Collective Memory in American Historiography." "Postmodernism and Chaos Theory in the Reconstruction of History."

What happened to Washington crossing the Delaware or the rise of trade unions or the planting of the flag on Iwo Jima? All gone, relegated to the old-fashioned and disgraced category of "narrative history" (i.e. history that makes sense.)

There is no narrative in history, of course, and to that extent old-fashioned history is dishonest. Real history wasn't a story. But it can be *made* into a story. That's what historians are supposed to do, to clean up the messy past and mythologize it, so we can all pretend to understand it and perhaps even learn something from the entertaining tales of the Pilgrim Fathers, Bunker Hill, Wounded Knee, and Watergate.

Without these story-like myths, all we know about the past is that it's dead. People in history have the rotten taste to be dead, which certainly won't happen to us. They were unsophisticated, wore funny clothes, listened to un-amplified non-digitalized music in the days when the only way you could get stereo was to have several musicians sitting in different positions in a room.

Worst of all they placed demands on us. For them we were the "posterity," that would achieve all good and wonderful things. When

Lincoln said: "We cannot escape history" he didn't mean the memory of the past but the judgment of the future: the judgment of posterity.

Now we *are* the future, and I think that's what gives us a bad conscience about history. Mostly, we have simply forgotten it, and those little bits we remember make us uneasy. Perhaps our problem is that we actually feel inferior to the past, less energetic, less worthy, even less educated, so we repress it like a bad memory. Would *we* fight a devastating war over slavery, with more than ten thousand deaths in a single day, when even one military casualty has become politically unacceptable? Would *we* listen to a president like Lincoln, who spoke in complete sentences and long, complicated paragraphs? Lincoln didn't do sound bites, or Tweets, and he scarcely ever smiled. He'd be off the ballot after the first primary.

The good news is that if history is history, we don't have to worry about how future generations will judge *us*. By not teaching history, we have neatly avoided the judgment of history, because we'll simply be forgotten in our turn. What a relief, what a liberation it is *not* to have posterity looking over our collective shoulder. Imagine the nasty, skeptical judgments that might be passed on our age by a future Alexis de Tocqueville, Voltaire, or H.L.Mencken. Imagine the first decade of the twenty-first century, seen through the eyes of Edward Gibbon - the author (as you may or may not remember) of *The Decline and Fall of the Roman Empire*.

THE GLORIOUS NINETEENTH
Certain dates serve as signposts in the fog of history, and the Fourth of July is one such date. Everybody knows that the Glorious Fourth commemorates the signing of the Declaration of Independence in 1776.

Like most of our historical knowledge, this is wrong. It's true that an unfortunate misunderstanding between Britain and her American colonies did blow up around that time. But the Declaration was not signed until July 19. This is a good example of the arbitrariness of history. The Declaration was adopted by Congress on July 2, which legally broke the tie to Britain right then. The proclamation on July 4, the public reading at Independence Hall on July 8, and the signing on July 19 were mere bureaucratic formalities. In fact, the first Independence celebration, in 1777, was held on the appropriate date, July 2. Congress later changed the date to the Fourth, for reasons that are obscure, but that may have had something to do with long weekends.

It may be that the exact dates of events in the past don't really matter except to historians. In any case this kind of precise knowledge seems to be a lost cause. A report from US Department of Education revealed an almost complete abandonment of history teaching in schools. The high school seniors tested were more or less incapable of distinguishing between World War Two and the Peloponnesian War.

Yet every nation, including this one, has a special patriotic date which is celebrated with varying degrees of enthusiasm. The English have their rather embarrassing Saint George's Day, observed or ignored on April 23; the Scots have Saint Andrew's Day, November 30; the Irish have St Patrick's Day of course; the French commemorate Bastille Day on July 14 when revolutionary crowds stormed the Bastille prison and released a rather disappointing total of seven political prisoners; and the Serbs like to celebrate the Battle of Vidovdan on June 28, 1389, which they lost.

So a National Day may be about a patron saint, a revolution, or a battle won, or lost – but most often it is about independence and national pride. Some commemorate a glorious moment, and others are just an excuse to keep ancient hatreds alive. A few nations cherish their grievances from hundreds or even thousands of years ago, passing the poison on lovingly from generation to generation, so that nothing can ever be erased or forgiven.

But not this nation: the Fourth of July comes without grudges or hatreds, which makes it a particularly fine national day. The generosity of this nation to its enemies has been legendary, and puzzling to other nations who suspect a devious plot. But there is no plot. It's just that the past is wiped off the slate as soon as it happens. When we say, "That's history," we mean that it is irrelevant, gone, and forgotten. Even the British have been forgiven for whatever they did, whenever it was. This benign historical amnesia is one of the most hopeful things about American culture, and we have the schools to thank for it. If nobody knows any history then history can't do us any harm.

THE WAY WE WERE

Fall is the season of reunions and homecomings. Families come together for Thanksgiving and the winter holidays, and for those who don't have a family, or don't like the one they have, there are many other ways of revisiting the past and renewing old ties.

The most visible and raucous reunions are college homecomings, when ex-students of various ages gather to remember the good old days. These are true festivals of nostalgia for lost memories of youth, endless parties, the kind of freedom that never comes again, and a close and reassuring community with plenty of football. Some may even remember the pleasure of learning, and wish they had learned more. Happy days, and not at all like adult life. A reunion brings it all back, if you can remember it.

Another attraction of homecomings and class reunions is our natural curiosity about our contemporaries. Who were the winners and losers in the career game, the marriage game, or the weight loss game?

The triumphalism and humiliation of reunions has provided the theme for hundreds of novels and a few movies, perhaps the most realistic being National Lampoon's comedy horror classic "Class Reunion" of 1982.

I have never understood the attraction of reunions, especially after seeing that movie. There is a picture of my school class, an untidy mob of scowling teenage boys, but I can't summon up much curiosity about them fifty years later. They are dim in my memory, but not so dim that I want to see them in sharp focus again. It might be interesting to know how many made a success of their lives, and how many were incarcerated. But we were no different from any other group of boys except for the accident of time and place, and the fact that we shared the same teachers. Perhaps our memories of those teachers had created a kind of bond, but it would be more the bond of a street gang against a common enemy than a community of scholars.

As we grow older the idea of reunion necessarily becomes more urgent. It's now or never. So, one recent year I went, for the first time and against my better judgement, to a reunion. It was the fiftieth anniversary of the British university where I taught for some years, and this tells you that it is one of the newer establishments of higher learning. Cambridge and Oxford are celebrating their six hundredth anniversaries about now. But fifty years meant something to us. Most of the faculty at the beginning were young, and now we are not, so a reunion was a rare chance to see those of my former colleagues who have survived. There were no sports, no tailgating (whatever it is, but it sounds dangerous), no parades or songs, but we gathered at a riverside restaurant in the beautiful village of Dedham, the survivors in many cases of forty years of teaching. I can't speak for myself but most of my former colleagues looked pretty good, and were as verbose and as argumentative as ever. It almost warmed my heart to meet them again, and relive for an afternoon that interesting period of my life.

Nostalgia strikes different people at different ages. In 2010 I visited the place where I had grown up sixty years before, even though it has nothing to recommend it as a destination. "You can't go home again" is one of those clichés that is, annoyingly, both true and untrue. Naturally you can visit a town, a house, a school, or some other physical object from your past. But what you can never revisit is the *person* you once were. The place is irrelevant, and so are the people. No matter how many diaries and photos and school reunions you collect, you can never have a reunion with yourself.

THIEVES OF TIME

The theft of time has become almost as much of an epidemic as the theft of smartphones. I don't have a smartphone, so that's not something I worry about. But I do have a small and diminishing amount of time, which I would rather not lose, and the world seems full of people who want to snatch it away.

We were in a lawyer's office, waiting to deal with a trivial piece of paperwork that should have and did eventually take less than five minutes. Our appointment was for 9 a.m., which came and went, along with 9.15, 9.30 and 9.45 before the great man deigned to see us just before ten, with no explanation, no apology for the fact that each of our days had been shortened by one hour.

During the same week, we wasted a great deal of time waiting for an electrician, who was hours late, and a plumber who didn't keep his appointment at all. So, I began to keep track, rather obsessively I admit, all the people and organizations who seem to take it as their mission in life to waste our time.

Doctors, of course, are notorious. Their appointment times are merely fanciful, like stock market predictions, and they reinforce the insult by having us wait, undressed, in a freezing examination room with nothing but depressing medical illustrations for entertainment.

Big companies have found ways to waste our time automatically, without any human intervention at all. When you need to get information from the humorously named telephone "help line" of a bank, a credit card company, or a computer manufacturer, you can be sure of losing a whole morning or afternoon. If you put the phone down for a moment you will immediately be assaulted by unsolicited calls from unknown people demanding money for a political party or a charity, or trying to sell you some nonexistent product or imaginary service.

It is tempting to unplug the phone and turn to the computer, but then you are at the mercy of the greatest time-wasting device ever invented – the internet. Everything that used to be quick and easy has become slow and difficult, verging on impossible, now that we have this wonderful resource. Booking a flight or placing an order, once a five-minute job on the phone or in person, can easily swallow up a frustrating hour once you enter the Alice in Wonderland world of the airline web pages. Of course, in time, we can eventually get anything from the web: all the truths and all the lies in the world are there. There is no shortage of anything except time itself. The question is: how can we save what little time we have?

Here's my idea. Your time and mine is definitely worth something. It's obviously not as valuable as the time of a notorious politician or an ephemeral TV celebrity, but it's worth *something* – let's say $50 an hour. When we keep an appointment or initiate a communication, the clock should start running at that moment. After an hour of waiting in the lawyer's office we should have the right, and indeed the duty, to bill him for $50 and expect payment. Two hours on hold with a software company, listening to vile music, should be worth $100. The thieves of time would get the message eventually: if you waste our time, it's payback time.

WE'LL DO THIS LATER

Procrastination is such a useful habit. I have always put off doing difficult or unpleasant things, and I'm glad I did – or rather I'm glad I didn't. I've been intending to write a novel, get piano lessons, and master the French subjunctive tense for over forty years, and I'm happy to say I have not yet done any of these things. The novel and the piano would have annoyed a lot of people, and the French subjunctive would never have done me any good at all.

Procrastination is usually seen as a weakness, but in fact it is a strength. Fools rush in, as the cliché reminds us. The opposite of procrastination, as identified by University of Pennsylvania psychologist Cory Potts, is *pre*-crastination, or rushing into things without a thought because you just want to get them done – impatience, in other words. For example, if Napoleon had put off invading Russia in 1812, or Hitler had hesitated before invading Poland in 1939, a vast amount of trouble would have been avoided. You may be able to think of other more recent political examples.

Socrates was famous for inducing a kind of intellectual paralysis in his fellow Athenians by constantly asking questions, then asking more questions about the answers. This technique reveals that most of the "knowledge" we act on is wrong, and most of our "informed decisions" are informed only by ignorance and wishful thinking. Such persistent questioning can be irritating. It was so irritating for the citizens of Athens that they killed poor old Socrates just for forcing them to think about things they thought were obvious.

Procrastination happens when the obvious is not obvious – in other words when we are uncertain. We share this habit with the higher animals; just watch a cat trying to choose between two comfortable places to sleep. The cat is thinking about it. He may think about it for hours. Procrastination is a product of the fact that we think. It's not strong or brave to rush into things without thought or hesitation, it's stupid. This is especially true of big, dangerous things like double bacon cheeseburgers with fries, international wars, and marriage. In fact, marriage may be the number one excuse for procrastination in the known universe, and a good thing too.

When I was a kid, parents and teachers accused me of procrastination practically every day. This was fair enough, in so far as I always did (and still do) like to think about things for a while before actually doing them. Latin homework was a good example. Sometimes I would consider for days or weeks before deciding not to do it, on the entirely rational grounds that nobody but priests had any use for Latin, and I was not cut out to be a priest. That's not indecision, and it's certainly not laziness: that's the brain doing its job. A moment's thought will reveal that most of the things we imagine we should do immediately could be done later or, better still, not at all.

My talent for procrastination is above average and has saved me from a great deal of foolishness, as well as untold hours of wasted time. I can put off a medical appointment or a home repair job more or less indefinitely. The future for me is a convenient filing cabinet where all these good intentions can be carefully arranged in order of importance, and then forgotten. Edward Young, the eighteenth-century poet, coined the phrase: "Procrastination is the thief of time." But that's the reverse of the truth. A good procrastinator never wastes a minute on pointless tasks, because he never starts.

The procrastinator is relaxed, calm, because nothing needs to be done in a hurry. The *pre*-crastinator is anxious, fretful, full of worries about the future and always trying to get ahead of time itself. American culture is future-oriented and therefore dead against procrastination. Everything must be done right now, or sooner. Procrastinators don't really believe in the future until it arrives. When it does arrive it immediately becomes history, and therefore not worth worrying about.

Try it, you'll like it. When it comes to procrastination, it's never too late to start.

GOING TO THE SHOPS

Most of us remember bits and pieces from our childhood, but not the whole tedious story. Those who do recall every detail seem to spend the rest of their lives in therapy. One of the bits I remember with pleasure is a ritual I shared with my mother three or four times a week. It was called "Going to the shops."

"Going to the shops." was not the same as shopping. Shopping was an entertainment, and I have never learned to do it properly. But going to the shops was serious.

London at that time was more like an extended series of villages. Every district had its own main street, and most of the residents bought their food and other necessities there, walking from shop to shop because few of us had a car, and in any case those old shopping streets weren't designed for parking. This ritual has stayed in my memory when so many other things have been forgotten, and I can remember those morning walks virtually shop by shop.

The first establishment we encountered after turning on to the main street was the best: Mr. Pask's bicycle shop, a dark cave of a place smelling of oil and rubber and full of infinitely desirable machines. There was a repair shop in the back, forbidden to customers. I had read in a book that the Wright Brothers had discovered the secret of flight in a bicycle shop in Dayton, Ohio, and I always wondered what Mr. Pask was doing in his hidden workshop. My friends and I favored the theory that he was working on a pedal-powered helicopter.

Next to the bicycle shop was a candy shop that sold loose candy from big glass jars and fizzy drinks in bright colors – disgusting and unhealthy, but always worth a visit. And then some rather boring establishments, a butcher, a baker, a fish shop and a grocer, each with its own rich odor, and where we always had to wait. Then there was a photographer whose place was almost as full of interesting sights and smells as the bicycle shop, a general electrical store, a wool shop much patronized by my mother, a shop that sold everything including army surplus items, fresh eggs, and radio sets, an old-fashioned hardware store, a shoe repair shop full of antique machinery and warm leather smells and finally a newsagent's shop that was a cornucopia of brightly colored magazines and comics.

Small businesses like these are losing or have long since lost the battle against the big box supermarkets on the edge of town. Now everyone wants one stop shopping with a basket on wheels. What I used to do with my mother in those distant days was more like ten stop shopping, and it was certainly not efficient. But we used no fuel, created no pollution, and we got a whole lot of exercise.

You can still find old-fashioned shopping streets in some small European towns. Along the main street of our nearest town in France, in spite of all the boutiques selling overpriced clothes and tourist trash, the shadow of the old main street is still visible: the hardware store, the photographer, the electrical store, the wool shop, numerous food and wine shops, pharmacies, newsagents, a peculiar place that sells only knives, dog leashes, and walking sticks, a laundry, a small bookstore, and even bicycle and shoe repair shops tucked away on a side street. The old shopping street offered us everything we could ever need, if we hadn't learned to need so much.

WORTH PRESERVING

There is something special about ancient places and things that are part of our history. The Roman Colosseum, the Alamo, or the Taj Mahal are accidental time capsules, which is why great efforts are made to preserve what is left them. History is profitable too. People will cross the world to see certain iconic places, which is why Machu Picchu and Venice are as crowded and busy as Times Square on a Saturday night.

We can't preserve everything. What we see now, above ground as it were, are the terminal remains of our heritage. Most of the things that human beings ever built or made have vanished – fallen down, rotted away, built over, or been destroyed by fire, floods and war. All we can do right now is to try to preserve the good stuff that has survived. We still have an astonishing number of historical sites, from the Stone Age onwards, enough to keep the most dedicated tourist busy for a lifetime.

This preservation of this heritage has become a minor industry. The UNESCO World Heritage List has over a thousand sites, including the whole historic center of Vienna and the ancient mines of Wallonia in Belgium, all claiming a place on your "must visit" list.

It is unfortunate that this careful program of preservation has, to some extent, been thrown into reverse by the wars in the Middle East. This has been greeted as an unprecedented disaster, but it is just the repetition of history all over again. The Huns, Goths and Vandals who tore apart the Roman Empire were the direct ancestors of the Islamic State. Wrecking old civilizations is a well-established tradition, or an anti-tradition tradition if you like. Barbarians don't like culture, it annoys them. The problem is that the wreckers are in danger of ruining the mass tourism industry.

World Heritage sites are far too spread out, and far too vulnerable to destruction. It's time to start moving our heritage to a secure location. It's a big job, but it will be worth it in the end. The French have shown the way with the caves of Lascaux, a World Heritage site which has been recreated as a full-scale model that can be moved from place to place, like an art exhibit. In principle, any historical site too big to move stone by stone could be recreated as a full-scale model, like the Venice resort in Las Vegas. Everything that exists can be copied: The Parthenon (although the Greeks might be willing to sell the real thing now), the Pyramids, Notre Dame Cathedral, and so on down the World Heritage List.

The sensible thing would be to bring all this reconstructed history together in one central location where there is plenty of space, and no competing cultural narrative – say in the middle of Kansas. In this way, a lifetime of tourism could be accomplished in a single visit, with a gigantic saving in fuel, pollution, and aggravation, and without having to speak any foreign languages or eat any disgusting foreign food.

As for the original buildings and monuments, every computer user knows that once you have made a copy of something you don't have to worry so much about losing the original. In any case most of these monuments are in poor condition and being rapidly worn out by millions of tourists. In London, for example, Buckingham Palace and the Houses of Parliament are both in danger of falling down. Think how nice they would look, all fresh and bright, in the Kansas sunshine. Tourists of the future will learn to love fake historical monuments with proper bathrooms nearby, rather than real monuments in remote, unsanitary and unsafe locations. As for the real ones, we will be sad to see them go, but what we lose in authenticity we will gain in security. It seems small price to pay.

THE NOSTALGIA INDUSTRY

Nostalgia is the warm feeling we get when we imagine the good old days. Television, and especially Public Television, is a wonderful source of ready-made nostalgia, with its apparently endless series of quasi-historical dramas, many of them British. The curious thing is that the times and places that viewers seem most nostalgic about were worse in just about every way than our lives now. This could be a kind of historical *schadenfreude* – gloating over how much better off we are than our ancestors. But I suspect that nostalgia is the opposite of complacency, a sad emotion. If the golden age was really in the past, what do we have to look forward to?

For ten years the television series Downton Abbey was the flagship carrier of international nostalgia. It came to an end in 2015, to great lamentation among its hundred and twenty million worldwide viewers, and immediately went into reruns. Fans are already gripped by a kind of pre-emptive nostalgia at the thought of seeing it all over again. It is a genuine cultural phenomenon. *The New York Times* even ran a four-page special advertising supplement, in case anyone missed the start of the repeat series. New or recycled historical series are already lining up to fill any potential nostalgia gap, including classics like Upstairs Downstairs. The production of decorative nostalgia is a kind of cottage industry.

Downton Abbey is a superior soap opera, beautifully produced, and a work of art in its own way. I watched most of the first series, and quite enjoyed it. But I couldn't bring myself to believe in it. My grandmother worked as a maid in one of those great houses at the turn of the nineteenth century, and her stories about it were more like Dickens than Downton. It was a cruel world, and a hard life.

Nostalgia never has much to do with reality. While enjoying these colorful tales we know full well that the past was very much like the present, only worse. But the idea of a Golden Age is endlessly seductive. Two thousand years ago the Greeks and the Romans looked back with nostalgia to the Age of Heroes. Five hundred years ago, during the Renaissance, Europeans looked back to the Golden Age of the Greeks and Romans, and so it goes. Every nation has its own tales of a glorious past that never really existed. History is a bottomless source of inspiring but unlikely plots, as Shakespeare knew very well. England in the fourteenth century was captivated by ancient and fantastic tales about King Arthur and his Knights of the Round Table. America has its myths of cowboys in the Wild West, although some seem to find the Puritans of New England more appealing. The followers of the Islamic State believe that the tenth century was pretty much ideal.

There are two ways to visit the past: through history and through fiction. In general, fiction is the way to go. A novel or a movie puts the chaos of life into proper narrative order. It makes sense, which it never did at the time. Serious history books are hard work. The best place to experience the reality of the fantasy is on television where we can admire the architecture and the costumes and not get too bogged down in the messy details. Movies often ask us to believe in historical characters, beautifully turned out with perfect hair and teeth, and no skin blemishes. The past was not up to Hollywood's standards, cosmetically speaking, and they can't resist the temptation to present us with characters from history who look like, well, film stars. Shakespeare said that the past is prologue, meaning that what happened then is intimately linked to what happens now. What we see now is not so much the past as prologue but the past as a long-running soap opera. History seems like a safe place because it has already happened, the plot is known, and there are no surprises. No wonder we view it with a sense of nostalgia – so charming, so elegant, so civilized. It may be empty escapism, but it's powerful magic just the same.

Not all fictional portrayals of the past are warm and fuzzy, of course. Some of them revel in the sheer horror of it, and I haven't seen an optimistic film about the *future* since Woody Allen's "Sleeper." If Hollywood is to be believed, the future will be all about apocalypses, barbarism, screaming teenagers, and giant armored vehicles racing across devastated landscapes. If that future ever comes, *we* will be remembered as the Golden Age. Who wouldn't prefer gentle dramas from a charmingly imagined past?

Nostalgia may be flourishing right now because the Baby Boomers are becoming history themselves, and prefer to look back rather than forward. Even the 1950s look pretty good as reflected in the rear-view mirror. But I was there, and it wasn't so good. For most people, life was much harder. Kids in school had to read real books and take real punishment, and grownups had to wind their car windows up and down by hand. Life was tough.

What I seem to remember, although it could be a false memory, is that in those days we looked forward very much to the future – the gleaming, prosperous, technologically sophisticated, more equalitarian future that we had been promised by our great leaders. The past was dark and dangerous territory, we didn't want to go there. We suffered, I suppose, from a kind of inverted nostalgia, a dream of the good new days to come. It is comforting to have once enjoyed that kind of naïve optimism. In retrospect, I feel quite nostalgic about it.

GOODBYE TO ALL THAT
Back in the long-forgotten pre-Amazon era, I spent some happy years working in a big university bookstore near Trinity College in Cambridge – the old Cambridge, not the new construction by the Charles River. The bookstore was a veritable warren of wisdom, with sections for Greek and Latin books, mathematics, art, literature, the sciences, philosophy, and an enormous history department. It was a happy hunting ground for professors, and for the more dedicated students, and we liked to think that it was in some sense the intellectual heart of the university.

It must be admitted that our stock, though huge, was limited. We didn't sell T shirts, gifts, greeting cards, CDs, magazines, mugs, or stuffed toys, but only books. Although the store was in a prime retail location it never occurred to the owners to sell anything else. It certainly never occurred to them to sell absolutely *everything* else, and to get rid of the books. But the wheel of history has taken another turn, and the bookstore at our nearby university here in New York has taken exactly that step. The books are gone. They will now be ordered from and delivered by Amazon. So, the store is no longer a bookstore but a delivery channel for those dreadful things called textbooks – educational fast food, and just as unhealthy.

Textbooks aside, you would think a university with a faculty of over a thousand would feel the need to have a flourishing general bookstore on campus or nearby. But the only independent bookstore close to the university shut down years ago. What happened to intellectual curiosity? Have even professors given up reading? Amazon is a convenient resource, I use it myself in the absence of a local bookstore. But it only works if you know exactly what you want. It is not a place where you can browse, read, and make discoveries, and the reviews are worse than useless.

I could scarcely believe in the idea of a university bookstore with no books, and paid a visit just to convince myself that it was true. There were piles of T shirts, baseball hats, backpacks, ear buds and all kinds of college branded merchandise, but indeed no books apart from half a dozen shelves of bestsellers and cut-price remainders at the back of the store. How many T shirts can anyone use in a four-year college career? Many of mine are more than twenty years old, and they still work well.

This trend from learning to leisure wear has spread way beyond New York. I walked into a bookstore at the University of Iowa when I was teaching summer school there, and walked straight out because I thought it was a clothing store. The books, apparently, were hidden away where they couldn't upset anybody.

A well-stocked bookshop, like a fine library, *is* slightly intimidating. It reminds us of all the things we don't know. Knowledge on the Internet is fragmented and invisible. If we don't search for it, it doesn't exist. The Internet never confronts us with our own ignorance, which is why it is so popular, and so politically dangerous. Real books are solid, visible, and hard to ignore. Yet now even some university libraries are beginning to get rid of their books and replace them with screens for students to goggle or Google at. This may the penultimate step towards the end of the five-hundred-year history of the printed book. It's too bad. But you can always read your T shirt.

TRAVELER IN AN ANTIQUE LAND

At school, we learned to recite a poem by Shelley called "Ozymandias" that began with the words: "I met a traveler from an antique land," and I had always wondered where the antique land *was*. When I came to Long Island I discovered that it was right there, down in the Hamptons, where selling antiques seems to be the main industry in whole towns and villages. There is a mysterious force, like gravity, that attracts old furniture and what are humorously called "decorative objects" to certain places. This force has not been definitely identified by scientists, but I think it is called money. It's much worse over in Europe, because there's so much more history and our ancestors had so many centuries to fabricate the antiques of the future, a surprising number of which seem to have made their way over to Long Island.

The extraordinary popularity of the Antiques Roadshow on Public Television has fostered the illusion that historic treasures lie all around us, just waiting to be discovered and turned into cash. The meaning of the word "antique" has suffered some damage in the process. The official definition is that antiques must be at least one hundred years old. The Oxford English Dictionary says: "Having existed since olden times, old, aged or venerable." But the frontier of antiquity is moving closer all the time. Most antique stores these days contain things that look perfectly familiar and serviceable to me, like manual typewriters, telephones with dials, and Kodak box cameras. Rusty garden tools, push lawnmowers and wind-up clocks are displayed like relics from an Egyptian tomb. It seems that anything without a motor or an electric cord qualifies as "antique," because it reminds us of the ancient days when life was full of brutal, physical tasks, like winding clocks and banging typewriter keys.

The word "treasure" is also used more freely than a strict dictionary definition would allow. Nothing I saw on my antiquing expedition to the Hamptons could, by the farthest stretch of the imagination, be called a treasure, or have been treasured at any time in the past.

Real antiques certainly do exist. Colonial objects are highly desirable and expensive. They are also remarkably common, which raises the question of their authenticity. The entire population of Long Island in colonial times would have fit three times into the Nassau Coliseum (16,000 seats). These few colonists had to work long hours at farming and fishing, just to survive. It's hard to imagine how they found time to make the vast numbers of genuine colonial antiques that fill the boutiques and auction houses of New England three hundred years later.

It is of course possible to enjoy antique shops without irony, and without caring in the least about authenticity. They offer such an intriguing window into the past. What must it have been like to have all this junk in your home? Our honored forbearers seem to have had a passion for glass and china objects of incredible ugliness, hideous lamps, comfortless chairs, and dreadful oil paintings. People really were made of sterner stuff in those days.

It is also intriguing to wonder about the antique stores of the future. How will our children's children imagine this century, as seen through the detritus of our busy lives? For all we know, when the twenty second century comes around, the same old rubbish may be recycling through the basements, yard sales and antique stores of the world for the hundredth time, and the present will look as tasteless in the future as the past looks in the present.

STUFF

The desire to make things clean and tidy in the springtime seems to be an almost biological urge. Like most biological urges, it should be resisted. Spring may be the season of renewal and new beginnings, but there's no point in going mad about it. The energy and optimism we feel at the happiest time of the year shouldn't be wasted on dull domestic tasks.

Cleaning is relatively easy if you can get somebody else to do it, but making a house or apartment *tidy* comes up against a fundamental problem of human nature, or perhaps culture. We simply have too much stuff. The giant retailer Ikea warned in 2017 that shoppers have reached "peak stuff." They don't have room in their homes for another coat hanger, let alone a coat, and instead they are wasting their money on "experiences" like travel and dining out. Tidiness means turning back the tide of stuff and aiming for the kind of minimalism you see in illustrations of Japanese décor: empty rooms furnished with almost nothing. It should be easy to achieve this: just throw stuff out. But it doesn't work that way for most of us.

The spare room that I call my study, where I pretend to work, is a fine example of what can be achieved when serious spring cleaning has been postponed for ten or fifteen years. Books, papers, CDs, files and bits of electrical equipment cover every surface, including the floor. None of these things can be moved for fear of disturbing the dust, which would activate my allergies, and ruin my one hundred per-cent intuitive filing system. It is a virtually perfect work space. Everything I need comes instantly to hand and nothing can get lost unless eaten by the mice.

"Stuff Happens" says the bumper sticker, and how true it is. Three garbage collections a week don't seem to reduce it, nor do charity contributions. We try to palm some useless items off on friends and relatives as holiday gifts. But it's no use because they do the same to us. Yard sales never work. You always end up with more stuff than you started with, because neighbors sneak around the back and dump their own stuff in your driveway. Losing stuff, like losing weight, is a lost cause. We can't get rid of it because we have reached saturation point. Everybody has more than enough, and nobody wants any more. In short, we have reached a steady state of excess, and we are prisoners of our stuff.

But we are willing prisoners. We adore our stuff and cling to it. That's why we need larger and larger houses, and commercial storage units lined up along every highway. A million years ago our ancestors moved out of caves because they had run out of closet space for their old animal bones and pieces of flint, and the process of accumulation has never stopped.

Some things are worth keeping for sentimental reasons. I still have my first teddy bear, called Rabbit (I was a short-sighted child), and he's not stuff. Nor are certain books that have followed me around for most of my life, not the boxes of faded color slides, nor the various anachronistic odd and ends in my bedside table like cuff links and collar studs. These things are valuable personal history.

In fact, when I look around the house, everything I see is valuable personal history – ancient cooking utensils, floppy disks, non-functioning cassette players - they're all fragments of my past life, like Rabbit, and they all might all come in useful someday. They are secure presences in a changing world. Even the human body renews itself constantly; we replace our physical selves about every seven years. So, nothing is permanent except our stuff, and nothing will remain of us except our stuff. We should treat it with proper respect.

THE CHRONICLES OF WASTED TIME

Recently I wrote two memoirs. I never intended to write even one, but here they are and each one is completely different. I reckon that, without stretching the truth, I could write at least two more, just as different as the first two. That's the elasticity of time, and the ambiguity of life.

Time is not our friend. It creeps past us on silent feet, one second after another. We never see it go, and it never comes back. Nobody ever stops to tell us: "Hey, pay attention, this is the best bit." The best bit of your life just slides past like all the rest, into oblivion. Shakespeare's chronicles of wasted time are the poems that record love and beauty in the past – celebrated now but wasted then.

Everything glowed with a gleam/And Yet we were looking away.
Thomas Hardy, "The Self Unseeing."

If time is not our friend, memory is positively treacherous. Some people remember every detail of their past lives, every meal they have ever eaten and with whom, and even more intimate details. It must be hard to live inside their busy heads. With every moment of their past engraved there, diamond bright, there's no way to escape into fantasy or selective editing. I both envy and fear the absolute recall and steady hand of a Proust or a Nabokov. The complete, unvarnished truth is not something that most of us want to live with, which is why Sigmund Freud invented The Unconscious - that convenient basement of the mind into which all the unwanted rubbish can be dumped.

Forgetting allows us to live our lives forwards, without nostalgia or regret. Most of us, I believe, are blessed with a kind of built-in self-editor that tidies up and improves the past as we go along. Nietzsche, going to extremes as always, once said: "No man with a good memory can ever be creative." The quote may not be exact, but it's an interesting thought. If you have a bad memory, everything is always new, including the leftovers you put in the refrigerator yesterday and rediscover with pleasure today.

So why a memoir, let alone two? And why now?

Age must be part of the answer. The desire to write a memoir typically arrives at about the same stage of life as arthritis. There is an irrational fear of forgetting everything, which makes little sense because, when we do lose it all, we won't know that we've lost it. This may be why some people suffering from dementia exhibit an eerie, tranquil happiness. Their personal slate has been wiped clean.

A slightly more rational reason is to leave a record of one's life, a justification, what used to be called an *apologia,* and I must plead guilty to that. There were some personal things that I wanted to say, and I'm glad I went ahead and did it even if nobody ever reads the books. We want the past to make sense, if only to ourselves, and the only way to do that is by careful and selective remembering and forgetting. Otherwise our stories are indeed the chronicles of wasted time, a chaos of tiny events that added up to nothing, and meant nothing. As Donald Trump used to say, when confronted by some unpleasant truth: "Sad."

Theme II

MIND *versus* BODY

There are people who strictly deprive themselves of each and every eatable, drinkable and smokable which has in any way acquired a shady reputation. They pay this price for health. And health is all they get for it.

MARK TWAIN

The chief function of the body is to carry the brain around.

THOMAS A. EDISON

THE KNOWLEDGE MAN

Denis Diderot is an almost-forgotten name in intellectual history, although everybody knows Mr. Google. But whenever we use an online search engine to answer one of our questions we are benefitting from the genius, bravery, and determination of Monsieur Diderot.

His idea, which was as simple as it was revolutionary, was to gather together all the knowledge in the world in a systematic way so that anybody could find information about anything. In other words, Diderot invented the encyclopedia.

It was a project on a heroic scale, completed in 1772 and filling twenty-seven large volumes containing seventy-five thousand entries. It was not at all popular among the rich and powerful of the time. The idea of spreading knowledge is never welcomed by people whose position depends on the ignorance of those less fortunate. Knowledge really is power. That's why universal education evokes such mixed feelings. On the one hand, it is the force behind economic and social progress. On the other, once people start thinking for themselves, who knows what might happen?

Diderot was said to have written ten thousand of the Encyclopedia articles himself. Some of them were so radical that the entire book was banned for a while. But now it is treated as an intellectual monument, and the French state honored the author in his tricentennial year.

When I was growing up, encyclopedia salesmen came from door to door. "The encyclopedia man" became a kind of joke, spoofed by Monty Python among others. My parents had two different sets in multiple volumes, one for adults and one for children – that is to say, for me, my very own encyclopedia. An encyclopedia in the house was supposed to guarantee that your child would grow up both intelligent and knowledgeable, and obviously it worked in my case. You can still find printed encyclopedias gathering dust in public libraries, but rarely on family bookshelves – the Internet has seen to that. I leave it to you to decide whether the Internet in the house will guarantee that your child will grow up both intelligent and knowledgeable.

The great thing about an encyclopedia in book form, and especially a big one like Britannica or Americana, is that you can read it, explore it, and get lost in it. One thing leads to another, and another, and another. You may start by looking up Diderot and end up reading about speculative fiction or Italian opera. I know, because it happened to me. Internet search engines simply seek out a target and hit it: here's your question, here's your answer, end of story. This is very practical and useful, but there's no adventure in it, and precious little chance of making strange or unexpected discoveries.

Intellectual giants of the past like Goethe, Nietzsche, Hegel, and Freud all admired Diderot, not just for his massive encyclopedia but for his subversive satirical writing. He was a man with a mission, to promote knowledge in all its forms without prejudice and without censorship. It is ironic to reflect that if he were to pursue the same passion today, three centuries later, he would probably be in as much trouble with the authorities now as he was then.

STARTING OVER

Every summer tens of thousands of young people are launched into a new life after college and, let's not forget, a few people who are not so young. There may be as many as two million students over thirty in higher education, and some are much older. A remarkable woman called Ingeborg Rapoport defended her doctoral thesis at the University of Hamburg, at the age of a hundred and two.

My own venture into higher education also came rather late, although not *that* late. I arrived at university long after the proper age, because I had been doing interesting things elsewhere, and found that I was by far the oldest student in my entering class. The younger students accepted me cheerfully, whether as an inspiration or a warning I don't know

I don't subscribe to the cliché that "Education is wasted on the young," far from it, the more the better. But I do believe that ignorance is wasted on the old. Life experience without knowledge leaves a person, as it were, half finished. Now, it seems, education for adults is coming back into fashion. Older people have more experience, more curiosity, and perhaps more time and money than they used to have. Shuffleboard gets boring after a while. Their minds tend to range wider, so they are ideally placed to make the most of the chance to learn something new.

Most of the energy and money in higher education goes towards young people, as it should. The standard assumption is that education should happen fast, in one compact package, and should be over by one's mid-twenties at the latest, when serious careers should begin and idle curiosity should end. But that may be a prescription for frustration and disappointment. By the age of twenty we have learned only a microscopic fragment of the things we could learn, and in any case, most of the knowledge acquired in college vanishes in a puff of smoke about half an hour after the Commencement ceremony.

The urge to return to education later in life may be purely practical – to get a qualification for example. But it may also be the intellectual equivalent of the mid-life crisis, the moment when we suddenly realize how little we know, and how much we are missing. Self-education is always possible, of course. There have never been so many learning choices available on and off the web, and every public library is a free university.

But self-education is hard and solitary work and, as Benjamin Franklin said, "He who teaches himself has a fool for a master." So, some choose to go back to school in middle life for the full learning experience, complete with lectures, tests, and long hours of study.

College administrators are having a hard time attracting traditional age students, and have launched what look like desperate searches abroad, sending out recruiters around the world like eighteenth century press gangs. They might do better to look closer to home for grown-up students who can afford their exorbitant fees, and who will cause less trouble with political protests and all-night keg parties. More education, right across the age range is better for all of us, because the ability to think for ourselves makes us less vulnerable to tricksters of every kind, commercial and political.

So perhaps we should give a special cheer of encouragement to the older students this year. Their graduation will be less a commencement than a recommencement - a second chance for them, and perhaps, in the long run, for us.

BETWEEN TWO CULTURES

Those of us who never had a proper education in science are reminded of our ignorance every time we switch on a computer, or a microwave, or even a light bulb. It might as well be magic, but it's not, and we have no more idea how these tricks are performed than we understand the flying broomsticks in Harry Potter. It is humiliating, and dangerous, because science is behind just about everything we use and depend on. Satellites spin in the sky above our heads, we get miraculous drugs from the local pharmacy, and make calls on phones that don't seem to be connected to anything, and we don't understand how any of it works.

The British scientist and novelist C.P. Snow wrote about this in 1959 in a famous book called *The Two Cultures*. The two cultures were science and art, and Snow was alarmed at how little they understood about each other. Nothing has changed since 1959. In fact, science has run so far ahead of scientific illiterates like me that we can only gape at it like the Pilgrim Fathers confronted by a video game.

I was painfully reminded of this by reading a memoir by the scientist and controversialist Richard Dawkins about his lifetime of research in biology. He writes well and most of his arguments can be followed by the scientifically retarded, but the underlying knowledge of things like phenotypes and genotypes, memes and genes, arthromorphs and biomorphs is simply not in my brain, so that his descriptions of research sound as much like mysticism or alchemy as the products of reason and logic. So, I must trust Professor Dawkins, and I do more or less. But if I trust him, without being able to explain why, I might trust anybody with any theory about reality. That's what's so dangerous. The more a few scientifically educated people know, and the less the rest of us know, the more science begins to look like some sort of elite conspiracy. Ignorance breeds fear, and into the empty space comes every dumb idea and idiotic belief that has ever entered into the mind of man – and believe me that's a long list.

Science doesn't leave much room for the opinions and beliefs we cherish. We love to have pointless arguments about the best basketball team or religion or political party or TV show, because it is fun to argue and we can always consider ourselves right. My opinion is as good as yours. But when it comes, say, to finding the elusive infinitely small particles that may be the basic building blocks of the universe, my opinion is definitely not as good as yours, and totally worthless compared to the opinion of a physicist. My idea would be to get a large magnifying glass. Their idea was to build enormous machines, like the Hadron Collider outside Geneva. Guess whose method is most likely to succeed.

Of course, science can't do everything: it can't tell us the right word to use in a poem or explain Beethoven's late quartets. There are different things to know, and different ways of knowing. But we need a better balance, more people like Alexander Borodin, the Russian composer who was also a research chemist, or indeed Richard Dawkins himself, a biologist with a wide-ranging knowledge of the arts.

We aren't all smart enough to be scientists, but it is important that we understand how and why science works, and magic doesn't. Even I know what a scientific proof should look like: observation, classification, experiment, repetition, comparison and so on. That's how we know that our knowledge is knowledge. If you don't believe that, you might believe anything.

SOLITUDE

We humans are a sociable species. That's how we survive. We have the self-protective herd instinct that tells us that it is safer to conform, follow the leader, and go with the crowd. This behavior can be seen in its purest form in your local high school, where 'fitting in' is practically a religion.

What makes us different from bees or lemmings is that we can and do break away from the herd, and think our separate thoughts. We are bees with a perspective on the hive, which allows us to evolve and to create. It also gives us a headache.

The times when we are separated from the swarm, mentally or physically, are potentially creative moments when we can reflect on what (for want of a better phrase) I have to call the meaning of life. Even though Monty Python made an international joke out of it, the meaning of life is still a pretty important question.

Solitude used to be available in public places, like airports or trains, where we existed in a kind of crowded limbo, cut off from our friends and from the strangers all around us. But limbo has been abolished by scientific progress. "Public space" has taken on a new meaning, now that we're all connected. It is an arena of beeps and ring tones and competing conversations yelled at full volume. Everyone is talking into thin air, or peering at a tiny screen while trying to press buttons the size of deer ticks. Nobody has the slightest desire to pause for reflection. That kind of solitude has become quite scary. We are never alone, unless the battery runs out.

Intimate couples split apart in public spaces. They turn their backs, each one absorbed in communication with someone else, somewhere else. The solitude of their togetherness is too much to endure. Or perhaps they are just following the prescription of the German poet Rainer Maria Rilke:

> *"I hold this to be the highest task for a bond between two people: that each protects the solitude of the other."*

Smartphones make it possible to escape the too-familiar other, but not the millions and billions of others. We can travel to the ends of the earth, but even the deserts and mountains are crowded. Resorts ironically offer "Relaxation and solitude," but you and they know that thousands of others will be sharing the same solitary experience on their phones, all day and all night.

Gabriel Garcia Marquez's novel *A Hundred Years of Solitude* is not really "about" solitude, except in so far as it follows the pointless and circular lives of the Buendia family, cut off from the wider world and progress. They are solitary in so far as they are ignorant, and their solitude is less a gift than a pathology of isolation.

Henry David Thoreau represents the more romantic, more intellectual view. In *Walden* he wrote:

> *"I never found the companion that was so companionable as solitude. We are for the most part more lonely when we go abroad*

among men than when we stay in our chambers. A man thinking or working is always alone, let him be where he will. Solitude is not measured by the miles of space that intervene between a man and his fellows. The really diligent student in one of the crowded hives of Cambridge College is as solitary as a dervish in the desert."

Solitude remains a romantic, poetic notion for creative people. Fortunately, it is rarely put to the test. But on a trip abroad one summer I was unable to connect to the internet for a week, I had no telephone, and the cell phone failed. We had no TV or radio either. We were cut off from the continuous chatter of the outside world, and achieved a kind of solitude by default.

It was disturbing at first, but then a profound peace descended. This, I supposed, was the magic of solitude that everyone writes about, but almost nobody can find. I could almost feel my blood pressure going down, I slept better, I was relaxed – and I couldn't write a word.

This may be what happens to people who hide away in isolated writers' colonies, hoping that peace and quiet will bring the inspiration that everyday life had failed to bring. Thoreau wrote often and lyrically about solitude, but he was constantly involved with people, with nature, and with his own philosophy. He was no more solitary than I am, sitting alone in my study, apart from two cats, the birds outside the window, and the radio playing a harp concerto by a composer with a marvelous name – Karl Ditters Von Dittersdorf. Is this solitude? I think not.

Real solitude over a long period must be very much like Death Lite, which is why solitary confinement is one of our cruelest punishments. No wonder we love to dream about it, but never to practice it on ourselves.

THE SUM OF HUMAN HAPPINESS

The pursuit of happiness is one of our inalienable rights, along with life and liberty. It's not just a right but a duty, although only half of all

Americans report being content with their lives. That puts the United States in eleventh place on the international happiness index, way below the Scandinavian countries, but much higher than the Russians, Spanish and Portuguese, who don't seem very cheerful at all. It's easy to understand the Russians, but I don't know why the Iberians are so gloomy. It must be all that sad guitar music. These differences are consistent over time. Happy nations tend to stay happy through good decades and bad. Depressed nations stay depressed, no matter how many cable channels or Happy Meals they get. Money has almost nothing to do with it.

The Founding Fathers were wise to specify the *pursuit* of happiness, rather than happiness itself. Sigmund Freud held the opinion that actual happiness was a form of neurosis in adult human beings, and that the best we should hope for was a delicate balance between mild cheerfulness and mild depression.

This delicate balance is sometimes hard to find. There is a long tradition that tells us to make the most of our problems and learn from them. I was forced to reconsider this piece of conventional wisdom after a major hurricane left us freezing and without power for ten days. We learned to live without modern technology and to re-learn some technologies of the past, which is where we seem to be headed anyway. But this was the only lesson I could derive from the hurricane experience, and it wasn't a particularly happy one. It's all very well to quote: "Sweet are the uses of adversity," but Shakespeare wasn't familiar with power cuts.

Our personal balance of happiness was running low when the power came on after ten days, at which point we rediscovered the old truism that the secret of happiness is to take pleasure in small things, like the possibility of a hot bath. In other words, we were delighted to have luxuries that we had already, but never thought about – small scraps of pleasure that briefly loomed very large, and quickly became ordinary and taken for granted.

If Freud was right, these little flashes of happiness are the best we can hope for. We should always be ready to seize them when they appear, and then be ready to let them go when their moment has passed. Certainly, we should pursue happiness, but *carefully*, in case we catch up with it, like an old beagle I used to have. She loved to chase rabbits, but she was alarmed by the prospect of catching one. So, she would always contrive to run just a little slower than the rabbit. The dog was happy to have a great chase. The rabbit was happy to escape. I was happy not to have a dead rabbit on my hands. For a moment, everyone was happy.

A THOROUGHLY MODERN MARRIAGE

The continuing popularity of big weddings is a source of joy and comfort to many and a puzzle to others who, like me, are happily married but never felt the need to announce the fact with an expensive stage show. Yet the fifty billion dollar a year wedding industry continues to flourish, and the institution of marriage is sustained by it. I suspect that the desire to have a wedding is often stronger than the desire to have a marriage. It might be better to separate the two, so that anyone who likes weddings can have as many as they can afford without being stuck with the co-star for the rest of their lives. Marriage is about biology, not theater.

Marriage is splendid, when it works, but it is never an easy choice. It goes against human nature. "Till death us do part" is a big commitment, especially now that we are all determined to live so long. Young men especially are accused of being commitment-phobic. Yet they readily make lifetime commitments to things like tattoos, body piercing, football teams and Harley Davidsons. What's so special about marriage?

It may be the idea of a thirty-year mortgage that gives them pause, or the trauma of wedding itself, or the fear that marriage and adulthood will be the equivalent of a police raid that closes down a long and enjoyable party. Those carefree teenage years can be stretched into decades, and it must be hard to give them up.

Young women are also becoming more attached to their freedom, and marrying later or not at all. Given that an average wedding costs $25,000 an increasing number of couples choose to bypass the whole white limousine and catering hall extravaganza and just live together no matter what their mothers say.

A wedding used to be a rendezvous with destiny. Now it's more like a throw of the dice. Many people must march down the aisle twice, or maybe three or more times before they pick a winner. There's no three strikes rule, which is good news for Mr. Trump, now on number three, and some people have a really hard time making the right choice. Liz Taylor, for example, had eight husbands.

This practical, unromantic trend in matrimony, first invented by King Henry VIII and then re-invented in a kinder, gentler form in Hollywood, has revived the old idea that marriage should have built-in time limits, rather like a car lease. You could turn in your partner in good condition with a limited mileage after three years, or take the option to make the contract permanent. Another suggestion is the time-limited marriage license, re-newable after a certain period, say every ten years, like a driver's license or passport. Renewal would be a simple matter, involving an eye test, a physical, and a brain function test. The Marriage Licensing Authority could refuse to renew a license in cases of obvious marital incompetence, and either partner could let the license lapse at the end of its term, and take off for Hawaii with a clear conscience.

Romantics naturally hate this notion of conditional marriage. But the happy result would be even more weddings, without the intervening traumas of divorce. More weddings would mean more hearts and flow-ers, more tears, more bad poetry, more family drama, and many more

shopping opportunities. Children could look forward to a regularly scheduled supply of new and indulgent step-parents, and nobody need ever
feel trapped in a relationship again.

This is a perfectly rational, workable and sensible proposal, like term
limits on Congress. Like all rational, workable and sensible proposals, it
stands absolutely no chance.

NOT QUITE WHAT WE SEEM

Do you ever get the uncomfortable suspicion that you are a fraud and an
imposter? I feel that way whenever I'm in Europe and I have to pretend
that I know what is going on. This must be a problem for everyone who
tries to navigate a foreign culture. In order not to look like an idiot you
must act as if you understand the language, the culture, the strange things
for sale in the market, and even the driving.

Nobody is fooled by this pretense, of course, which makes it harmless
and even quite amusing. But there's something disturbing about the way
we – and I mean human beings in general – are so very ready to pretend to
be something that we are not, and to be have talents that we don't possess.

I've been pretending to read a book by a French psychoanalyst,
Roland Gori, called *The Making of Imposters*. The good professor, who
may or may not be a real professor, argues that social expectations are
so high in this competitive world that people in search of success are almost forced to fake the necessary knowledge and expertise, as well as to
profess a character that they don't really possess. They exaggerate their
qualifications and suppress their real personalities to fit in and get on. The
psychologist calls them "Imposters despite themselves," and argues that
they live in an unhealthy state of constant anxiety and fear of exposure.

This really comes as no surprise. The idea that we play more or less
false social roles was old news in Shakespeare's time, and has been

intensively studied by sociologists in our own time. When it comes to the human character there are layers beneath layers, and facades beneath facades. Every day it seems we read about another politician, scientist, doctor, attorney, religious leader, or businessman, or woman, being exposed as a fraud. Professor Gori's book suggests that this has become an epidemic, because so few of us can live up to society's high expectations.

Gori highlights something so commonplace and so true that it is almost shocking: people are not what they seem. Who hasn't felt like an imposter at some time in their lives? Unworthy in love, for example, not fully competent to do our job, not really believing the things we are supposed to believe? My own low point was when I was drafted into the army and had to spend two years pretending to be a soldier – possibly the worst performance ever seen in military history. People in the public eye like political leaders and entertainers must be particularly vulnerable to the feeling that they are impersonating an unreal imitation of a counterfeit version of themselves.

The book *The Making of Imposters* offers some self-help advice. The happiest and healthiest people are those who do not choose or need to pretend. Gori tells us to face up squarely to our own pretenses and try to overcome them. "To know that you are an imposter," he says, "Is the best antidote to being one."

So, I'll start right now, cards on the table. I haven't really read all three hundred twenty pages of *The Making of Imposters*, but only a review of it in a French newspaper. There, the truth is out in the open, and I can rejoice in my new authenticity. But don't expect me to keep it up for long.

GIFTED AND TALENTED

Wolfgang Amadeus Mozart is the poster child for the whole category of gifted and talented children. He started playing the piano at the age of three, and composing at the age of six. When he was eight years old, the

45

little boy amused himself by writing his first symphony for all the instruments of the orchestra.

History seems full of such astonishing child prodigies: the mathematician Blaise Pascal, the poet Alexander Pope, the artist Pablo Picasso, and hundreds of others. It's a mystery where their gifts came from, but what they had in common was an early rather than a late start. They focused on one passionate interest from childhood, and stuck to it in spite of everything, even in spite of being labeled as odd, or even abnormal.

There's no way of measuring how many geniuses appear in any given place or time, but these days they seem quite rare. It may be that, in an egalitarian society, a true genius learns to hide his or her superiority, just as the driver of a Ferrari must keep it down to fifty-five miles an hour on our restricted roads, even if it can easily go at two hundred. Genius, like speed, may attract unwelcome attention.

All parents naturally want their children to be special, and some make intense efforts to get their offspring into gifted and talented programs. Garrison Keillor, the host of Prairie Home Companion, liked to joke that all children in Lake Wobegon were above average. The joke is that only half of all children can ever be above average and the rest are inevitably below average, even in Minnesota. Only a tiny number are born with an extraordinary talent. But, in reality, not many parents want their children to be *that* different, let alone unique like Mozart. Fitting in may be more important than standing out. The goal is not so much to create a genius as to open the doors to those professions that combine high pay, high prestige, and the smallest possible amount of physical effort. That's good enough, especially if the neighbor's kids don't do as well.

Modern childhood is so extended that there's not much chance of making an early start on a career, except perhaps in sports or entertainment where precocious talent is easily recognized and potentially profitable. Most young people are not expected to be capable of anything useful until they have been processed through the whole educational machinery from kindergarten to PhD. Even if a child does have a special gift, by graduation time he or she may have forgotten what it was. Grades and credits and distribution requirements and multiple-choice tests have knocked any taint of genius out of them.

What would happen to a Mozart today? The chances are he wouldn't find a music program in his school, and in any case Mozart scarcely ever went to school. As a hyperactive, mischievous boy he would probably be given drugs to calm him down, flunk out of school from sheer boredom, and end up working in the fast food industry. I sometimes wonder how many mute inglorious Mozarts there are, flipping burgers out in the suburbs.

I once asked my mother if I had shown any special talents at the age when Mozart was composing symphonies. She thought about this, for rather too long in my opinion, but finally admitted that I did sleep much more than the average child. So, I must accept that I am part of the vast majority whose special gift is to have no special gift. It's quite a relief really. At least I haven't wasted my genius and, as a consolation prize, I can always listen to Mozart.

SELF PORTRAIT

The trendy word of the decade seems to be "selfie," which I understand to mean simply a photographic self-portrait. Why this idea should suddenly be so much in vogue is hard to explain. Cameras were equipped with time-delay shutters for taking self-portraits as early as the 1850s, and I was certainly using one in the 1950s. However, a fashion is a fashion, and we must do our best to understand it.

My first reaction when the word "selfie" popped up was that it indicated a sudden plague of pathological vanity, perhaps caused by air pollution or genetically modified French fries. But when Hollywood stars and presidents start taking selfies it obviously must be more serious than vanity. We need to look deeper for an explanation.

People have always loved to gaze at pictures of themselves, although a visit to any portrait gallery will make you wonder why. When photography came along it was a godsend. Everybody could take as many self-portraits as they wanted, and we did. I have hundreds of old family snapshots, usually taken on vacation. They show us not how we are, but how we were, which is just as well. It's like Dorian Gray in reverse: our pictures stay young, but we do not. As we get older we take fewer photographs, and those are usually shot from the middle distance and slightly out of focus. The camera doesn't lie, unfortunately, and I doubt that the vogue for selfies will follow today's young enthusiasts into their senior years.

One part of the selfie craze seems to have to do with sharing. Social media sites offer few coherent words but they are full of pictures, sometimes updated every day. Some sites like Flickr seem to be virtually nothing but pictures. Nobody wants to look at your old photograph album, but you can spread your selfies through cyberspace whether cyberspace wants to see them or not.

Everyone seems to believe the cliché that a picture is worth a thousand words, but the opposite is true. Selfies in themselves say nothing, except "Look at me, I'm here, I exist." They literally flicker across the consciousness leaving no trace. They're not *worth* a thousand words, they *replace* a thousand words. I could send you a picture of my cat but, I would need to add several thousand words of supplementary description, history, praise, and character analysis. Otherwise you would see nothing but a cat.

Words take time. They slow us down, force us to consider information, and exercise the memory. The historian Daniel Boorstin observed fifty years ago that images had become more important than words in our culture, taking us back towards pre-literate time and making us much less thoughtful and more open to emotional manipulation. He should see us now, and "see" is the operative word. I am hoping that words will one day come back into fashion, but I'm not optimistic. As we gaze into the multiplying mirror of our self-images, we may no longer have the words to express the awful realization that the joke is on us.

SAFETY FEATURES

Our car was recalled by the manufacturer. It wasn't one of those urgent recalls you sometimes read about, when a particular make and model is discovered to be a death trap, but just a minor repair to the braking system. The car, like its owner, has reached the stage where occasional visits to the repair shop are inevitable.

The part that was supposed to be replaced was a piece of brake hose, although it turned out that mine was in perfect condition. The worst thing that can happen if your brake hose leaks is that you lose stopping power, which is certainly alarming and could be fatal. But in this case the chance was very small, and in any case drivers of my generation are accustomed to brake failure, although not exactly complacent about it. In the days when brakes were operated by cables, those cables quite often corroded and snapped. The early hydraulic brakes were not much better. Driving was full of surprises.

Cars built before the 1960s, and often kept on the road for a long time, were more challenging than modern cars: steering could fail, lights went out unexpectedly, engines cut out all the time, fires were quite common, and of course there were those unpredictable brakes. These vehicles encouraged prudent driving. In the case of one British car I drove regularly, made in 1934 and already ancient when I owned it, it was necessary to plan stopping well in advance, and scan the roadside for something soft, like a thick hedge, in case the brakes failed completely. At the time, I was living in a village at the bottom of a steep hill, so every evening commute was an adventure.

Modern cars are less like death traps and more like mobile couches. This has come about through technological progress and legal regulation. There are, as far as I can discover, almost a thousand government regulations covering vehicle safety. Air bags, lights, safety belt, crush protection, and of course the all-important brakes are legislated in enormous detail, and about seven hundred thousand lawyers are poised to pounce on any mechanical failure that might possibly have caused an accident.

All this creates what feels like a secure driving experience, although driving is still by far the most dangerous thing we do. But I can't help wondering whether it reduces our level of alertness, and therefore our ability to respond to the unexpected. A three-thousand-pound metal box on wheels travelling at fifty miles an hour and guided with one lackadaisical hand on the wheel by someone talking on the phone, is not actually a very safe place. We expect one hundred per-cent protection from every danger, and that may be dangerous in itself. It makes caution or even common sense seem unnecessary, and it would be wiser in many cases to recall the idiotic drivers rather than the cars.

There are so many vehicles on our crowded roads, and so many distracted drivers, that it may not be a good idea to make us feel so cozy and safe, and to suggest even subliminally that nothing bad can happen in this lovely shiny vehicle. It can. Just look at the wrecks piled up behind any body shop. Now, as in the earliest days of motoring, the main safety feature is the driver – awake, alert, watching the road, and ready for anything.

THE LAST GASP

When the sun begins to peek out, however reluctantly, and the temperature crawls up to a tolerable level, I always have the irrational feeling that I should be more active instead of spending my days reading, writing and feeding cats. A lot of senior citizens in search of eternal youth are fiendishly active these days. They go to the gym or the swimming pool every day, or run ten miles at dawn or do Tai Chi or Kung Fu or Pilates (whatever it is) or Jazzercise or one of the other tortures invented for the elderly.

Far from being healthy this seems like a plot to hasten us on our way and save the Social Security budget. Earlier generations didn't act like this. When they reached retirement age they stopped, quite literally, and took it easy. Bodies get old and creaky, just like machines. It makes no sense to hammer our bones and muscles when they are already three-quarters worn out. It's like putting a classic car in the Indianapolis 500 when it should be in a museum. My grandmother, who barely moved for the last thirty years of her life, lived to be a hundred, and my mother, following the same regime, lived to a hundred and three.

So, the urge to be active is objectively and medically irrational, but nevertheless it is hard to resist in springtime. It impelled me to enter a sports equipment emporium that happens to be next to the place where I buy my office supplies. If I was thinking at all I was thinking that there might be some harmless and painless sporting activity suitable for persons of my age.

At first glance, it seemed more like a shoe store than a sports store, with enough footwear to equip a whole nation of athletic centipedes. A bored young man explained to me that no kind of sport can be attempted without the right kind of hi-tech shoes. They even had special shoes for walking, although I have been walking in ordinary shoes all my life. There were shoes for golf, shoes for cycling, shoes for tennis and basketball and gymnastics. Somewhere in the back of the store there were probably shoes for tiddlywinks, and quite possibly shoes for playing video games. Another essential for the sporting life, I discovered, is the right clothing. A good half of the store was given over to workout suits, polyester tights, and other garments in rainbow colors.

The remaining sales space displayed real sporting equipment, most of it complicated and expensive. I examined the bikes because I used to enjoy cycling, but I don't think I could learn to ride one of these amazing machines with fifty gears and a mass of accessories including a tiny computer that will tell you how fast you have travelled, how far, and perhaps why. A bike alone is not enough: you need a helmet, a hydro pack whatever it is (presumably a bottle of water) and a chain big enough to secure Fort Knox. The only equipment in the store that looked user- friendly were some hula hoops left over from the 1950s and a box of colored beach balls, but I don't see how these would fit into my lifestyle.

Clearly the sporting life is not for folks of my age. We would look silly in the outfits and we couldn't afford the equipment. I'll stick to my old regime and just take my regular walk in the park in my regular clothes, wearing my regular shoes.

FEEL MY PAIN

Everybody loves a mountain, especially if they can drive up to the summit instead of climbing. The most popular and highest mountain in the southwest of France is called Mount Aigoual, standing a little over five thousand feet, which has two excellent roads leading to the top. Our little Fiat just made it, and we were rewarded with a spectacular panorama. What took away some of the pleasure was the pain and suffering of the many cyclists who, for mysterious reasons known only to themselves, had decided to *ride* all the way up the mountain, a distance of twenty-two miles, not a single yard of them flat. There were dozens of cyclists, perhaps hundreds, all bathed in sweat with agonized faces and leg muscles that stood out like steel cables at breaking point. Nobody, as far as I know, was forcing them to do this. It was their own choice.

I can see that coasting *down* the mountain would be fun. When I was a kid my friends and I used to ride to a nearby hill and puff our way up to the top, just so we could come zooming down again. But our hill was only about a quarter of a mile long, probably no more than fifty feet high at the summit. That was all the pain and suffering we needed at that or any other age.

Human nature is unfathomable, although Sigmund Freud among many others tried to fathom it. Psychologists have long recognized the existence of masochism, the ability to get pleasure from pain. It seems to explain a lot about human nature, although we might be happier if it explained less. The world is full of examples. In addition to the cyclists we saw people resolutely *walking* the twenty-two miles up that mountain, carrying heavy backpacks. The trek takes eight hours. The diagnosis seems obvious, the treatment less so.

Painful activities are extraordinarily popular – marathon running, all kinds of athletics, eating healthy diets, camping, and so on. I read about a forty-six-mile off-road triathlon in Sweden that must be a kind of benchmark for miserable experiences. "It's about taking as much pain as possible," said one of the organizers. Indeed, enthusiasts like to say: "Feel the pain" with a kind of pride. But plenty of people with arthritis feel the pain – there's no virtue in it.

Pain is not just a pleasure for young people. Before climbing the mountain in our Fiat we had visited a famous spa nearby. This offered cures for just about everything, including old age, with a combination of sulfur baths and massage, with the additional option of being covered in honey as a special treat. The mixed stink of sulfur and honey in the place was quite literally nauseating, so we stayed only long enough to see a row of already-processed victims, people at the far end of life but still keen to suffer, sitting hollow-eyed on plastic chairs, wrapped in white robes, and obviously glad that the torture was over.

This may be the answer of course. We enjoy suffering when it stops, when we get to the top of the mountain or climb out of the sulfur bath. It's the anticipation of relief that gives us courage, and the anticipated sense of superiority. Not for me though, I don't like pain. I go to considerable lengths to avoid it. But am I missing out on the pleasure of pain? Should I be torturing myself, just for the fun of it? It's the kind of question that gives me a headache, but an aspirin should take care of that.

WALKING ALONE

After what seemed like a long time crawling around on the floor I learned to walk at the age of about fourteen months, and I have been walking ever since. I liked walking from the start. It was more dignified than crawling, and faster, and allowed me to see and grab more things. Some medical authorities have even suggested that walking may be good for our physical health, although we should probably reserve judgement on that.

There is some reason to believe that walking is good for our *mental* health, although most of the evidence dates from an earlier period of history when people used their feet more than we do now. This may help to explain the astonishing creative and intellectual brilliance of certain famous characters in the past. How did they achieve so much? It certainly wasn't because they had good medical care, or even good general health. What their biographies show is that many of them did an astonishing amount of walking, not only from necessity but also from choice. Here's a short list.

The peripatetic philosophers of ancient Greece who walked from city to city all over Asia minor, the poets of the Romantic Age like Wordsworth and Blake, the philosopher, Jean Jacques Rousseau, Henry David Thoreau who wrote a book about walking, Ralph Waldo Emerson, Charles Dickens who was reputed to walk twenty miles a day, Robert Louis Stevenson, Virginia Woolf, Vladimir Nabokov, the composers Brahms, Beethoven, Tchaikovsky, and Dvorak – the list could be extended almost indefinitely. They were all walkers on a heroic scale.

Walking is deeply unfashionable these days. It's not unusual to see apparently fit people maneuvering aggressively for the parking spot closest to the supermarket door as if their lives depended on saving half a dozen steps.

But deliberate walking for exercise has not yet died out, and the habit may even be on the increase as health-conscious baby boomers reach an age when they must give up jogging or take up permanent residence with their chiropractor. Some people like to walk in the suburbs where they can study the three varieties of suburban architecture and enjoy the thrill of danger that comes from having no sidewalks. Others prefer to walk in the city so they can get their minimum daily dose of air pollutants and carbon monoxide. A few prefer the torture machine called a treadmill, so they don't have to go anywhere. For myself I prefer the country, or any place where no buildings are visible in any direction. Human habitations and traffic distract the mind, in a way that nature does not.

Distraction can ruin a good walk. That's why it's important to walk alone sometimes, because the whole walking experience is about being with yourself and paying attention to the world around you. The very ground under your feet becomes part of the experience, if only you pay attention, *quietly*. You can't walk *and* talk *and* think all at the same time, which is why cellphones are so popular and why so many walkers come in pairs, chattering like birds every inch of the way. Talk is the white noise that saves us from thinking.

The mechanical business of walking and the freedom of being outdoors, taken together, seem to expand the mind. There's no competition, no speed, no hurry, no rules, no disturbance. What could be more conducive to creative reflection? That, I am sure, was the secret of our astonishingly creative ancestors. They walked a great deal, and therefore thought a great deal. The philosopher Nietzsche wrote: "Do not believe any idea that was not born in the open air, and of free movement." But enlightenment is not guaranteed. You can take a long peaceful ramble in the country and come back with your head as empty as before. It happens to me all the time. But then, at least, I had a nice walk.

SPA PACKAGE

I spent a few days in England in a resort town at the height of summer. Finding a hotel room wasn't easy, but eventually I connected by phone with a helpful receptionist at one of those faded grand hotels the Victorians built all along the south coast. They had a room for me, and we discussed prices. For my short stay, she said, the best deal would be something called the all- inclusive "Spa Package." I made the reservation, without thinking about it very much or indeed at all.

It was only as I approached the hotel that the phrase "spa package" came back to haunt me. I've no objection to a spa of the type frequented by Jane Austen's characters, with afternoon tea, gentle walks, and long relaxing naps. But spas, like everything else, have become more rigorous, and I had heard about these so-called health spas that some hotels have installed to drum up business. They sounded like bad news to me. I had visions of being grabbed by determined women in leotards as I stepped through the door, stripped, boiled in a Turkish bath, thrown into a cold pool, and then massaged to within an inch of my life while being anointed with strange aromatic oils. I also began to worry about the food that might be served in this establishment. A spa package might include a healthy diet. There's nothing I fear more than a healthy diet – I'm just not well enough to survive it.

My body and I weren't happy about any of this. We like a quiet life. So as soon as I had checked into the hotel I locked myself into my room and lay on the bed. If the spa people came for me I would pretend to be dead. But they didn't come, and after a while I felt brave enough to examine the details of my spa package, which had been handed to me at reception. It turned out to be almost harmless.

The Turkish bath and cold pool were there, as I had feared but, apparently, they were voluntary. In addition, I was offered a long menu of services that I found utterly mysterious, including exfoliation, a skin hydrator body wrap, Indian head massage, and restorative mud envelopment. I paused for a moment over the gent's manicure, but I can do that myself in three minutes.

Some familiar favorites from the nineteen sixties were also on the spa menu, including reflexology, various massages, and all kinds of things labeled "holistic" and "natural," although they didn't sound natural to me. When I finally crept down to have a look at the spa there was a definite feeling of *déja vu*. Soft New Age music was playing, the rooms smelled of incense, and the threat of yoga hung in the air.

The staff, who were quite friendly and not at all frightening, tried to persuade me to stay and take advantage of my spa package, but I know my limitations. I returned to my room, un-improved and un-anointed, and no more natural than I had been before. When dinner time came around I was delighted to discover that there was not a single healthy item on the menu.

Altogether my spa package was a great bargain.

A GOOD LONG READ

The phrase "A good long read" was often spoken with nostalgia by my busy parents. It was something they dreamed about, but rarely achieved except around Christmastime and on summer vacations.

Most middle-class Victorian families had servants, so everyone except the servants had a lot of time on their hands. Unlike us nineteenth-century home owners didn't spend their days on domestic and garden chores. They read a lot, and they loved long books. Authors were happy to write them, not least because they were paid by the word or the page. Dickens, Thackeray, Hardy and the rest routinely published novels of eight or nine hundred pages or more, to say nothing of Monsieur Proust with his mind-numbing three thousand pages. In the modern age, with so many distractions and our much shorter attention spans, these huge volumes are a challenge. I recently finished *Middlemarch* by George Eliot (904 pages) and *The Way we live Now* by Anthony Trollope (844 pages) and I feel as though I ran two marathons, uphill all the way. They are both fine books, but the stories evolve at such a stately pace that it's hard to remember the complicated plots and all the characters when the reading must be spread out over a period of weeks in the intervals between work and domestic chores. How wonderful it must have been to simply sit and read, knowing that dinner would be prepared, the carpets swept, and the children cared for without any effort on your part.

There have been some fine twentieth-century practitioners of the long, long novel – Tom Wolfe for example, and David Foster Wallace. You find their books abandoned in hotel lounges or discarded in yard sales and charity shops. You can see how someone might think such a book would be good for the long winter evenings. But how long could any evening be? Modern novelists are up against the scurrying realities of modern life when reading even a few pages is a victory against the odds.

Everyone loves a good story, but it needs to come to an end before we forget the plot. Sometimes one good story begets another, and another, and another, until we have that most satisfying of all fictional experiences known as a series. This form of the writer's art is still alive and well. We have a fine backlog of multi-volume tales from writers as various as Anthony Powell, P.G. Wodehouse, John Updike, and Georges Simenon, to say nothing of the Harry Potter series that surprised everyone by getting millions of children addicted to reading something longer than a hundred and forty characters. A series is addictive without being overwhelming. It allows us to enter a world of strangers, who don't remain strangers for long, and can be encountered again and again for a lifetime, with new discoveries to be made at every reading. Because we get to know the characters we can spread our reading over weeks or years without ever losing interest or forgetting the plot. They become friends, co-conspirators in our bid to escape our own mundane reality.

Finding a series of books that we love is like discovering a second life. The characters and settings become as real as those in our own lives, and perhaps more so. Every year I give myself the gift of the historical novels of Patrick O'Brian. If nothing disturbs my concentration I can just get through all seventeen books by the first day of January, then return to volume one. That's what I call a good long read.

ANNO DOMINO

I am tired of birthdays, and time, and its relentless habit of moving on, one second after another, until the next birthday arrives. Einstein believed that time was an illusion. All my old aunts clung to this theory. They celebrated birthdays until they were thirty-nine, and then they stayed at thirty-nine for the next several decades. But I have no faith in relativity. Time seems all too absolute to me.

I have been told, by some very senior seniors, that age used to command respect, although their memories may be playing tricks. Old people get less respect nowadays than old cars or old furniture, which at least may have monetary value. When did you last see an old person, however well-preserved, valued at tens of thousands of dollars in the Antiques Roadshow?

I have also heard that, in ancient times, old people were allowed to just relax and dodder about, taking naps and pursuing amusing hobbies. Confucius said:

Old age is a good and pleasant thing. It is true you are gently shouldered off the stage, but then you are given such a comfortable front seat as a spectator.

That's history too. Now we are expected to be eternally on-stage, eternally active, like the near-geriatric Rolling Stones, and adventurous like those octogenarians who climb Everest or sail alone around the world when they could and should be reading a good book in a well-padded rocking chair. Retirement has become just another name for career change. The only advantages of age that I can see are discounts (very occasional and very small) and Medicare, which is just a device, like a field hospital on a battlefield, for turning exhausted seniors around and sending them back into the fight.

Young and not-so-young readers may like to note the eight crucial signs of impending seniority. They have nothing to do with chronological age. If you are in a hurry you can start these behaviors at any time. They will start anyway, so you might as well get ahead of the game.

1. Walk with your hands behind your back. A stranger once stopped me on my walk and pointed this out. "That's a sign of age," he said, and he was right. Even before I qualified for Medicare my hands started drifting behind my back as if drawn by invisible strings. Observation shows that I'm not the only one.
2. Schedule your life around doctor visits, and discuss your schedule and complaints with other patients in the waiting room.
3. Read the obituaries, and then forget them.
4. Read the small print in pharmaceuticals ads, even if you don't take that medication, yet
5. Lose things, especially reading glasses, names, and bright ideas
6. Take a certain misanthropic pleasure in meeting people who are younger than you, but in worse shape.

7. Fall over for no special reason. My old cat does it all the time, so I can't be far behind.
8. Finally, get in touch with the curmudgeonly side of your personality – everybody has one. Complain about old age and modern life, the ungrateful younger generation, and everything. It's the only real compensation for the cruel joke of time.

When you look ahead to your Golden Years and ask: "Am I there yet?' just refer to my handy check list of senior life. Personally, I prefer not to think about it.

Theme III

BEING MODERN

Progress might have been alright once, but it has gone on too long.

OGDEN NASH

Progress means bad things happen faster.

TERRY PRATCHETT

A TECHNOLOGICAL *COUP D'ÉTAT*

Those of us who were born before 1940 have seen a lot of changes. We arrived on the scene before television, before penicillin, polio shots, frozen foods, Xerox, contact lenses, videos, and the pill. We were here before radar, credit cards, split atoms, laser beams and ballpoint pens, before dishwashers, tumble dryers, electric blankets, domestic air conditioning, drip-dry clothes, and before anyone seriously thought of going to the moon.

We got married first and then lived together (how old-fashioned can you be?) We thought Fast Food was what you ate in Lent, and that a Big Mac was an oversized raincoat. We existed before house husbands or computer dating, day care centers, group homes or disposable cameras. We never heard of FM radios, CDs, artificial hearts, word processors, or young men wearing earrings. For us a "chip" was a piece of wood, or a fried potato, "hardware" meant nuts and bolts, and "software" wasn't even a word.

Who would have thought, even twenty years ago, that television would come down the wire and the telephone would be wireless? Who could have predicted students who don't study, accountants who don't account, or scientists who cheat on their experiments? Who could ever have predicted that young people would not always be clean, respectful, moral and hard-working, the way we were?

We've had to absorb all these changes without the option of saying "no." Change is supposed to be good, change is supposed to be progress, in the way of which nobody is allowed to stand. That's the way human beings are: we work on something until it is perfect, and then continue to "improve" it until it's not perfect any more. Classical music was perfect, for example, about 1855 the date of Brahms's First Symphony. The novel reached its height in 1927 with Proust's Remembrance of Things Past. In my opinion, cars reached perfection in 1965 with that year's Aston Martin DB6. We just can't leave good things alone.

The manual typewriter was perfect in 1939. When I was about twelve years old my mother gave me an old Underwood model from that year. Believe it or not, I still have that typewriter, I still use it, and it has never crashed or lost any data. My data is always right there, on the roller.

But despite all the changes we were a fortunate generation. We had the luck to miss the First World War, to be too young for combat in the Second, and to grow up in the decades of peace and rising wages. We benefited from a mighty surge of scientific and technological discoveries, including new medical treatments that allowed us to live longer and (with chemical help) more cheerfully.

But history played a sad trick on us. Computers came crashing into our lives in the 1980s. We tend to forget how extraordinarily recent personal computers are. We already imagine that we can't live without them, but we did until 1981 when the first true PC was put on the market by IBM. Thirty years later these aggravating machines have infiltrated everything from medicine to grocery shopping to personal privacy, without planning and without resistance, like a science fiction nightmare come to life. "Virus" is the exactly right word to describe this invasion. We can identify it, but we can't cure it.

Kids launched into the new cyber-world with glee, and apparently without any need of learning, as if the computer was a natural part of their brains that had been lost, and now was found. Those of us who were already middle aged or older struggled, complained, and finally surrendered to the inevitable. The computer I am using now is one of five that I own. I don't like any of them, and they don't like me. But my work and my life are inextricably tied up in these pesky gadgets, and I don't see a prospect (short of death, the final logout) of ever breaking free.

Age brings wisdom to some of us, if we're paying attention. But *knowledge* is something else. Dealing with a family crisis takes wisdom. But when your computer screen goes blank, no amount of wisdom will help. You can be as wise as Solomon, and the screen will stay blank. We need knowledge, and sometimes it seems that we have less and less useful knowledge as we get older. We learn something and, before we know it our knowledge is out of date and any ten-year old kid knows more. I used to know how to fix cars, tape recorders, radios – but not any longer. Seniors are eternal freshmen in the world of high technology. The only consolation is that exactly the same thing will happen to today's smug kids, and probably even faster. They will have to start asking *their* kids.

Since those early days, the electronic revolution has engulfed us entirely. There are about seven billion smartphones in the world, and nobody ever seems to switch them off. The so-called social media have transformed and degraded the business of news and the racket of politics, and cyber warfare has become a reality. There are critics and unbelievers, of whom I am one. But we have about as much influence as atheists in the Catholic church in the fifteenth century. Computers in their many forms are now the official gods of the world religion of modernity. Like the gods of the ancient world they are eager to extend their powers over everything and, also like the gods of the ancient world, they don't care in the slightest what happens to us in the process.

THE GHOST IN THE MACHINE

I always enjoyed machines because I understood them. My childhood hobby was dismantling any machine I could get my hands on, although my talent at putting things together again was less well developed. Sometimes I would apply my screwdriver to household items like the iron or the gramophone, with disastrous results, or I would buy army surplus items from a store down the road – small generators, field telephones or gear systems. My goal was to understand everything by taking it apart. It was just as well I didn't go into medicine as my mother wanted, although I might have made a good pathologist. As my confidence grew I began to make my own machines by combining parts of others. One I particularly remember was an elaborate time machine that I built when I was about eight, hoping to use it to travel ahead in time and therefore to short circuit the tedious business of growing up. In the event I short circuited the electrical system and got a nasty shock. To my great disappointment I had failed to project myself into the future, and was still only eight years old. Also, I was in serious trouble with my father, who had to repair every fuse in the house.

Later I acquired motor cycles, and eventually cars to work on, and began to learn some real mechanical skills. Then, in the 1980s, the great electronic curtain came down and everything became a black box, untouchable and incomprehensible. It must have been much the same for grooms and coachmen when the horseless carriage was invented – their competence simply vanished along with their ontological security. I am rather glad to have lived at a time when I could fix my own car, develop my own photographs, type my own letters without finding an electrical outlet, and even build a simple radio set. But my sense of competence didn't last beyond middle age. This battle of the generations has been decisively won by those born after 1980.

It is an utter waste of time to grumble about the baleful effects of progress, but everybody does it and I don't want to be left out. Technological progress is the closest thing we have to the "Life Force" promoted by Bernard Shaw and others in the early 1900s. It is more powerful than we are and it is unstoppable, no matter how much we would prefer to stop it. We don't like to cope with too many new things too fast, and the past two centuries have given us more new things to absorb than all previous centuries combined. It has been a mixed bag: steam power and internal combustion, electricity, flight, antibiotics and anesthetics, radio, film and television, and now computers. The latest thing always seems the most dramatic and dangerous because we understand it the least, and that's where we are now with the so-called information revolution. Older folks like me have many ironic things to say about the excesses of computer technology and its hypnotized consumers, even as we use the stuff ourselves. But we have reached our level of incompetence and hate to admit it. Scientists can pick up signals from the Voyager space craft four billion miles away, but on some days I can't get my e-mail to pick up messages from across the street.

There's a reason why the bestselling line of instruction books for computers is called *For Dummies*. Most of us have no idea what goes on behind those cute icons on the screen. Their secrets are as secure from the casual user as those of the CIA or the Vatican Curia. A few adepts know the secrets, of course. The vanity of those who are computer literate is boundless, and to some extent justified. But because they are so few the whole web has begun to feel and operate like one of those ancient conspiracies – the Illuminati perhaps – who were believed to use their secret knowledge to control the world.

Every generation deserves a slice of good luck. My own age group was born into a period of relative peace and prosperity, while those who immediately followed benefitted from the sexual revolution and the abolition of child discipline. But the impact of what we might call the Silicon Valley generation looks like being more profound by far. Not only have they created an entirely new kind of elite, with incalculable fortunes based on technological knowledge and access to information, but they have literally changed the way the world works.

This makes the tech-savvy younger generation very annoying. Young people have been annoying from the very earliest times, when the first generation of *homo* sapiens grumbled that the second generation had no respect for its parents, couldn't sharpen a stone ax properly, and had no idea how to cook a dinosaur, let alone how to wash up afterwards. More than two thousand years ago Plato, quoting Socrates, wrote:

> *"Our youth now love luxury. They have bad manners, contempt for authority; they show disrespect for their elders and love chatter in place of exercise; they no longer rise when elders enter the room; they contradict their parents, chatter before company; gobble up their food and tyrannize their teachers."*

Things were never what they used to be, and we are all deeply attached to the world and the culture we were born into. Every big change seems like an historic catastrophe, and the past will always seem to be lost from one generation to the next.

But perhaps computers have shifted the generation gap to a new level. They have made thoughtless consumerism practically a duty, promoted political manipulation and disinformation on a scale the old Soviet leaders could only have dreamed of, created super-fast and out-of-control financial markets, and weapons that allow us to wage war by remote control. Their clever algorithms choose which movies we watch and which books we read. This is the first rumbling of a digital earthquake that will make most human skills and occupations redundant by the end of the century.

Multiple studies have found that time spent online strongly correlated with loneliness. Social media may make it worse. Computer addiction is a big issue, and the poisonous effects of violent video games are well documented. Computers haven't abolished drudgery, and certainly not paper which multiplies insanely as we print everything for fear of losing it. However, they have almost abolished the need for memory. Every trivial question is instantly checked out on a smartphone. We are in a conspiracy against ourselves, the essence of which is that we accept technology as fate, and convenience as the next best thing to happiness.

None of these trends is brand new, but the computer revolution has put them into overdrive. The internet is the ultimate greedy institution, offering expensive and opaque ways to do simple things like keeping appointments, balancing a check book, or buying a real book. We are headed for a future where we will work online at home, receive our salaries electronically (and have them paid out again automatically to cover the connection charges), and spend what is left online. No actual living will be necessary.

The internet is also having a devastating impact on literacy and learning, as any teacher will tell you. Even in university students are no longer expected to read whole books or articles: fragments are posted on special websites, so it's not even necessary for them to get out of bed and go to the library. In 2005 the University of Texas at Austin was reported to be getting rid of its books and installing "information centers." But there is a huge difference between browsing a library and calling up data on a screen, which is unlikely to lead to anything new.

The internet is not an infinite realm, let alone a magical one as some users seem to believe. A few years ago, it was estimated that the whole worldwide web would fit on five thousand high-capacity disks which would fit into a closet. I can never quite forget that closet full of disks. It is all too finite and offers a claustrophobic kind of freedom, and even more limited by the fact that almost everything in it is geared to sales and commerce. The internet is one huge advertisement for itself. My guess is that, unless and until it crashes and evaporates for technical reasons, rolling back this particular example of progress will prove to be the most thoroughly lost of all lost causes.

FROM HARDWARE TO SOFTWARE

My father had a talent for do-it-yourself home repair, and I inherited fifty percent of it. Like him, I instantly notice when something goes wrong in the house. Like him, I can usually figure out exactly what needs to be done. Unlike him, I almost never get around to actually doing it.

But sometimes I have pretended to try, and my first stop was always the local hardware store. Hardware stores were staffed by competent men, like the heroic surgeons in TV dramas, who would calm my fears and save me from the horrors of domestic decay. Of course, this screen door can be saved, they would say. Certainly, the old cistern can be nursed back to life. And no, the laundry machine doesn't need a quadruple bypass, just this small plastic washer. The traditional hardware store was like an old-style doctor's office, where ageing suburban homes could be diagnosed and the correct medicine prescribed. Do you have one of those things that closes the drain in the hand basin? Is there a way to stop bugs coming in around the edge of the air conditioner? Every problem had a solution.

In hardware as in health, the right advice at the right moment can save us from something much worse. If I had taken the advice of the hardware store man, I wouldn't have spent a week cleaning up after the last flood in the basement. If I had paid attention and replaced the lock on the garage when he told me, I might never have been trapped in there one winter day with the outdoor cats and no heat. On other occasions I could have avoided a painful electric shock from the outdoor lights, and having the bird feeder fall on my head.

The old-style hardware store is going the way of the friendly local doctor's office. The giant warehouses that have replaced them are more like HMOs - cheap, but totally impersonal, and you never get to see the same hardware person twice.

The traditional hardware store was a place of magic and mystery. It smelled of linseed oil, varnish, and exotic chemicals. The narrow aisles were stacked with boxes, containing heaps of free range nails, screws, bolts and nameless gizmos in all sizes, odd-shaped pieces of plumbing, electrical sockets, switches and connectors - whole houses deconstructed and reduced to their component parts. Along the walls were serious tools: big drills, heavy hammers, wrenches and saws that had "Real Man" written all over them, not like the toy tools you find wrapped in plastic at the home improvement warehouse.

An old-fashioned hardware store was as masculine as a lingerie store was feminine. Members of the opposite sex came in warily, not knowing what to ask for or how it would fit. Now women have been liberated into new forms of domestic slavery like home repair. hardware boutiques and superstores flourish, patronized by incompetent males and un-confident females, and nothing gets done.

One day, my local hardware store vanished, transformed into a video store. I drove a few miles to the next, which had metamorphosed into a French restaurant. Inevitably, I ended up at the home improvement warehouse out on the highway, where I spent twice as much time finding my few items, and got no advice whatsoever. These places are a hollow mockery of the true hardware emporium. Who needs screws and nails bubble-wrapped in hygienic little boxes? It's as bad as a supermarket. If things go on like this, suburban children won't know where screws and nails come from any more.

These elaborately bubble wrapped gizmos are discouraging. They look good on the shelves but, once their protective plastic is violated, they are revealed as pathetic and useless. Unopened, they can stay in the garage forever, causing no more guilt than a can of beans. But you can't ignore a pile of 2" No 8 screws, bought for the specific job of replacing the draft excluder on the front door. It's like the difference between a romance novel and a plunge into a singles bar.

The traditional hardware store was one of those vanishing social spaces, where you could listen to other people's crazy questions, and even join in the guessing game of answering them. The purchase of half a pound of nails could involve a conversation, a battle of wits, some jokes, and a sports commentary. But this is nothing compared to the time you can waste wandering up and down the aisles of the superstore, trying to find a live human being who is articulate in some recognizable language.

Many young suburban males are not comfortable in hardware stores. Their interests have drifted from hardware to software, and they don't know one end of a drain-cleaning rod from another. Like me they have forgotten the useful skills of their fathers, such as pretending to fix leaks in the roof and pretending to re-hang the door. So, the few surviving hardware stores languish for lack of customers, and the entire old housing stock is visibly collapsing around us. The reason why big ugly developments are swallowing up the last acres of open land is that men can't fix their old houses, and they can't admit this to their wives, so they move to new houses. We can only guess what will happen when the new houses start falling apart.

INTERMEDIATE TECHNOLOGY

For writers of a certain age, the most nostalgic sound in the world is the irregular clatter of an old manual typewriter, being used by somebody who can't type. I have a bunch of typewriters, fully-functioning antiques that provide a reassuring link to the past. My favorite machine is a Royal, manufactured about 1949. I got it in a garage sale ten years ago, and have used it almost every day since.

The reign of the manual typewriter was quite short. The first crude machines appeared in offices in the 1870s, and the first electric typewriters in 1935. By the 1980s, typewriters were history. For my generation, though, the clack of a typewriter was and is the very sound of romance. In movies or radio dramas, the appearance of a brilliant writer or a heroic journalist was always signaled by this very sound.

It was important that these characters couldn't type. They were hacking out the words painfully, letter by letter, so that you could *hear* great writing being committed. There's nothing romantic about high-speed typing. Earlier generations of writers composed in near-silence. Most of the great literature of the world emerged from under a scratching pen. When the typewriter appeared, many writers condemned it as a barbaric device that would probably usher in the end of civilization, and certainly the end of literature. But those of us who grew up with typewriters never missed the romance of the fountain pen. The clumsy machine was like a superior alter ego, turning our awkward phrases and spidery calligraphy into real *writing*.

My first typewriter came into my life quite unexpectedly when I was fourteen. It was donated by my mother's employer, the benevolent proprietor of a chain of London pubs, who had heard that I wanted to be a writer and made this gift, presumably out of sympathy. It was an Underwood, manufactured sometime in the late 1920s, and retired after a long, hard life in the office, but built like a tank.

For years I wrote everything on it and its more streamlined successors: reports, letters, stories, books, theses. My first wife god bless her was a great believer in hard work. In the evenings, she liked to hear the sound of typing from my room. But sometimes I preferred to relax, read, or take a nap. So, I recorded a cassette tape of an energetic typing session, which ran for an hour and a half, and I played that every evening until she caught me. That trick would never work with a computer.

I never learned to type properly. As a very young journalist, I found that good typing was not admired. It was not, as we would now say, cool. Journalists were not supposed to be stenographers, we just got it down with two flying index fingers helped by the occasional thumb on the space bar and adventurous stabs with the other digits. On a good day, before the pubs opened, I could manage sixty words a minute. Not all those words were in the Oxford English dictionary, of course.

Considered simply as a writing machine, the manual typewriter has many advantages over the computer. It allows us to pause and think, for hours if necessary, in absolute silence, without humming at us or suddenly flashing up a screen saver as a guilty reminder of idleness. A manual typewriter, like a good friend, knows the value of quietness. It slows us down and, in those long pauses, grammar and spelling, structure and style can be considered. They *must* be considered, because it's so tedious to fix mistakes. When we are ready to start work again there's a palpable sense of drama and action. The burst of noise says: something's happening.

A manual typewriter is more or less cat-proof. I've had alarming things happen to my computer because of cats walking over the keyboard or playing with the mouse. And, although I can't prove this, I swear that nobody could write such nonsense on a manual typewriter as is routinely churned out on word processors.

Somewhere along the way, I lost the original Underwood, but I found its twin in another garage sale. Five other manual typewriters are lurking in the basement. I was more than ready for the Year 2000 computer crash, but it never happened. I've not given up hope. When Armageddon finally comes, I'm sure that the old Underwood will survive. I like to think that it will be the only machine on the planet in a condition to take down my comments on the interesting period immediately afterwards.

NEW AND IMPROVED

Whenever any product or service is advertised as "New and Improved," the truth is almost invariably the exact opposite. There's even a name for this in England: Hutber's Law, which states succinctly that improvement equals deterioration. Even the geekiest geek quails at the prospect of a new and improved computer operating system. He knows it will take months to get back to where he was before with the old, unimproved software, at which time another improvement will already be on the horizon.

The most common improvements we see these days involve the replacement of human beings by computers. The humorously named "customer service lines," where at least you could yell at somebody, are replaced by incomprehensible and labyrinthine web sites were the FAQs never include *your* question, and the "contact us" feature should be called "contact them," because they *never* contact us. Human beings in general are being improved out of existence, or at least out of work. We swipe our own cards and pump our own gas, check out our own groceries using machines with annoyingly unctuous mechanical voices. A few years ago, this was a nightmare future conjured up by science fiction writers: now it's here.

This process of backward improvement has been going on for a long time. When my family first had a telephone at home we just picked up the receiver and asked for the number. If we didn't know it the operator would find it for us. Now a simple phone call involves an expensive and fragile gadget the size of a matchbox with about a hundred tiny buttons and an instruction book the size of a club sandwich. If you ever do get through to anybody, it is like a buzzing, echoing conversation from outer space. And anyone who thinks that the experience of long-distance travel has improved lately has obviously not gone beyond the end of the street for twenty or thirty years.

It's not just in the high-tech world that we find this kind of backward progress. Simple kitchen implements like corkscrews and can openers have been dis-improved regularly for years, so that a really state of the art gadget can be almost impossible to figure out without a degree in engineering. We have an ultra-modern, elegant kitchen towel dispenser. It takes two hands to operate it, and the paper often rips, or the whole thing comes unstuck from the counter. So, I usually leave the paper roll just standing there. It's not elegant, but it works.

Nothing is immune from Hutber's Law. Things that were marvelous just because they were mysterious are "improved" until they become dull and ordinary: The King James Bible and the Latin Mass are two obvious examples. High definition TV has allowed us to see in excruciating detail just how bad television is. Musicians can't resist improving on transcendent composers like Beethoven by adapting his symphonies for the didgeridoo or the steel drums. No film maker or operatic director can resist re-making and ruining a classic.

The Luddites never got the credit they deserved. We have swallowed the idiotic trope that newer equals better, and it serves us right.

STAND BY, TURN OFF, RESTART

An annual event in America, less regarded but perhaps more informative than The State of the Union Address, is National Screen Free Week in April. This could be an extremely difficult and challenging time for computer addicts, but it isn't, for the simple reason that nobody pays the slightest attention. National Screen Free Week is one of those publicity stunts, like National Inventors' Month, National Immunization Month, National Toddlers' Month, and National Breastfeeding Week – all of which start on the same date.

National Screen Free Week began originally as National PC-Turnoff Week when a few people over fifty still remembered what a PC was. It was, of course, a Personal Computer, the kind most of us had and still have at home in the form of a laptop, a tablet, or a smartphone. Banks and government organizations have *im*personal Computers, which are larger, more powerful, and much nastier. Those keep running 24/7, no matter what. But once a year we are encouraged to switch off our home computers, and more importantly our children's computers, for seven whole days.

You can see the problem. The computer in all its forms is not just a gadget, like a popcorn popper. It has become *the* indispensable household tool. The computer has absorbed the functions of the television, the toy box, the bookshelf, the telephone, the post office, and (dare I say) the church into a single, bland, plastic box. We can no more switch it off that we can switch ourselves off – indeed, for some addicts, the second option would be easier than the first.

I came late and unwillingly to computers. Like a primitive tribesman presented with a radio, I assumed that they must have been created by a kind of dark magic. But they are addictive just the same. Little by little my whole world has squeezed down so that it fits on to a small screen. My friends and colleagues, my writing, my research, and my hobbies are all lurking in there somewhere. I don't play video games, but that's only because my reflexes are too slow and I have cats to play with instead.

How much more engrossing computers and smartphones must be for kids who grew up with them. They've never had to struggle with clumsy books or board games, or walk down the street to talk to their friends, or play outside on the hard ground under the hot sun. Childhood has been put online, where it is less strenuous, quieter, and very much less dangerous.

I thought I had seen everything until I saw a tiny toddler being wheeled along in a stroller with a video screen attached to the shelf in from of his/her face. The screen was playing cartoons heavily loaded with commercials. The child ignored all the distractions of the busy street, including the parents, and the parents ignored the child. Complete mutual isolation had been achieved.

Now the activists of Screen Free Week want to take it all away for a whole week, forcing kids to go outdoors in the unhealthy fresh air, and indulge in a list of "fun" activities that are listed (guess where) on the web site. These include such anachronistic pastimes as making a scrapbook, having a picnic, writing a letter, and taking a walk. If these don't convince kids that their smartphone is essential to life, I don't know what will.

The most interesting proposal made by the Screen Free organizers is: "Give your kids the gift of boredom." I think they are on to something here. Boredom is an essential life skill for young people, who will need to survive a lifetime of boring schools followed by boring jobs. Boredom will give them time to think, to get a better perspective on themselves, and maybe even to be more creative. Boredom teaches how to be alone, and solitude is an almost forgotten art.

On the other hand, boredom proverbially leads to mischief. We have a lot of computer-addicted children in the neighborhood. If I believed that Screen Free week really was going to happen, I would be worried about vandalism by little internet-deprived troublemakers. But it won't happen, not in our suburban street. Every home and garden is saturated with high-speed wi-fi connections. We might as well put a voluntary ban on breathing.

SPAMMED OUT

It's a great shame that the name of the wonderful pink luncheon meat, Spam, has become so sadly degraded. Real Spam is the food of the gods. Electronic Spam comes from the other place.

Last Monday, when I checked my e-mail after the weekend, I had 102 messages. Normally I just delete those with meaningless or teasing subject lines. But this time I stopped to look at each one, to see why I am so popular.

They broke down as follows: just about half of the total were promotions for pornographic web sites of one kind or another; twenty-three were for Viagra; fourteen were for other medications including Prozac, Valium, and Zoloft; and seven were for personal services unmentionable on public radio. If this is a portrait of the needs of American manhood it's a pretty pathetic one.

Just for variety I had two messages from Nigerian gentlemen who promised to make me rich, one from something called the Christian Coalition, and two that warned me that the British have abandoned themselves to Satan. But that's old news. Buried in this avalanche of sleaze, profiteering and madness were two messages related to work, and two from personal friends.

What have I done to deserve this? Who said I needed Viagra, or Prozac, or pornography? Has my age triggered some geriatric exploitation program in the depths of the internet? It's depressing and time wasting, and it's beginning to make e-mail not worth using. Just when you think you have cleared all the junk away you get a pop up message advertising a program to get rid of pop up messages.

The simple solution would be to get rid of e-mail. But it has wormed its way into our lives in more ways than one. Sending messages written on paper would seem eccentric at best and subversive at worst – and of course you could never hope to get a reply.

Young people are, as usual, ahead of the rest of us in solving this problem. They have long ago switched over to instant messaging, which bypasses the spam problem because it is a person-to-person connection. Like most people of my age I am naïve about instant messaging but I have often observed young people intent on a small window in the center of the computer screen, typing like mad, pausing, and typing again.

Well, I have looked into it and I find that instant messaging is a way of talking to one's friends – not necessarily friends who are far away, but friends who may be in the next room. It seems that conversing face-to-face has become incredibly retro. If young people do happen to meet in person they must rush off in opposite directions and each find a computer so that the conversation can commence.

This is because you can't *speak* the language of instant messaging, not least because it seems to consist mostly of vowels. Words and phrases have been stripped down to a kind of shorthand. "BRB" means be right back; "HW" means homework, obviously not being done at the moment; "TTYL" means talk to you later, and so on. There are also "visual signals" that can be inserted into these messages, but I didn't enquire too closely into them.

This system clearly has many advantages. It saves a lot of keystrokes, and grammar and punctuation simply vanish. Also, I'm told that it saves a lot of embarrassment. It is the language of flirtation and gossip in schools and offices everywhere, and only the initiates can read the code.

I was talking to a student who was doing this, in the intervals of playing a game on another computer and talking on her cell phone. She was happy to explain.

"I'm just talking to my friends," she said. I asked where these friends were, thinking they might be Peace Corps volunteers in Croatia or Afghanistan. "They're right here, on campus," she said. "Why don't you just talk to them in person?" I asked. This was met with a look of such utter blankness that I felt embarrassed. Talking to your friends face to face is, apparently, seriously odd, verging on perverse. I asked another silly question: "Can you convey abstract ideas, such as 'Man is born free but everywhere he is in chains'?" She raised her eyebrows and went back to typing something that looked like GRK PLS BOR NAF. The answer seemed to be no.

So, I'm not convinced that instant messaging is an entirely satisfactory substitute for the language of Shakespeare. I spent some time trying to render Hamlet's soliloquy into an instant message. The first line was easy, but after that I got stuck. If it comes down to a choice between using this impoverished language and deleting fifty Viagra ads every day I will get out the old typewriter and take my communications business back to the U.S. Post Office.

JK (Just kidding)

VIRUS ALERT

I picked up one of those nasty viruses that seem to come out of nowhere and make your life miserable for a week or two. I was sniffing and sneezing in front of the computer screen when the phone rang and a well-known voice from the radio station said "You've got a virus."

"I know," I said, "It's nice of you to be concerned."

"Your *computer* has a virus," said the voice unsympathetically. "You've sent it to us. Switch the thing off."

I switched the thing off, resisting the temptation to spread the disease to some of my least favorite people and institutions. Not without a sense of relief, I turned to my forty-year old manual typewriter and the wired telephone, both of which were virus-free and working perfectly.

But I wasn't allowed to get away with this low-tech efficiency for long. I was urged on all sides to do something about my toxic computer, although I protested that the virus would probably go away by itself in about ten days. Mine always do.

I'll spare you the details of the recovery process. I was forced to get some new anti-virus software and wait ages while it scanned through 42,000 files (42,000, can you believe it?). It identified fifteen different viruses, and eventually removed them. A lot of my e-mail vanished in the process, which was a bonus.

The next time I switched on the computer, the very first thing that appeared on the screen was the message: **VIRUS ALERT: IMMEDIATE ACTION REQUIRED.** This was the so-called NIMDA virus, and my brand new anti-virus software was powerless against it. I was told to download a "patch" whatever that is, from Microsoft, whoever they are, but the instructions for doing this were three pages long and, to me, utterly incomprehensible. I've decided just to live with NIMDA, like a persistent hacking cough.

Scarcely a day passes without a real or fake virus alert, passed on by credulous friends or even by some semi-serious organization like the phone company. It's no mystery who is responsible. There's a long tradition in America of boys smashing mailboxes, and this is the modern equivalent. As in the old days, the culprits are mainly young men with a bad attitude and time on their hands. A few of the viruses do come from abroad, but most of them are home made in some teenager's suburban bedroom.

I don't know about you, but I don't find this very amusing. It is simply vandalism, although there must be some skill in it. I wouldn't know how to create a computer virus, and I think we should be concerned that so much talent is being wasted. In a time of national decline and uncertainty, these kids can find nothing better to do than smash electronic mailboxes. So, I have a modest proposal. The modern, high-tech military can use their talents. When they are identified, these young hackers should simply be drafted and sent to the center of the action, carrying armor plated laptops. Their mission would to be create confusion and chaos in the enemy's e-mail, assuming he has any. The young nerds will also encounter some really interesting viruses out there, the kind that attack more than their hard drive.

With luck, the electronic vandals would return from military service matured and changed for the better. For the first time, they would deserve the thanks of their country. Some of them, like my vanished e-mail, might never be seen again.

RESET PASSWORD

Like most people I start my working day by avoiding work. Instead I read my e-mail, and then delete it. Or I just delete it, which saves time. But the e-mail program demands a password, and the other day my mind went blank so I had to do something useful instead. The secret code came back to me in time but I worried that this was the proverbial first straw in the coming hurricane of forgetfulness.

The experts who concern themselves computer security insist that we should have different passwords for different things, change them fre-quently, and not write them down. They must be meaningless strings of numbers and letters, or they will be too easy to crack. If you use your cat's name, for example, evil criminals may capture your cat in the street and torture him until he reveals it. Passwords must be obscure to be secure.

That's all very well for those whose brains are young, un-cluttered and efficient. But that condition doesn't last long. It occurred to me, as I stared at the blank password box that, quite soon, all sixty million baby boom-ers will forget their passwords. I'm a generation ahead of them, and I can guarantee it. My passwords are vanishing into the mist already.

This will be much more serious than the Y2K problem that was false-ly predicted in the year 2000. We need passwords for everything: cell phones, e-mail, the wireless connection, data storage, every web company and service we have to deal with, on line banking, on-line shopping, on-line bill paying, and just about everything. Even the house security system demands a password, and I live here! Once we start forgetting these passwords our lives will shrink, piece by piece, until we are reduced to the pathetic state of folks in the 1970s, who didn't have any passwords. It's hard to imagine how we lived without them. Imagine just reading your mail or checking your bank balance without a password.

The web companies have accommodated the frailty of human memory in a minimal way, by offering a little button near the password box that says: "Forgot your password?" There is something condescending and critical about this, like your old school teacher saying: "Forgot your homework?" If you click on this icon it usually presents you with another memory test, like your grandmother's maiden name or your parakeet's birthday. If you can't remember the password, you certainly can't remember these. You are stuck, and have no choice but to join the line of several thousand other senior citizens who are on hold, trying to call Bombay and reset their passwords.

My habit is to make passwords out of objects in the immediate vicinity of the computer, so I can look around for inspiration. But I still must remember which object: is it the jade plant today, or the wireless router, or the model number of the printer, or the stone owl that sits on the desk? It's anybody's guess, really, and often you are allowed only three guesses before the site blocks you out. In a fair and just society seniors would be allowed more guesses according to age. I would like at least ten.

This password culture suggests that nobody trusts anybody about anything. I'm sure it contributes to the universal paranoia. Before we were all caught in the World Wide Web, less than thirty years ago, only spies like James Bond, and master criminals like Professor Moriarty needed codes and passwords, because they had so much to hide. Now, it seems, all of us have everything to hide: so many secrets safely hidden behind so many passwords, if only we can remember what they are.

DEATH ON THE SMALL SCREEN

The internet is loaded with violent language: Ram Force, Mega Power, Virus Smasher, and so on. There's little that is gentle or beautiful, and nothing at all that is thoughtful or reflective. Right down at the lowest level, where culture shades into barbarism, we find video games.

I confess that I know nothing about videogames except what I hear and read, but that has never stopped me from offering an opinion. Priests make a career out of condemning sins in which (we hope) they have never participated. Some perfectly charming and intelligent people I know play video games. Have I misjudged their character, or their hobby?

Two things make me hesitate. The first is the torrent of articles, books and TV interviews featuring people who really *do* know what they are talking about, who state categorically that most of these games are phenomenally nasty, violent, anti-social, and sick, and who worry seriously about their effect on players of any age. Video-addicted adolescents have already committed occasional acts of mass violence, and there will be more. There seems no doubt that the anonymous anarchy of the internet brings out the worst in some people, on social networks as well as in video games.

The second thing that inclined me to the anti-game camp was a visit to a video game store in suburban Long Island, where I found indeed that most of the offerings (as described on their covers) were phenomenally nasty, violent, anti-social, and sick. I was offered the chance to play a game on one of the store's machines, and lasted about two minutes before I was briskly annihilated by rotting zombies from outer space.

Based on this limited information it does seem to me that "gaming" constitutes a kind of parallel universe or second life that offers an illusion of catharsis, especially to young boys who are always full of hateful and violent thoughts and intensely frustrated by the contrast between their favorite action movies and the tedium of suburban life. It is an adolescent masculine world, to the extent that in 2014 we were hearing reports of virulent hate campaigns against female gamers and game creators. Women, it seems, ruin the fantasy.

We all need to play, and we all need a bit of escapism from time to time, so perhaps the phenomenon is perfectly normal and healthy, a harmless substitute for real-life games of war and murder. The jury is still out, and probably playing video games in the jury room.

A DAY IN THE SECOND LIFE

The closest I ever came to playing a video game was a computer experiment I indulged in a few years ago. It wasn't exactly a game, but it was the closest I had ever come to living online. I wanted to find out how far computer graphics could create the sense of escaping into a different world and a different identity

Until a few years ago the only way to obtain a complete new identity was to be placed in the Federal Witness Protection Program. But then along came a computer game called "Second Life" (now part of ancient history) and we were offered the power to create a whole new version of ourselves, and a new world to live in.

The publicity and hype surrounding "Second Life" became so intense that even I couldn't ignore it, so I loaded the thing into my computer. Over the years my computer and I have grown to resemble each other, like a man and his dog, and neither one of us takes kindly to novelties. We grumbled and beeped our way through the installation process, which included choosing an identity for my virtual alter ego, or Avatar. An Avatar is an incarnation or reflection of a person or a god. I decided that I wanted to be reincarnated onscreen as Professor Thorstein Veblen, a maverick Norwegian/American sociologist of the last century who had a good eye for absurdity and was very popular with the ladies. Veblen, I thought, would have an interesting time in the virtual world.

My next task was to create his onscreen appearance, which wasn't easy. In real life Professor Veblen was short, unprepossessing and unkempt. But these choices didn't seem to be on the computer menu. Reluctantly I was forced to make him taller, slimmer, younger, and much more attractive than Veblen or myself. Then I had to choose clothes for him, which was another puzzle. Veblen's clothes in real life were a mess and everything in the electronic wardrobe was smart and fashionable. So, I got him started with jeans and a t-shirt. You can customize the outward appearance of your Avatar in great detail. Many seem to be in a state of perpetual makeover, flickering in and out of their clothes. This seems perilously like playing with dolls.

At this stage, I ran into a real problem. I wanted my Second Self to be, above all, much *smarter* than me, as smart as Professor Veblen in fact, otherwise what would be the point? But no matter how I searched I could not find a way to improve his mind. Clothes, cars, toys and even land can be acquired in the virtual world, but apparently not intelligence or education.

There was nothing to be done but let Veblen loose as he was, and he appeared on my screen walking across a place called Orientation Island. There were a lot of women walking with him, all young and slim, and some very lightly clothed, and I encouraged Veblen approach them with the intention of discussing his social theories. But they seemed bored, and just walked away. I made him fly, hoping this would impress the ladies, then accidentally dropped him in the ocean. With apologies I fished him out, and left him sitting alone on the top of a cliff.

You could easily waste a whole day in Second Life, but I hadn't got any work done that morning, and nor had Veblen. I switched him off, feeling obscurely guilty, and left him sitting there disoriented on Orientation Island. I'm glad I visited my Second Life. It makes my First Life seem very rich and full indeed.

THE INCREDIBLE JOURNEY
The old laptop we were using in France was corrupted by anarchic Gallic computers on the local network, and went more or less permanently on strike. It is easy enough to buy a new computer in France, of course, but then we would have to cope with the keyboard which, in the European style, starts top left with AZE and ends bottom right with VBN. This deviation from the odd but familiar QWERTY arrangement is enough to drive a person mad. Personally, as a lifelong hunt-and-peck typist, I would much prefer keyboards to follow the alphabet from ABC to XYZ, so I would finally know where to find things and double my typing speed.

So, to keep a long and tedious story short, we delayed the purchase until we could make it during a visit home. Here we placed an order with an American manufacturer for an American laptop with a normal if not very logical keyboard, and waited.

The first surprise was an e-mail that said that our computer would be "built by February 16." In these bad economic times I had assumed that they must have hundreds of unsold computers sitting in boxes waiting to be shipped. But this message about building it suggested something even worse: they can't afford to keep any inventory at all, so they are making them one at a time when they get an order, like an old-fashioned craft workshop. Some highly trained, highly paid technician at corporate headquarters in California was assembling all the little bits and pieces – chips, drives and keys and so on – and gluing them together just for me. I felt both flattered and embarrassed, like a man who has ordered a bespoke suit but doesn't quite feel that he deserves it.

Punctually on the appointed day came another e-mail saying that the building of our laptop had been completed and that it was being shipped via a big express service whose name you know. There was a tracking code with which we could follow its progress from California to our home in the Long Island suburbs. I can never resist these things, so I started to check the progress of the package. Surprise! It wasn't coming from California at all, but from a place called Kushan, which turned out to be a city in South China. Next time I looked, a few hours later, it was in Shanghai, and the very same evening it had arrived in Anchorage Alaska, which seems to violate some fundamental laws of space and time. But we must assume that a bit of time travel is mere routine to these express delivery services.

By early next morning our frozen long-distance laptop had very sensibly migrated southwards, but overshot the mark and arrived in Newark New Jersey, where it languished for a while, presumably enjoying the scenery. A couple of days later it was delivered to our doorstep by a young man who, considering how far he had come, looked quite fresh and cheerful. When I slid the laptop out of its box it brought with it the chill of Alaska, and perhaps just the faintest whiff of Kushan soy sauce.

This is one of those moments when globalization becomes real, and not just an abstract word. To have our modest laptop built and shipped all the way from the far side of the planet, at the cost of who knows how much carbon debit, literally brought the global madness home. And it's just one stage in a continuing process. As wages rise in Kushan we will find that our stuff is being made in Ethiopia or Somalia, or wherever labor is cheap and unemployment is high. But here's the good news: eventually, the relentless logic of the market will bring all these jobs back home.

CELL MATES

Our old cell phone finally died. It was ancient as these things go, large and black and rather like a regular phone without a wire. I took it back to the phone store. The place had moved since I was last there, perhaps because of the shifting of the earth's tectonic plates over time. The young man stared at my phone with incredulous amusement and showed it to his senior colleague, the equipment service manager. "Have you ever seen one of these." "No" said the equipment service manager, shaking his head so hard that his earrings jangled. I refrained from saying that he was probably still in kindergarten when I got this beauty.

The phone had worked, at least I think it did. I used it so seldom that it might have been dead for years. My policy with cell phones is to keep them switched off. It saves the batteries, and you can almost always find a real phone when you need one. Also, I keep the number secret, which cuts down on incoming calls.

However, my phone was now so old that I qualified for a free replacement. Of course once I had accepted this they launched into their sales pitch, and I had a long battle to avoid all the "extra features" they were trying to sell me to improve my life: phones that allow you to call anywhere in the world, phones that allow you to call strange creatures from other planets (although no special equipment is necessary for that - you can just dial Washington on your regular phone), phones that browse the internet, and even phones that take pictures like a camera and allow you to send them. These are apparently very popular with young people, although I can't think why. Perhaps art students like to share particularly fine pieces of art they encounter in obscure galleries.

I finally escaped with the basic free phone, which the salesman clearly regarded as a defeat. In terms of size my free upgrade was more like a downgrade. The new phone was about a quarter the size of the old one, with buttons too small for my fingers and a rather striking bright blue screen covered in cabbalistic symbols. The manual was five times as big as the phone itself, and it will clearly take me years to figure out all the "features."

The manual told me that I should run the battery down to zero three times before the phone would be completely happy, which meant I had to switch it on. It was on for days and the battery showed no signs of running down. This was probably because nobody knew the number, so there were no calls.

When I finally made a call myself I discovered that, in spite of its formidably high-tech appearance, my new cell phone still sounds as if voices are coming from the bottom of a very deep well somewhere in Nebraska. The sound crackles and fades and vanishes, so I've adopted a conversational style first developed by my mother. She is very deaf, but politely pretends that she can hear what other people are talking about. In imitation of her I've taken to saying: "That's right" or "Very good" from time to time, or if I catch a negative tone "Don't worry" or "It will all sort itself out."

This seems to work, although it occurs to me that, in that echoing, electronic void, callers probably can't hear me either. It's interesting to speculate, now that these phones are so common, on the possible consequences of this dialogue of the deaf. One can imagine how a few missed or garbled words could destroy a relationship, or a business deal, or even a terrorist plot. The cell phone introduces an interesting element of ambiguity into the human comedy, and it's worth recalling that God threw down the original Tower of Babel and confused the languages of the world because too much mutual understanding would only lead to trouble (Genesis 11: 1-9). There may be more to this cell phone phenomenon than we thought.

IMAGINARY FIENDS

Every new communication technology has its critics. Plato believed that writing would lead to the death of memory, and he was right. No doubt the quill pen was denounced as an instrument of the devil when it was first invented. Typewriters were despised by authors like Bernard Shaw. The telephone, radio and television were all confidently expected to destroy civilized society. Computers have been universally vilified for making us slaves to e-mail and the Microsoft/Apple monster. But no communications gadget has attracted more sheer loathing than the cellular telephone and its even more anti-social offspring, the smartphone.

The use of wireless phones in emergencies is not what annoys most critics. It is rather their use *all the time* in situations that are not only not emergencies, but that are not worth talking about in any way whatsoever. It's not just noise pollution, it's trivia pollution. *This* is why we make the landscape hideous with microwave towers? The technical means are ludicrously out of proportion to the social ends, like using a stealth bomber to settle an argument in a schoolyard.

The mobile phone is not merely an annoyance in public places. It is an insidious, revolutionary device for abolishing solitude, silence, and thought. Being alone with our thoughts, painful as that can sometimes be, helps to develop individuality and internal independence. We all need solitude and quiet sometimes, especially creative and spiritual people, although I read that Franciscan monks in Assisi are being fitted with pockets in their habits to accommodate cell phones. So much for the contemplative life. A little solitude helps you to think for yourself, to know yourself better. The ability to connect to friends or family any time anywhere makes us much less like independent individuals than a single extended amoebic chattering creature. I talk, therefore I am.

When we are all instantly and intimately connected, life can have no surprises. Travelers don't arrive unexpectedly at your door after an absence of months and an uncertain journey, as they might have done in 1850. They arrive with multiple previews, like a new TV series, announced every step of the way by their own built-in publicity system: "Hello, we're at the airport." "Hello, we're just waiting for the baggage." Hello, we've picked up the car." "Hello, we've stopped for coffee on the Interstate." "Hello, we'll be there in half an hour" By the time they do arrive, we don't want to see them anymore.

Twentieth century novelists invented stream of consciousness writing, which demonstrated once and for all ninety-nine per cent of conscious thought is boring. If we say our thoughts out loud this becomes obvious. The result is not conversations, but the unedited static of disconnected brains that don't have anything to do.

This may be purely a generational thing, a different wiring of the mind. Young people seem able to use several communication channels at once. I came upon a student working at my radio station who was writing a term paper on a laptop. He also had another computer running with instant messages flying back and forth, a third computer for web pages, a regular phone, a cellular phone he was using for text messaging, and the radio was playing. "What we really need in here is a television," I said, as a joke, and he agreed.

Smartphones have been a huge success with the younger generation, even more so in Europe and Asia than here. Part of my reaction is sheer envy. How do they find so much to talk about? How do they get other people to listen to their stream of inane chatter, apparently for hours at a time? Somebody must be on the receiving end. How do they persuade anyone to call *them?*

Perhaps it is a symptom of the nervous anxiety that seems to define America in this century. Parents are fearful of some nameless threat, and so are children. The perpetual chatter of the social network becomes a psychic safety net. *The New York Times* reported that some college students stay in constant communication with their parents through cell phones and special 800 numbers. What kind of college experience is that?

You might as well have your mother living in the next room. Sometimes it feels as if the whole world is living in the next room. We have so many ways to communicate, that the temptation to do so is almost irresistible.

By slow stages, scarcely even noticing it, I too have become addicted to the clever technologies of communication. I have a wired phone, a simple cell phone (never switched on), an answering machine, a fax machine, two e-mail addresses, an internet connection, cable TV, a regular radio, and short-wave radio for foreign broadcasts. If I want to reach out and touch someone I can, at least electronically. If I want to know about anything from Caesar's Gallic Wars to the latest video game software, I have it at my fingertips. Some people have begun to collect data on themselves, attaching gadgets to their bodies that monitor heart, breathing, paces walked, calories absorbed and so on, in an ecstasy of technological narcissism. The e-mails pile up, with their daily surfeit of bad jokes, terrible prose, hysterical 'do it now' messages, fake medical miracles, fake virus alerts, and the hosts of imaginary friends generated by social and professional networking sites - friends without human contact, conversation, touches, hugs, or gifts.

While our attention is on the computer the voice mail is squirreling messages away, today's *New York Times* has about a hundred pages, and I can never finish the much bigger Sunday issue until Wednesday. The fourteen unread magazines in the rack add up to 1,245 pages, I counted them; the seven unread books by the bed total another 1,791 pages; and as for the list of books to be read one day, don't even ask. I have some student papers, and three long chapters of a textbook to read before tomorrow morning. The college mailbox adds a steady flow of memos, newsletters, and more textbooks. The US mail delivers heaps of catalogs, charity solicitations, and even the occasional real letter, written with a pen, from some old friend from back in the dark ages.

By the end of the century, or much sooner, we will have personal communications devices implanted into our aching heads at birth, with satellite uplinks, so that we can live in a mental whirl of a zillion web pages, entertainments, advertisements, games, and instant messages. The definition of a servant (or slave) was someone who could be summoned at any time. Now we are all servants, tied to our masters, spouses, children, creditors, sales people, and assorted con artists and criminals 24/7. Officials, like teachers and doctors are now wide open to communication from everybody, creating an impossible overload of demands, expectations, complaints and threats. Switching off is an almost aggressive act. We suffer a kind of Stockholm syndrome with our electronic devices. They are our jailers, we are their prisoners, and we have come to love them.

PROFESSORS IN THE CLOUD
One trend in higher education now is online teaching. Powerful new technologies mean that teachers and students no longer need to meet in boring old classrooms. They can communicate knowledge wholesale over the internet. Many colleges and universities, including Harvard and Stanford, are getting into the online teaching business by offering what are called MOOCS or Massive Open Online Courses.

These courses have audio, video and interactive elements, and virtually everything you would find in a real college classroom except living, thinking human beings. It seems like a rather impoverished substitute for an educational experience, to sit alone at a keyboard, remotely connected to a teacher who doesn't know you. But what is so excellent about these online courses is that many of them (so far) are free. Having benefited from a one hundred per cent free education myself, I wish everyone else could have the same opportunity. It is the most valuable thing a young person can get, and we should give it away for nothing. Half the world's problems are caused by ignorance and superstition (the other half are caused by greed and selfishness, but that's a dilemma without a technological solution).

There is a lot of idealism behind this open access movement. It builds on the theories of the philosopher Ivan Illich who argued in the 1970s that education should be taken out of the schools and colleges and put back in the hands of the learners themselves.

There are also a few snags. Student motivation and concentration are hard to guarantee when everyone in the virtual classroom is only a click away from his or her e-mail, or a video game. Accurate testing and evaluation are almost impossible. Above all, education has become a very big and profitable business, and free online courses are a threat to those profits. Socrates in his time got in trouble for wandering around Athens dispensing subversive wisdom at no charge – in fact the authorities had him executed. If he had set up a proper school with hefty tuition fees no doubt they would have treated him as a model citizen. The free distribution of information has never been popular with those in power.

Free and open education on the internet would turn society upside down in more ways than one. Only a very few superstar professors would need to be employed, and the rest of us, along with huge numbers of educational administrators and managers, would have to find new careers in the fast food industry. The institutions themselves – four thousand bricks and mortar colleges and universities – would become empty shells, because students would be following their courses at home, lying on the couch. College sports would become mere video games, binge drinking and bad fraternity behavior would be things of the past.

For those of us who care nothing for grades or credits, the pursuit of knowledge has never been easier, and that's good. However, it offers a dim prospect for the academic community, and for all the young people who plan to go to college and have a thoroughly good time. But they shouldn't worry. Quite apart from the institutions, the professors and the football coaches, millions of parents have an interest in stopping this move towards internet education. Parents of teenagers live for and dream about those four years when their dear offspring will leave home to pursue the intellectual life. However good and idealistic it seems, we just can't take that away from them.

HARD LABOR

For most American families Labor Day is not about the history of the American Trade Union movement, but that's what it *was* about for a hundred years. Labor Day was supposed to celebrate the dignity of labor, and now that tradition has faded. For several years in a row the traditional Labor Day march in New York was cancelled due to security concerns or lack of interest. It has been revived as a shadow of its former self, more like an all-purpose carnival. Only about one in ten Americans now belongs to a union. Who needs them anymore, when we have almost arrived in the automated future, when all the work of the world will be done by non-unionized robots?

We're not quite there yet. For years it seems we've been hearing reports of the golden age when computers will relieve us of all life's drudgery. For example, one report predicted that we will have fully automated kitchens, so that we can call home from work and order our evening meal to be prepared by smart machines.

Wait a minute, what's this about calling home *from work*? If these machines are so smart, why aren't *they* working, instead of fooling around in the kitchen? Computers and automation were supposed to create the leisure society, but the opposite has happened. Now we shop from work, as plenty of office workers do, visit the library and do research from work, carry on our personal relationships from work, and even order up house cleaning and gardening from work. Presumably we shall soon be able to take care of our children and cats from work, and even enjoy our vacations at work. There will be no need ever to leave the office. If we do make the mistake of coming home, the new technology allows us to continue working from there, and never ever to be disconnected from the demands of our masters. The Duke of Marlborough once said: "As for living, our servants can do that for us." If he were around today he might say: "Our computers can do that for us."

The irony is that we have the power already in our hands to abolish or enormously reduce most routine work. The professions - which, let's face it, are mostly mystification, repetition and sleight of hand - could easily be automated out of existence with today's technology. Banking and finance, most aspects of law and medicine and education, and all administration and politics could be managed much better by computers than by human beings, however highly paid.

At the beginning of the last century, when trade unions were flourishing, optimism about technology was at its height. Edward Bellamy's best-selling novel, *Looking Backwards,* published in 1887, predicted what life would be life in the twenty-first century. Top of the list of dramatic changes was: *no work.* People in our century, Bellamy predicted, would spend their lives in cultural and creative pursuits, and live joyfully with their families 24/7. Karl Marx predicted much the same thing. Even as late as the 1950s, science fiction writers were portraying a future age of leisure. Now, it seems, we are heading for an age of no leisure at all. So much for human prophecy. A computer could have made a much better guess.

NO PLACE TO HIDE
The world has never been a very private place. For most of human history we have lived huddled together for protection in caves, villages, towns and cities. Only the very rich could afford the luxury of being alone. So, we are by habit a gregarious, curious species, and we like to know our neighbors' business. The more we know about the people around us the more comfortable we feel, so long as what we know is fairly harmless. Being at home in a village or a city is largely a matter of learning something about our neighbors, but not too much.

This changed with the invention of suburbs. In the spread-out sub-divisions, ordinary families can have all the privacy they can stand. Each separate suburban home is a cave of secrets. There are people all around us, but they might as well be Martians for all we know about them. So, in places like Long Island and Connecticut, we have become accustomed to a high degree of privacy, and most of us are happy with that. If suburban life had a motto it would be: "None of your business."

Whenever there is no problem, technology will step in to create one. We are now in the midst of a full-blown hysteria about privacy on the internet. Not only are there prying gadgets everywhere – tiny voice recorders, video cameras, and GPS transmitters that can follow our every step and misstep - but the whole internet has become a world of personal secrets waiting to be discovered.

This is not about security for things like financial information. We all need that, although it too seems to be a lost cause. But what amazes me is how many people post all kinds of intimate, personal stuff on the web, or send it via e-mail, and then complain bitterly when strangers take an interest in it.

What is remarkable about these complaints is the sense of fatalism, as if we absolutely must post every detail of our personal lives on the social media. We can't choose not to, any more than we can choose not to eat or breathe. Once on the internet everything becomes public property. It seems perverse to complain when unauthorized people to take a look, whether with the aim of selling you something, or checking your political opinions, or simply using your private life as entertainment. But nobody *has* to post all their intimate secrets on the web, it's purely voluntary. If for example you choose to post embarrassing pictures of yourself – which, as a humanitarian, I would never do - it must be assumed that people will look, and probably laugh.

For some of us privacy is not a problem, because we have no secrets worth knowing about. But if your life is more like a daytime soap opera, or late-night Playboy movie, and you must share it, I recommend taking a giant step backwards in time to old-fashioned and even historic communication methods such as a letter, a private conversation, or even a call on a wired phone, if you can find one.

You might also check the dictionary for an old-fashioned word: "reticence," meaning the habit of keeping private things to yourself. Chances are that you don't know many intimate or scandalous things about your grandparents. But not because they were paragons of virtue or even because they had no internet to broadcast their secrets. The fact is that your grandparents probably *did* know the meaning of reticence.

NO MORE SECRETS

Spying is a very ancient profession. Two thousand years ago ancient Rome was full of spies, employed by emperors, powerful senators and priests to keep a secret eye on the population and sniff out any hint of treachery or unorthodoxy. They were kept busy, but they had limited techniques at their disposal: listening at doors, bribing informers, and simply watching the people they suspected. It must have been hard and unproductive work to be a Roman spy, and everybody hated them.

Things have changed. Long Island had its own patriotic spies in the Revolutionary War, and they are now treated as heroes. Indeed, in our more enlightened age the spy has become a positively romantic figure, from Mata Hari to James Bond and George Smiley. They belong to another and more glamorous world, a world of secrets where the fate of nations may hang in the balance over a missing formula, an intercepted message, or a kidnapped leader.

Real spies are more mundane and even sad figures, like Jonathan Pollard or Aldrich Ames, or the legions of bureaucratic operatives employed by the CIA or MI6. However even these old-fashioned snoopers may soon be out of a job. We are all in the game now. Everybody can spy on everybody else. Whenever anything dramatic happens it seems that there is always someone standing by ready to record it on video. Millions of people must spend their whole lives just waiting, smartphones in hand, for the right moment.

It's not just the smartphones. For a long time, there have been miniature voice recorders that will allow you to record any conversation secretly. Those strangely intimate discussions that you hear while standing in line at the post office, and rash promises made at the end of romantic evenings, can be preserved forever and produced in court if necessary. I have one of these recorders myself, a tiny thing that weighs just a few ounces. I intended to use it for noting down clever ideas, but never had any, and in fact use it for prosaic reminders like "Buy more cat food."

After the easily-concealed voice recorders came miniature digital cameras, then cameras hidden in cell phones, then vest pocket video cameras, then video cameras in cell phones. It's only a matter of time before almost every object we use or look at will be booby trapped with a video camera. Beware of anyone wearing sunglasses, a brooch, a badge, or a watch, carrying a pen, a thumb drive, or anything down to about an inch in size that could hide a camera. Soon they will be down to the size of the Higgs Boson particle.

Another clever gadget goes a step further. This is a metal box that you can attach inside or under a car, and which will report where the car goes and how fast, where it stops and for how long, and who knows what other incriminating information. Combine this with a few strategically placed hidden video cameras and you could pretty much follow every moment of another person's life as it happens. This is such a monumental invasion of privacy that it takes your breath away. We will all be on camera, all the time. No moment of indiscretion, stupidity, or humiliation will go un-recorded, and it will be posted on Face Book for the world to sneer at. There will be no more secrets.

The police are equipped with video cameras, and no doubt criminals will soon have them too, CCTV is everywhere, satellites in the sky and drones overhead can track our every move. This universal snooping is bound to spread. If we can do it, we will do it. Doctors will record patients and vice versa, everyone will film encounters with real estate agents, financial advisers, car salesman, boyfriends, and everyone who would prefer not to go on the record with rash promises. Teachers of the future may face whole classrooms full of cameras. Every student will have one, from kindergarten on up, and the teachers had better have them too if they intend to say anything not in the textbook. In my time as a teacher I was in the habit of making off the cuff, ironic, and usually politically incorrect remarks, but I would never dare to do that now. Back then students used to laugh at my comments, now they might start a riot, or a lawsuit, or sell the video to Sixty Minutes.

Looking on the bright side, in the long run this universal mutual spying may produce a perfectly disciplined society, like North Korea or Orwell's Airstrip One, where nobody will dare to step out of line. The only question is: who is going to watch those trillions of hours of incredibly boring video, and who will watch the watchers themselves?

HOW BIG IS YOUR DATA?

We hear lot these days about something called "Big Data." It's a macho-sounding thing. Anything called "Big" usually is, like big business or the big bang theory. But what does it mean?

In the world of research everybody likes to claim that they have Big Data. It's not enough just to have a bright idea while standing in line at the supermarket checkout. You need a theory that is backed up by millions upon millions of numbers, which is what Big Data means.

When I was doing research in the social sciences thirty years ago I had a lot of small data: personal observations, interviews, newspaper clippings and so on, and I would juggle these odds and ends around until I reached some sort of conclusion. This is no longer good enough. Now I would need a mega gigabyte computer, a huge amount of stuff to put into it, and an algorithm to tell me what it all means. The result might be the same as what I could figure out with my notes on scraps of paper, but when it comes to scientific credibility there's no comparison. Big Data wins every time.

What is rather creepy about this is the way we have all become gathered up into these big datasets without knowing it. Every purchase, every phone call, every social media encounter, every medical record, even every book taken out of the library becomes a grain of sand in the Big Data mountain. The government uses some of it for "security" reasons, as we now know all too well, and business uses most of the rest to sell stuff. Only a fraction of Big Data is used by researchers looking to answer Big Questions about the human condition and the meaning of life.

It's not so much a privacy issue, because most Big Data is anonymous. It's the uneasy feeling that, far from being unique individuals, we are just… well…data for somebody else to use for politics or profit. We're all statistics, we know that, but a datum seems smaller and more trivial than a statistic. Statistics are useful, and often amusing, and almost invariably wrong. They tell us, for example that 70% of Americans who own running shoes never run, and that the average English person drinks 3.77 cups of tea a day. It was not for nothing that Mark Twain coined the phrase "Lies, damned lies, and statistics."

Big Data, made possible by hugely increased computing power, is old-fashioned statistics writ large and without the deniability. It brings together such gigantic numbers of facts that it may actually hit on the truth sometimes. For example, there's a book called *Dataclysm* by Christian Rudder, that explores what Big Data can tell us about human behavior, mostly dating behavior. It turns out that most of it is obvious: pretty women get more dates, people who share the same interests are more likely to get along, and so on. You could get the same answers by asking your mother. Other Big Data studies from the General Social Survey and the US Census have shown that people are less trusting than they used to be, and slightly less happy, and that newspaper readership is declining. Who would have guessed it?

I have every respect and sympathy for researchers who spend their days laboring over screens full of long numbers. It's not half as much fun as research used to be, although I'm sure it is more scientific. It is almost embarrassing to recall that what we used to call research involved things like reading books, going out into the real world, talking to people, and trying to figure out what on earth was going on.

EVERYDAY IMAGES

My camera is a large, clunky, complicated, and fragile thing that that I use only to take photographs, which I then print and put into albums. This tells you that both my camera and I have become historic objects in our own lifetimes.

Photography has changed as it has simplified. There must be more pictures being taken every day now than were taken in the entire annals of the photographic art. Most of them seem to be blurred shots snapped at arm's length with cell phones, casually, and without preparation. The resulting self-images are "shared" on the Internet, so I'm told, although this has never happened to me.

The sharing of pictures has a long history. Indeed, the very purpose of a picture is to be shared, otherwise what use is it? The first artists who scratched images on the walls of prehistoric caves presumably wanted other cave persons to admire them. The whole story of visual art is an invitation to look and be impressed. Wealthy families used to hang big portraits of themselves and their ancestors that said: "See how rich and handsome we are."

Photography brought a kind of democracy to images. We can all have family portraits now, and selfies too. Until recently personal photographs borrowed from the painting tradition: they tended to be posed and quite formal: stay still, stand up straight, smile. That's why old family photos don't look much like real people at all. But now the image has been, as it were, liberated: anything goes. What the old and new photographic technologies have in common is that the camera lens turns always towards us. We focus on ourselves and our special moments, in a kind of perpetual shutter-clicking Vanity Fair.

What we miss is everything else. Professional documentary photographers like Cartier-Bresson, Diane Arbus, and Walker Evans, set out to capture the essence of the world they lived in. But when I look back through *my* old photos the world we lived in is simply not there. It seems that we were always at the beach or some tourist site, always celebrating Christmas, always smiling, always standing up straight. I'm sure that there were gaps between those smiling moments, perhaps even times when we were working. Where are the pictures of ordinary things, ordinary activities? I would love to have pictures of my mother in her kitchen or my father working at his hobbies. But it seems that, like me, they were always on vacation.

We typically record the big, happy event, but forget the ordinary events that follow. The wedding but not the marriage, the graduation but not the job, the dinner party, but not the state of the kitchen afterwards, sunny days on the beach but not the dermatological complications that come later. It's almost as if we are embarrassed by the ordinariness of ordinary things, by the banality of everyday life. We only want to remember those bright moments when the red carpet was rolled out and the paparazzi were waiting.

What I hope is that the present mania for snapping pictures of everything, everywhere, all the time will, by benign accident, produce a much more complete archive of everyday life in all its confusion and tedium. Then, when the present generation grows old they will be able to open their digital mobile uploads and show their unbelieving grandchildren what life was really like in the old, old days, when the camera *never* lied.

HANDS OFF

We spent several hours in the cabin of a brand-new state-of-the art Boeing airliner, trying to hear a stream of announcements that were all but inaudible. Half the passengers were anxiously cupping their hands behind their ears, trying to decide whether the muttered electronic voices were announcing doom or dinner. The cabin crew paid no attention whatsoever.

Before this we had spent a couple of hours in one of the world's busiest airports, listening to a long series of garbled instructions and warnings from speakers above our heads, not one of which we could hear. Then we got on a French high-speed train, another state of the art device, which whisked us along at a hundred and forty miles an hour. Many no doubt interesting announcements were made through the public-address system along the way, but we couldn't make out a single word. In the super-modern stations at the both ends of the line it was the same story.

Yes of course I am going deaf, isn't everybody? Old people go deaf because of age, and young people go deaf because they listen to loud and awful music. In public places we all need clarity and volume, not mystery announcements, read *sotto voce*, very fast, and apparently in Portuguese. What if they were trying to tell us something important, like a safety emergency or a visit by ISIS or that the bar had run out of peanuts? We would never know it.

When you trust your life to these high technologies you may wonder why they can't get this one simple thing right. But this is the distinctively human contribution, not the fatal flaw but the necessary flaw in what might otherwise be a perfect system. The ancient Greeks understood that perfection is the enemy of progress, because in a perfect system nothing can ever change. It would be boring. So, when things seem in danger of going too well, human beings must step in to mess them up. "What was that," we ask each other after each garbled message, and we are engaged and entertained by the mystery. Think how dull travel would be if all the public announcements were clearly enunciated and audible.

This is what Arthur Koestler called "The Ghost in the Machine," the human factor. Consider the surreal spectacle of a great airliner, weighing three quarters of a million pounds, rushing down the runway and being thrust into the air by ninety thousand horsepower engines gulping thirty gallons of fuel a minute, and violating all the rules of gravity and common sense. We know that a sort of engineering miracle has been achieved, but not a *perfect* miracle. The whole improbable machine is being controlled by computers just like the one that drives you crazy at home, and the cabin crew are up there making inaudible announcements over a Mickey Mouse PA system and trying to fix the coffee pot. Although the robots seem to be in charge, human beings are not quite useless. There is always some whimsical touch that only we can add. That's our place, in the shadowy corners of the automated world, and always will be because we are the masters of creative imperfection and, unlike the robots, we do have a sense of humor.

MON SEMBLABLE, MON FRÈRE*

There has been flurry of interest in robotics and automation. This is one of those stories that comes and goes. People have been fascinated by automatons since the time of Leonardo da Vinci, and science fiction writers have been speculating about robots and artificial intelligence since the 1920s. But now reality has caught up with imagination, and these futuristic devices are no longer in the future. A lot of people have begun to wonder how we are going to live with robots, and how they will change our lives. The title of one book says it all: *The Rise of the Robots: Technology and the Threat of a Jobless Future* by Martin Ford.

Our human obsession with robots is uneasily balanced between fear and hope. We hope that they will take over the nasty, boring and dangerous parts of our lives. Researchers at Columbia have developed a machine that will do ironing, and robot lawn mowers are everywhere. The machines have already come very far, taking charge on production lines, in operating theaters, and in aircraft cockpits. Instead of tedious research we have Google, instead of literacy we have spellcheck and grammar check and soon, instead of watching the road ahead, we will have self-driving cars, so nobody will ever have to stop talking on the phone. It will be interesting to see what happens in the transition period, when half the cars are automated, and half are not.

Some of us, inspired by the darker side of science fiction, have an uneasy feeling that robots are sinister things, especially when they assume the form of fake human beings without human feelings. But that should be the least of our worries. Anything that replaces human work with mechanical work is a robot. It comes from a Czech word meaning "forced labor". The question is: who is being forced?

Robots are on the way to mastering every human skill from surgery to teaching and grading student essays. Recently a Google machine called AI beat a champion player in the ancient and fiendishly complicated game of Go. In a few generations, we may have a super-computer clever enough to almost understand the Federal tax system. Economists have estimated that, when everything that can be automated has been automated, between a third and a half of all jobs will vanish. We will have nothing to do and no paycheck to do it with. Nobody seems to have noticed that robots don't pay taxes like human workers, or that people without paychecks will have no way of buying the goods and services that robots will so efficiently create. It seems unlikely that robots will also provide unemployment benefits or charitable contributions to the poor.

An even more insidious thing about these devices is our attitude towards them. Little by little we come to trust them, and even like them because after all they seem to be doing something for us, even if we are actually doing it for them. I already find myself saying "thank you" to automatic gas pumps and cash dispensers. What if we learn to love them? How long will it be before some especially talented devices are worshipped? It's already happened with Apple products whose users are almost evangelical.

It is natural to have strong feelings about things that are important or close to us. Kids adore their stuffed animals, and grownups get angry at their computers. It is the basis of the ancient religions called 'animist,' in which believers may pray to a nearby mountain, or a graven image, or any object they think is sacred. The only problem is that, whether you put your faith in a totem pole or a clever machine, your prayers are never answered.

*"My likeness, my brother" (Baudelaire)

BIG BROTHER IS STILL WATCHING
The other day I received a surprise message from the British police, informing me that I was being fined thirty pounds for a traffic violation. It seemed that, two months ago in the provincial town of Colchester, I had strayed into a bus lane. The proof was enclosed with the police letter: three photographs taken from different angles showing my rental car crossing a completely empty bus lane on a completely empty road. I can

even remember the moment when this happened. I had swerved right into the bus lane to make an awkward turn that I had almost missed. The car was probably in the forbidden lane for half a minute or less and, as there was no other traffic in sight, I felt that it was perfectly safe to indulge in this piece of automotive wickedness.

But I had forgotten the eyes in the sky, the closed-circuit television cameras that seem to watch our every move. Britain has more of these spying devices than any other nation. One estimate is that there are almost six million of them, roughly one for every ten citizens. You only need to look up in a street, in a store, or in any kind of public building, to see the glass eye of the camera looking back at you.

This unexpected police attention was annoying on several levels. It wasn't so much the fine, because the pound had fallen so low that thirty pounds was not much anyway. But the business of setting up these cameras, and maintaining them, and monitoring them, and tracing the vehicles, and printing photographs, and sending letters imposing fines, must surely be enormously expensive as well as a monstrous waste of police time. There are plenty of real criminals in Britain to keep them occupied, without worrying about trivial traffic violations on empty roads. There are plenty of mad and dangerous drivers too, but perhaps they move too fast for the CCTV cameras to get a clear picture.

Spy cameras are multiplying here too. I've noticed them perched on traffic signals at several local junctions. This is vintage George Orwell stuff. In his dystopian novel 1984 the spy cameras are everywhere, and Big Brother is always watching. But since we are being watched everywhere all the time, how about a bit of recognition for those of us who sometimes do the *right* thing? I can remember occasions when I almost came to a full stop at a stop sign, or when turning right on red, and I have also been known to observe the speed limit. I am a model of a law-abiding citizen most of the time, but I get no credit for it. What about some rewards as well as punishments, a credit system for good drivers who get caught by the cameras doing the *right* thing? It would work rather like air miles. Credits would be deducted from any fines or points we might accumulate on our license in careless moments. In all modesty, I must say that this is a brilliant idea to reinforce good behavior, and I hope to see it adopted soon by police forces everywhere.

Meanwhile I contemplated the fine Would the British police try to extradite me and throw me into the dungeon of Colchester Castle which, incidentally, is one of the oldest castles in Britain? It wasn't worth the risk. I paid the fine, and next time I'm over there take care to drive on the left most of the time, and watch out for the bus lanes, and remember to smile for the camera.

FOR A GOOD READ, CLICK HERE

Summer reading is one of those traditional pleasures, like family fun, that exists largely in the realm of fantasy. The decline of reading in general is well documented. About a quarter of all American adults claim not to have read even a single book in the past year. But that leaves seventy-five per-cent who have read at least one, even if it was only *The Art of the Deal*. The paradox is that, as the reading habit declines, the number of books continues to increase. About three hundred thousand books were published in 2017, and sales went up. At this time of year, the newspapers and magazines hit us with their "Summer Reading Supplements," each one thicker and more daunting than the last. One such supplement, from a fairly well-known New York newspaper, was thirty-seven pages long, and reviewed or recommended over a hundred books, which works out at more than one for every day of summer. How much reading time do you expect to have?

In France the pressure to be a reader is even more intense. The summer book supplements are heavier, more intellectual, and more daunting. A survey came up with the heretical finding that a substantial majority of

French people believe that books are better than the internet, which is such a stunning rejection of progress that it can scarcely be believed. But it's true that, on a train or in a café, more French people can still be seen calmly reading books than swiping anxiously at their smartphones.

This raises an intriguing question: in what sense if any *are* books better than the internet? Personally, I love books because I am a relic of the past, but I know that computers and portable devices can deliver little packages of information and entertainment faster and often cheaper. You can even find my podcasts on your phone, which is a very high recommendation indeed. So why bother with a clumsy, old-fashioned technology that is four thousand years old and destroys an alarming number of our vanishing trees?

To answer this unwelcome question, I did some research. This consisted of sitting in the room where I usually work, staring at the computer screen for a few minutes, and then revolving on my chair to look at the books on the walls.

The answer, when it came, was obvious. Books create guilt, while the computer and all its mobile companions do not. There is just one computer in my room, and potentially it can bring me most of the knowledge in the world. That's the thing, "potentially." There are a few hundred books, and they are here already, on the shelves, on the desk, and on the floor. Some I have read and some I haven't, but they are *here*. And by being here as solid physical objects they remind me of all the things I don't know, but should. By contrast the blank computer screen is totally forgiving, it doesn't make me feel bad about the vast blank spaces in my mind. But a book will sit there glaring at me until I read it. When it comes to ignorance your friendly, undemanding computer is a co-conspirator, an enabler. If Freud was right, civilization depends on guilt. We should never, ever, lose our guilt about not reading books.

Theme IV

THE VOICE OF AUTHORITY

Politics is the art of running the circus from inside the monkey cage.

H.L.MENCKEN

If one cannot reform the world One can at least laugh at it.

E.M.FORSTER

I am not fit for this office and should never have been here.

WARREN G. HARDING

DISCLAIMER – WHAT DO *I* KNOW?

My view of American politics is detached, like the perspective of a spectator in the back row of the stadium who does not understand the rules of the game or even what game is being played. As far as I can tell from that distance American politics is closely modeled on American football. There are two teams (parties), distinguished only by random symbols and colors. The players, who are mostly rather heavy, run up and down and deliberately crash into each other. From time to time they all fall down in a heap. They seem to be pursuing an odd-shaped ball which passes from one team to the other and is carried up and down the pitch and sometimes wildly kicked into the air. I believe this ball represents the government of the United States. The men in striped jerseys represent the justice system; the men in suits the oligarchs who fund the two teams, and the public is behind barriers on the sidelines. There are also cheerleaders, representing the core party faithful, including journalists and pundits, who root for their teams so the rest of us don't have to.

The viewpoint of a bemused spectator is not ideal, but it's all I have. Nearly everything important that happens in politics or football is hidden from me, and from everyone else who is not dedicated to the game, by clouds of mystification and ignorance. The observations below, made over more than thirty years, are essentially those of what I believe is called a Monday morning quarterback – the ignorant blowhard who always know what the opposition is doing wrong, and how to put it right. So here, with few apologies, is my diagnosis of politics in twenty-first century America. There is no prognosis – I wouldn't dare.

POLES APART

Back in the olden days when I was a schoolboy there were many things about adults that I found mystifying. High on the list was their habit of dividing up people, ideas, activities, and just about everything else into good or bad, right or wrong, friend or enemy. Ours was a small school with only about three hundred boys, but even so we were randomly divided into four artificial groups called "Houses," indicated by a colored border around our caps. I was in Charter House, with a green cap. We were encouraged to despise, compete with, and generally set ourselves apart from boys in the other "Houses," both in sports and in academics. The four groups had everything in common except the colors on their caps.

Many mysteries of adult life became clearer to me as I grew up, but not this one. It seems that the entire world is artificially divided into mutually suspicious teams, tribes, parties, gangs and sects: Sunnis and Shiites, Democrats and Republicans, Mets and Yankees, Muslims and Hindus, black and white, Capitalist and Communist. Whose side are you on, our side or their side?

This primitive habit mind is older than history, and it must have begun in the Stone Age when language was undeveloped and very few people had a good grounding in logical or analytical thinking. The tribe over the next hill was different, and therefore dangerous and bad. Your own tribe was familiar, and therefore good: time for a fight.

We flatter ourselves that we have progressed since then. We have psychology, sociology, public education, and public radio. Yet our popular culture seems to be stuck in the stone age, obsessed with enemies and conspiracies. Lord of the Rings, Star Wars, Harry Potter, Superman almost every video game – they're all about the mighty conflict between good guys and bad guys

There is a name for this foolishness: Manichaeism, a set of beliefs that arose (would you believe it?) in Iran in around the third century AD, when barbarians were invading Europe and the Roman Empire was falling apart. The basic doctrine of Manichaeism was that the world could only be understood as the scene of a constant struggle between good and evil forces. This philosophy was very popular and still is, although the Church declared it a heresy more than a thousand years ago. It was particularly congenial to third century Iranians, as it is to eight-year old boys in any century. But the modern world is too complicated to be run by either of these groups. Motives are always mixed, ideologies are always confused, nothing is ever what it seems, and solutions are always incomplete. To state the obvious, politics is not a game, let alone a video game, let alone a discredited theology from the Dark Ages. It's more serious than that.

Fortunately, when I was at school, we kept our heads and refused to believe the nonsense about 'us versus them' that was fed to us by our teachers. But I must say that those of us in Charter House were *never* on the dark side, while boys in the other houses were often stupid, disobedient, and even wicked. We beat them at cricket too. But Charter House was a special case.

THE EMPIRE OF THE EXTROVERTS

The labels "introvert" and "extrovert" have been around for a hundred years to describe two personalities we all know well. Introverts are reticent, quiet, and enjoy being alone. Extroverts are sociable, generally louder, and more talkative. These are stereotypes of course, but where would we be without stereotypes? Most of us have no trouble in accepting one or other of these labels for ourselves, and for me it's easy. On a test of introversion, I once scored a hundred per-cent, which is the best I have ever done on any test.

There are many disadvantages to being an introvert. We have been beaten up at school, ignored by waiters in hundreds of restaurants, and interrupted in a million conversations. We haven't complained about this of course, because introverts don't like to complain. In a world full of boisterous extroverts we even feel a bit embarrassed to be so calm and unaggressive. But we received encouragement a few years ago from a book by Susan Cain called *Quiet: the Power of Introverts in a World that Can't Stop Talking*. It seems even more relevant now than it was then.

The author argued that the loud and confident character is not necessarily more admirable than the quiet and thoughtful one, although the former is usually more powerful and better paid. Introverts don't have to be anti-social hermits, or shy people with an inferiority complex. They can be actors, or politicians or even cheerleaders. It's just that introverts don't go to the party after the show, and they don't want to run the show. They like to be quiet, sometimes. This book made introverts feel better, but it didn't change anything. Extroverts were too busy imposing their opinions to read it, and in any case, they don't care. Noise is good, and our masters' voices get louder all the time.

We do need our extroverts, and not just in the circus. They are the fund raisers, the protestors, the leaders, the movers and shakers whether we want to be moved and shaken or not. Consider how dull the world be if it was run by reflective, quiet introverts rather than noisy, active extroverts. War would end at once of course, it's far too noisy. Politics would become less of a shouting match and more of a thinking match, with a corresponding loss of drama and hysteria. But it's not going to happen. How would a bunch of introverts take power without creating a lot of fuss? It would be embarrassing even to try, and the extroverts would scream and yell until the only way to get any peace would be to let them run things again, as usual. We might as well let them get on with it - not that we have any choice.

THE FALL OF THE MERITOCRACY

We trust most people most of the time, because trust makes life easier and more civilized. But never in history has it been safe to trust everybody all the time. Look at what happened to Voltaire's character Candide, who believed everything he was told and was always disappointed.

My generation has been too trusting, and is now paying the price. Our faith in our fellow man (and woman) has been worn thin by millions of advertisements that are indistinguishable from lies, decades of telephone scams of every conceivable kind, and more recently by a deluge of trickery and criminality on the internet. We are the daily target of credit card scams, time-share scams, tax scams, and identity theft scams. If you can imagine a way of cheating, somebody else has thought of it already, and tried it on you. Who are these people? They can't all be sinister Russians, there aren't enough sinister Russians on the planet.

This is small stuff, though annoying. Our naïve faith in human nature has taken a beating right across the board, from the bottom to all the way to the top. For most of our lives we assumed that scientific research must be rigorously honest, and that bankers were sober and trustworthy people. We believed implicitly that school grades, athletic performances, prescription medications and company accounts were more or less what they appeared to be. Not anymore. TV programs like Game of Cards and movies like the Wolf of Wall Street tell us: "This is how it really is, these are your leaders, get used to it." Only Pollyanna herself could fail to get the message.

A sociology professor called Michael Young predicted this collapse of trust more than half a century ago, in a book called *The Rise of the Meritocracy*. We were blindsided by the word "meritocracy." It had a fine ring to it, suggesting to the naïve mind that the best, most capable and most trustworthy people would rise to the top – a true hierarchy of merit where superior qualities of character, knowledge, and honesty would be rewarded. Nobody could argue with that.

I still have my copy of the first edition of *The Rise of the Meritocracy*. It is in brand new condition, which shows that I didn't read it carefully. If I had paid attention I would have understood that Young's vision of the future was more depressing than inspiring. He created a fantasy of life in the near future when the cunning strategy of the elite was to *really give* equal opportunity to everyone. All the smartest and most aggressive people of every race and class and both sexes were elevated to the top, and all those left behind (the vast majority, the ninety-nine percent) were without any power or voice. This was a meritocracy without merit, a self-perpetuating elite of manipulators, technocrats, power brokers, and money managers. There was nothing noble or superior about them. It was Social Darwinism in its purest form – the survival of the fittest.

"At its most basic, the logic of 'meritocracy' is ironclad: putting the most qualified, best equipped people into the positions of greatest responsibility and import...Our near-religious fidelity to the meritocratic model comes with huge costs. We overestimate the advantages of meritocracy and underappreciate its costs, because we don't think hard enough about the consequences of the inequality it produces." (Christopher L. Hayes)

In 1958 Michael Young predicted the rise of a ruthless hereditary elite as our inevitable fate. But he didn't foresee that such an elite could be so sleazy and incompetent that it would undermine its own authority. Now we have become cynical enough to understand what is going on, but it may be too late to do anything about it.

What the survival of the fittest guarantees, if it guarantees anything, is that those who rise to the top are precisely the ones we would least want to have at the top. But it's useless to complain, we are up against a law of nature here. It is all a question of who or what can do best in a particular environment. A penguin won't survive long in the Sahara Desert, or a friendly mouse in a house full of cats. The primitive world favored warriors who were brave and fierce; we seem somehow to have created a culture that favors tricksters and cheats. But at least we are permitted (so far) to make fun of tricksters and cheats. We have evolved from a meritocracy based on courage to one based on cunning. It may not be morally uplifting, but at least it is a lot safer.

What kind of society produces a Jordan Belfort, the Wolf of Wall Street, or a Bernie Madoff, a Ken Lay of Enron, Bernie Ebbers of Worldcom? Our kind of society produced them, and allowed them to succeed. We must face the fact that our present elites and leaders are those best adapted to this society as it now exists. It's a chilling thought because that makes the rest of us seem like penguins in the Sahara. If the heat doesn't get us, the lack of fish will. Young did not predict that the rise of the meritocracy would follow the universal rule: all that goes up must come down. In his view, it was a one-way street, leading to economic totalitarianism.

Professor Young had only one answer to this: create a revolution. In his pessimistic book, the revolution fails. It's important to remember that the entire story is a fiction.

HELP WANTED

There are too many choices - too many foods in the supermarket, too many cars, too many religions, and too many lifestyles. We can waste our whole lives making choices, none of which will make any difference in the end.

From time to time, by some strange failure of the market mechanism, the situation is reversed: we are faced with a *really* important decision, like whether to have children or cats, or whether to pay income tax or emigrate to another planet, and we find that we have no choice at all.

Election day is one such painful moment. How is it that there are a hundred different brands of cereal in every supermarket, but when it comes to Presidential candidates there are only two: All Bran and Corn Flakes?

No wonder so many people just throw up their hands and cry "None of the Above."

In the past, disgruntled citizens sometimes took drastic action. On the fifth of November 1605, a disaffected voter called Guy Fawkes, with some friends, tried to blow up the British Houses of Parliament with King James and all the great politicians of the day inside. He failed. The British celebrate this date every year with bonfires and fireworks. Whether they are celebrating Guy Fawkes's failure or regretting it has never been entirely clear. Tempting though it is, the Guy Fawkes strategy is not the legal or the democratic way to change a government.

Nonetheless, the present system has clearly failed, and I would like to suggest a better way of choosing a President, which can easily be put in place by the year 2020. In a word: *advertise*. Full credit for this brilliant idea must go to my old friend C. Northcote Parkinson.*

Parkinson pointed out that almost all job vacancies are filled by advertising, so why not this one? In a single stroke, we could get rid of the political party machines, the primaries, the party conferences, the debates, the ghastly lying advertising campaigns, the tedious speeches full of false promises, the election itself, and the legal battles afterwards.

Of course, an advertisement for the President's job would have to be to be very carefully worded. An ad. that simply said: "Wanted, President of the United States, salary $200,000," would bring in far too many applications. Even I would apply, and I can tell you that you wouldn't want *me* in that job. Prince Charles would probably apply, being unemployed. Perhaps you *would* want him.

According to the great Parkinson, the ideal Help Wanted advertisement would be written to attract one single applicant, who will be the perfect and only person for the job.

WANTED: PRESIDENT OF THE UNITED STATES. Hours of work 12.05 am to 11.55 p.m. 365 days a year. Male candidates must be tall but not too handsome. Female candidates should be of medium height and well-preserved. Attractive family with cute pet essential. All candidates must be virile and virginal, honest and devious, strong but not dominating, experienced but not expert, warm, generous, and utterly ruthless. Candidates must have no recorded past life whatsoever. Ability to read complete nonsense from a teleprompter while smiling sincerely at the same time is essential. Candidates must believe in America, baseball, mother, apple pie, and God in that order. Candidates must have no other firm convictions whatsoever. The successful candidate will have a foolproof plan to reduce taxes to nothing while maintaining all existing government programs (especially defense), and reducing the budget deficit to zero while providing a universal free health service. Candidates who fail to achieve all these goals within one month will be shot. Salary will be decided by popular referendum under the Gallup rules, and will be linked to performance. In case of unsatisfactory job performance, candidate will be required to pay back any salary previously received, and will then be shot. All unsuccessful applicants will be shot. Resumés, on a postcard please, to: Search Committee, 1600, Pennsylvania Avenue, Washington DC.

That should do it. If the wording is exactly right, only one candidate will come forward, probably someone on parole from a state mental institution, and he or she will be the best President we ever had. There would be no need for an interview, or even references. The candidate could move right into the White House.

If this idea is adopted, as I'm sure it will be, the fiascos of the past few years – and especially the shameful years 2000 and 2016 - could be forgotten. Public confidence in the system has now sunk so low that the change would come not a moment too soon. During the most recent campaign, a teacher I know on Long Island held a mock election in her class of 8th graders. They refused to vote, saying it was a complete waste of time. Sometimes 8th graders really do know best.

Note: Readers can follow up this reference in Parkinson's Law *by C. Northcote Parkinson, first published in 1957. See especially chapter two: "The Short List, or Principles of Selection" and the advertisement for Prime Minister of Ruritania. I have tried to stay as close as possible to the principles laid down by the genius Parkinson.*

HEROES FOR OUR TIME

President's Day is a day of remembrance. We must remember to go to the bank on Friday, because it will be closed on Monday, and not forget to make the most of all those never-to-be-repeated sales. There is so much to remember that the Presidents themselves are often forgotten. But they were rather special Presidents. We don't have a national holiday for Chester Alan Arthur, or Grover Cleveland. But the banks close and the sales open for Washington and Lincoln.

George Washington was commander in chief of the Continental army during the revolutionary war - a rebel against the king, to put it plainly - and the first President of the United States. Abraham Lincoln was the sixteenth President, who really made the mythical journey from log cabin to White House, and was elected at just about the worst moment in the history of the United States. He preserved the Union, and freed the slaves.

These were two men of heroic stature. The word "hero" has a strange, archaic ring, although we know what it means. "A brave, illustrious or much-admired figure," says the dictionary. The tabloid newspapers use "hero" rather too freely to describe any citizen who shows some physical courage in a situation where cameras are present. But, in general, people must wait until after they are dead before being so labeled. The same applies to becoming a "great statesman" or an "immortal composer." These are essentially post-mortem honors, because living people could never live up to them.

We need heroes, and we need symbols, but we prefer them to be firmly in the past. Washington or Lincoln would have no chance of being elected to the Presidency today, or even to the local school board. Washington, with his grim unsmiling face and his austere character would be an image-maker's nightmare. Lincoln, with his complexity, his deep ambiguity, and his alarming tendency to talk in complete sentences, would have the selection committees running for cover.

Washington and Lincoln are heroes of historical memory, pillars of nostalgia. Nothing is more boring than the present, nothing is more uncertain than the future, and nothing is more reassuring than the past. The past is settled. We know the plot and can rerun it again and again, like an old movie. George Washington will *always* win the battle of Yorktown. Abraham Lincoln will *always* save the Union in the last reel. It's not like the morning TV news, when anything can happen.

We who are alive today have the task and the duty of providing such heroes and such satisfying stories for future generations. We don't seem to be doing too well. Where shall we find the heroic figures for our great grandchildren to admire in the coming decades of the twenty-first century?

Not among our politicians, that's certain. Their heroic resistance to term limits, campaign finance reform, pollution control, arms reduction, and a genuine balanced budget won't earn them any respect in the future. I doubt whether the tomorrow's heroes will be soldiers, either. The perpetual wars of choice waged overseas for the past hundred years have embarrassed and disgusted most reasonable American people, and most of the rest of the world too. Reverence for the military went out with the Vietnam War and the Gulf War. Rebels have not been admired or fashionable in America since 1776. Washington was the last American to become a hero by attacking the government.

It would be nice to think that our age has produced spiritual leaders who will be the heroes of a more enlightened future, men (and women) who have risen above materialism. Jim Bakker? Pat Robertson? Oral Roberts? I think we can forget about them. What about intellectuals? In the eighteenth century, thinkers like Voltaire and Rousseau were internationally celebrated. Will this happen again? The signs are not encouraging. There aren't many possibilities left. Heroes of business and finance? Mr. Gates? Mr. Buffet? Will posterity admire them quite as much as they admire themselves?

It seems that the only heroes we can offer to the future are our celebrities. We have plenty of them, and who else is likely to qualify? Future generations won't have to ask *why* a given celebrity was once so famous. Fame itself was the only qualification. Our great grandchildren will never be disappointed in the heroes and heroines of our age, because they never really existed.

ALL TOO HUMAN

The role of modern Presidents is not unlike that of the gods of ancient Greece and Rome. The gods represented certain fundamental ideas or principles, such as war, art, love, or wisdom. They interfered in human affairs whether humans liked it or not. The gods were supported or hindered in their activities by a Parthenon of lesser gods, very like Congress. At its most imperial, the role of the President corresponds to that of Jupiter or Zeus the chief god of the ancient world, whose symbol was the eagle and who was very fond of using thunderbolts and otherwise throwing his weight around. The men who framed the Constitution were educated in the classics, which is why Washington DC looks and works so eerily like ancient Rome. The founders knew all about the Olympians, and they never quite abandoned the imperial idea, even as they created a democratic Constitution.

All Presidents inherit the uneasy compromise embedded in that Constitution. They are expected to be amiable and Olympian, democratic and commanding, all at the same time. They must seem to be flexible, while expressing no uncertainty about anything. Whether it's a university or a nation, the President must give a plausible appearance of being in control of everything, while denying responsibility for anything that goes wrong. But that's what we the voters seem to hope for and expect – a reasonable imitation of Zeus, who is really just a regular guy.

That's why Presidents like to be pro-active. It allows them to focus on the few things they can do, and ignore the enormous number of things they cannot do. War: we can do that. Peace in the Middle East, a sound economy, term limits on Congress: forget it. Some Presidents have admitted out loud that their power isn't what it seems to be. Eisenhower, when he got to the White House, complained that he had had more power in the army. "I just sit here in the Oval Room," he grumbled, "And tell people to do this or do that, and nothing happens!"

What we tend to forget about the gods of the ancient world is that they too were not really very powerful or effective. They argued amongst themselves, got carried away by their emotions, made stupid mistakes and were, in short, all too human. Zeus, Athena and Apollo among them made an appalling mess of the Trojan War, for example. The ancient Greeks and Romans recognized and accepted this fallibility. It came under the general heading of "fate," dispensed by the three Greek goddesses Clotho, Lachesis and Otropos. We need to be equally realistic and fatalistic about our leaders.

How much "leadership" do we really want? The trouble with great leaders is that, like the ancient gods, they are unreliable. They can lead to the top of the mountain or over the cliff. Mediocrity, uncertainty, and confusion at the top may be easier to live with, and safer than heroism or self-glorification.

Alexis de Tocqueville, a French aristocrat who came to America in 1835, liked the idea of democracy but feared that voters would never choose a candidate with superior talent or intelligence, and so democracy would produce nothing but weak and indecisive leaders. H.L.Mencken took up the same theme in the 1920s. If we keep voting for Presidents who seem just like us, he warned, we will end up with a President who *is* just like us, a regular, confused, inadequate guy, the absolute opposite of a mighty, powerful, thunderbolt-throwing god Zeus.

That's the beauty of democracy. Who needs Zeus?

SCARY CLOWNS

One of the more bizarre news stories of 2017 was a plague of scary clowns. A few young men, who were clearly somewhat deranged, were dressing up in clown costumes and going around scaring adults and children with creepy and threatening behavior. Real clowns were naturally outraged by this phenomenon. Clowns are meant to be fun, joyful, and above all harmless. I used to love seeing them at the circus when I was a kid, with their slapstick stunts and collapsing cars and gloriously messy cream pies.

Times have changed, it seems, or perhaps we have just gone backwards into a darker time. There was always a sad and slightly sinister clown, known as the *Auguste,* and the clown in history was an ambiguous figure. Some were simply funny, getting their laughs by wild and grotesque antics, and doing prankish things we would like to do ourselves, like delivering a pie in the face to just the right person. Others followed the tradition of the court jester, whose job it was to speak truth to power by making satirical jokes. But clowns have always had a darker side. Disguise itself has a dark side, because what is a disguise if not a lie? At carnival time, masks are often used as a cover for bad behavior.

If clowns are scary it is because they are irrational and unpredictable. Their crazy antics blow the whole notion of consecutive logical thought sky high, which opens the door to laughter, but also to madness. Clowning is an emotional thing, and emotion is always easier and more satisfying than rational thought. Their funny wigs and strange colored faces are part of the act. Nobody really looks like that, and when somebody does it is unsettling. When someone acts like a crazy clown we generally treat them humanely, with medication or therapy. When all else fails, we lock them up.

So, the bad clown is back, perhaps inspired by figures like the Joker in the Superman movies, or Stephen King's *It,* or a general tendency for culture in the twenty-first century to regress to the fifteenth. Clowns are dimly related to the supernatural. They come from the dark side, like witches and evil spirits and those little monsters who will come to our doors on Halloween demanding candy with menaces - smaller and (perhaps) more innocent versions of the scary clown.

Halloween is, in this sense, a clownish festival left over from a more credulous and superstitious past. It was a stroke of genius by the framers of the Constitution to schedule Election Day immediately after Halloween. We are in the right frame of mind. We can no longer tell the difference between fact and fantasy. In fact, the two events are quite similar. The candidates dress themselves in improbable disguises and go around making threats and asking for handouts. We, the voters, are supposed to admire the costumes and not make any rude comments about how transparent they are. Elections are about illusions and blackmail, power and money, so they are never an edifying spectacle. If you see a scary clown during the election season pay no attention, on no account take him seriously and, if he won't go away, try a cream pie.

A VERY SPECIAL DAY

Everything and everyone seems to have a special "Day" - the Groundhog has one, and the feminist leader Susan B. Anthony has her Day on February 15, followed immediately by Lithuanian Independence Day in case you didn't know. But not all "Days" are equal, even among the Saints. The Days of St. Nicholas and St Valentine, for example, get more attention than all the rest of the congregation of saints put together. Some would argue that the only really important Saint's day belongs to Saint Patrick.

The degree of excitement surrounding a special day seems to be in direct proportion to its sales potential. Super Bowl Sunday is huge, for example, as are Christmas and Valentine's Day. But President's Day (February 21), while historically important, is a low-energy, low-profit event. There are some sales, and a day off for bank and post office employees, and that's about it. This lack of commercial possibilities seems to mute the celebrations. Nor do we make a great fuss over February 12, which is the anniversary of the birth of Charles Darwin.

Darwin has arguably had more influence on the way we think that all forty-four Presidents put together, plus all the kings, prime ministers, emperors and dictators who ever strutted across the world stage. With his world-changing book *The Origin of Species*, Darwin helped us to understand why leaders lead, and why followers follow, and what all those Valentine's Day hearts and flowers are really all about. This is important stuff, whether you agree with it or not.

We all have our own personal hierarchy of importance when it comes to big anniversaries and national events. The guys behind the counter in the post office, who are my main source of information about the real world, will be discussing the Super Bowl weeks after the event, but they will ignore Darwin Day completely. When Post Office re-opens on February 22 they don't have much to say about President's Day either. Which is a pity because Presidents are important, possibly even more important that quarter backs although I know it's sacrilege to say so. Quarterbacks only have to carry one ball. A President must carry hundreds, and is counted a failure if he fumbles a single one.

When George Washington took on the job in 1789 there were fewer than four million Americans in this vast continent. Now there are close to three hundred million, a nation so big and complicated that it seems beyond the possibility of government. Yet forty-five ordinary human mortals, some of them very ordinary indeed, have tried to govern it, and perhaps they deserve more credit than they get for attempting the impossible. If we had our priorities right we might put a lot more energy into historically important events like Presidents Day, celebrating it perhaps with a general amnesty for past Presidents and a ritual payment of back taxes by all our patriotic billionaires. And it wouldn't do any harm to focus more attention on intellectually important anniversaries like Darwin Day, which could be commemorated with seminars, lively debates, and educational trips to the local zoo.

This is a perfectly sensible and rational suggestion. But there's nothing less popular on this earth than a perfectly sensible and rational suggestion. This is the first lesson that every new President learns.

A LIE FOR ALL SEASONS
Irony is my favorite form of humor. It begins with the recognition that things are not what they seem, and never were. "Thy Wars brought nothing about/Thy lovers were all untrue" as John Dryden wryly expressed it three centuries ago. And when it comes to the great, the famous, the heroic figures of any age, we always discover sooner or later that the Emperor *never* had any clothes.

But, as delightful as irony can be, it is possible to have too much of it. Consider George Washington - soldier, statesman, first President, patriotic icon. In the days when history was taught in schools, every child knew the story of George Washington and the cherry tree. Young George, running amuck with a chainsaw, lopped off one of his father's favorite trees. When accused of the crime, the boy is supposed to have said: "Father, I cannot tell a lie," and confessed.

This story may even be true. George Washington was a very exceptional human being. As a child, he wrote down one hundred and ten *Rules of Civility and Decent Behavior*, which we can still read with profit today. They include such gems as: "When in company, put not your hands to any part of the body not usually discovered," "Put not off your clothes in the presence of others," and "Cleanse not your teeth with the table cloth." This is all very good advice for those of us who want to be accepted in polite society.

But consider that phrase, "I cannot tell a lie." It sounds so strange to us now. If young George Washington had grown up in our time he would never respond to the vandalism charge with such a simple confession. He would automatically denounce it as fake news and call an attorney. He might take the case all the way to the Supreme Court. Confession may be good for the soul, but it is not recommended by legal experts, because it is fatal to the legal profession. If you are of a certain age, you may remember watching old movies in which criminals, captured by the heavy hand of the law, would say things like: "It's a fair cop, I confess, I can take my punishment."

This satisfying *dénouement* never appears in modern crime fictions, and for a very good reason. We are more sophisticated now, and we have discovered how profoundly unsatisfying, uncomfortable, and indeed unprofitable the plain truth can be. Nobody loves a truth-teller. The composer Johannes Brahms was famous for his frankness, and widely disliked because of it. There's a story that, on leaving a party, he said to the hostess, "Please forgive me if I have, by chance, forgotten to offend one of your guests." The truth always hurts.

This is what the critics of President Trump failed to understand. We are perfectly happy with lies, because we have learned to discount them, and even enjoy them as a kind of entertainment. Airline employees look us straight in the eye and tell us that the plane will be here in half an hour, when they know and we know that it is grounded in Calcutta for the foreseeable future. Doctors say, "You're doing very well for your age," although usually they avoid eye contact when they say it - something to do with the Hippocratic oath I suppose. Every year we see tens of thousands of advertisements, virtually all lies. Every four years we have an election. And then there's sex. I think it's fair to say, to misquote Winston Churchill, that never have so many lies been told by so many to so many, and been so little believed.

Thanks to a healthy tradition of investigative journalism in this country the most blatant political lies are exposed quickly, although the word "lie" is rarely used. If young George Washington denied cutting down the tree today he would have been accused of a "mis-statement" or an "incorrect interpretation of the facts."

Lie and liar are toxic words. They mean exactly what they mean. Members of the British parliament are forbidden to use them in debate, although they are often be needed. Politicians are reduced to silly locutions like "terminological inexactitude" or "economical with the truth." That just don't have the same stinging impact.

If things go on like this we will begin to lose faith in everyone and everything: our lawyers, doctors, TV anchormen, the unrepeatable President's Day discounts, the messages on the Valentine cards we got last year and, heaven help us, even our politicians. But do we really need a truth teller? The idea of a George Washington in the White House telling us all the truths we don't want to hear would be a nightmare. What we want, and will no doubt elect in 2020, is a kind of dissimulator in chief who will have perfected the art of telling us what we *do* want to hear. There should be no shortage of highly qualified candidates.

POLITICS FOR THE REST OF US

Enthusiasm for politics has never been lower. There is less public trust than there was at the time of Watergate, and if you're too young to remember Watergate don't depress yourself by looking it up.

This credibility gap between politicians and voters isn't new. We can date it precisely from March 4, 1789, when the first Congress met. Satirists from Mark Twain to H.L.Mencken, Will Rogers and Steve Colbert have made careers out of the obvious irony that government by the people for the people is in fact government by politicians in spite of the people.

In this all democracies are much alike. In France in the early 2000s, President Nicolas Sarkozy launched his great project to change the habits of the nation. The French have an enviable lifestyle that many people go there to enjoy, and more would like to imitate. They have sensible working hours, long paid vacations, health care, a rich cultural life, and almost an excess of what we might call, for want of a better term, *joi de vivre*.

The President decided that he wanted the French to be more like Americans: to work harder, worry more, forget about job security, and so on. This would save the French government a lot of money. M. Sarkozy planned to make France over in his own image, and he was a workaholic, an authoritarian, and a bundle of neuroses. Sarkozy may love America, that's his business. But the last thing the French people needed was to be forced into the stressful American way of life. The President's unpopularity quickly exceeded all previous records, and he was tossed out of office in 2012, and failed dismally in his effort to make a comeback in 2017.

Too many politicians want to change the world to suit their personal tastes. They call it leadership. But democracy is supposed to work the other way around: *they* should do what *we* want. That's what "representative democracy" means.

Off year elections, when the voting apparatus is already set up, would be a perfect opportunity for the rest of us to get into the game. Propositions, citizen initiatives, referenda, call them what you like, but we could take non-binding votes on dozens of specific issues about how we want to live, and what kind of country we want to live in. Politicians can wriggle around opinion polls based on small samples, but not the undeniable voice of the whole electorate. Most people I'm sure would love to cast their votes for specific policies on health care, the war, taxation, and dozens of other things. We don't know what the outcome of such votes would be, but they would create dreadful headaches in Washington, and in every state and electoral district in the nation. That alone would guarantee a one hundred per cent voter turnout in every future election.

CREATED EQUAL

We've come a long way since the dark days of the 1950s when men and women were as fixed and unthinking in their roles and prejudices as Democrats and Republicans. Now we have women CEOs, women astronauts, and even Presidential candidates. But equality? Not yet, although equality was written into the Declaration of Independence. "All Men are Created Equal," wrote Jefferson, temporarily forgetting about women. But what did he mean? What did he think he meant?

When Alexis de Tocqueville came to America in the 1830s he remarked that the passion for equality knows no bounds here. He didn't mean economic equality, like those rotten communists, but equality in some vague idealistic, almost metaphysical sense. Indeed, equality is perhaps the most relative of all relative concepts. It's obvious that human beings are not equal to more highly evolved creatures like cats. It's equally obvious that we humans are not equal to each other, because equal means "the same," and any high school dropout can see that we're not the same. We start unequal, we finish unequal, and we are never ever equal in between Every year, on August 26, we are reminded of this conundrum by National Women's Equality Day, which celebrates what was supposed to be a great equalitarian moment, the Nineteenth Amendment that gave the vote to women on that date in 1920. Who could have guessed what a disappointing gift the vote would turn out to be? At the time, politicians were terrified that women (a majority of the population) would take over the Congress and create a feminist revolution. This, as you may have noticed, failed to happen. It failed in a *big* way, like President Clinton's plan to provide universal affordable health care, or President Bush's plan to turn Iraq into a liberal democracy.

Women have been voting and standing for office for ninety-seven years, but their progress in the realms of power has been grindingly slow. In 2017 women made up fewer than twenty per-cent of members of Congress – just a few bright spots in a sea of dark suits. The most credible female Presidential contender in 2016 was derailed by a spectacular set of dirty tricks, some of them orchestrated by Russia. It didn't feel like equality.

There's some truth in the old feminist joke that women will never be equal to men because they find it so hard to get down to men's level. Politics is a long way down. So, who will make the adjustment towards equality? Will men give up their hard-won insanity, developed and nurtured through thousands of years of senseless wars? Or must women, just in order to be equal, sink to the same juvenile level?

The big changes didn't happen in politics, where the power is; they happened at work, where the money is. Women rushed to do the jobs that men did because, compared to housework and childcare, paid work seemed infinitely more interesting and dignified. But, as any man could have pointed out, if asked, most paid work is not liberating. It takes up all the time you might otherwise use having a life. Women's lives in the twenty-first century look more like a Road Runner cartoon than glossy magazine vision of gracious living. At home, we've been launched down the slippery slope from two-parent family to one-parent family to the no-parent family.

Sexual equality is hard because the trade-offs are so unpredictable, and so treacherous. Adam and Eve were the first and perhaps the only truly equalitarian couple: they both followed the same fashion in clothing, both worked side by side in their garden, and no doubt they both did the dishes. But they were cast out of paradise to labor all the days of their lives without health benefits, because curiosity drove them to eat of the fruit of the tree of knowledge: not an apple, of course, but a lemon.

ETERNAL REVENUE
From time to time, and especially in April, most of us have wondered why taxes exist. The answer, of course, is that we must have taxes to support the government. This leaves us with the question: why does the government exist? That's easy. If we didn't have a government, nobody would collect the taxes.

In primitive societies, there were no governments, and therefore no taxes. But as soon as kings and chiefs and emperors appeared on the historical stage they acquired an exaggerated sense of self-importance, and a taste for expensive things like gold and jewels, fine foods, rare fabrics, and huge palaces. Naturally, they soon ran out of cash. There were no dot.com investments in those days, to create instant wealth, and such important people certainly didn't want to work. So they had to find a reliable source of income.

About five thousand years ago, some early financial genius noticed that the peasants sometimes had a bit of food to spare, or a few pennies left over at the end of the month, and it was child's play to take it away from them. If you could relieve a large number of peasants of small amounts of goods, it could add up to rather a pleasant lifestyle for the people at the top of the social pyramid. Taxation was born.

In the beginning, the collection system was simple. When a king or a great lord ran out of cash, he would send out a raiding party to strip the nearby villages of everything they had. There were no thirty-day extensions. Anyone who objected to the assessment was simply killed. The taxmen would ride back to the castle with their booty, and that was that.

This slash-and-burn system of tax collecting had many advantages. It was nasty while it lasted, but it was soon over. The king's men might come at any time, but they might not come for years, so April wasn't always ruined. There were no forms to fill in, and no audit to worry about, because there was never anything left to audit. And these episodes of random violence induced a healthy respect for the power of government, something that seems sadly lacking nowadays. Above all, primitive tax collection was cheap. There was no huge bureaucracy, not even a computer network, if you can imagine it. A few thugs, a few swords and a few horses accomplished what the IRS struggles every year to accomplish – the traditional transfer of wealth from the poor to the rich.

The ancient Romans, as you might expect, had a more organized, bureaucratic system. The state licensed individuals called "Publicans" to go out and collect tax money, from which they would take a commission. They worked like bounty hunters, and you can imagine that they were less than universally popular around the Roman Empire.

But many of us I'm sure would prefer the system used by the ancient Greeks. Most of their taxes were indirect, based on the possession of conspicuous things like houses, flocks of sheep, servants, and so on. The more you owned the more you paid, and most citizens paid nothing. If you were *very* rich you might be asked to put up something extra when there was an urgent need, for example to support a war against the

Trojans. Those with large fortunes were also expected to contribute to public works, which might mean building a temple, a ship or a school, or supporting a music group or a theater festival. This, of course, gave the rich great prestige as public benefactors.

Here is an idea whose time has clearly come again. In the past few decades the poor have got poorer and the rich have got very much richer. Let *them* pay for all this expensive government stuff. The rest of us would admire and praise them for it, of course we would.

In contrast to ancient Greece our modern system of tax collection is a masterpiece of waste and redundancy. Governments have learned to confuse the issue by creating such an intricate smokescreen of rules that we spend all our time worrying about the "how" of paying tax, and never have time or energy to ask "why?" One reason why is that, like the peasants of medieval times, we don't have much choice. America's most famous tax rebel, Henry David Thoreau, hid in the woods to avoid taxes. But he was hauled off to jail anyway.

Thoreau had the right idea. He thought that taxes should be voluntary. Citizens should pay for what they wanted, no more and no less. April 15 would be like a gigantic charity appeal, with every arm of government bidding for your dollars: the Pentagon would like lots more missiles, the three million federal bureaucrats would like higher salaries, NASA would like to drop more expensive space probes into deep holes on Mars, and so on. Alongside each item, we could choose to contribute $5, $10, $25, or nothing. That would be a truly democratic tax system.

Governments hate voluntary tax schemes, of course. They have an irrational fear that, given a choice, citizens might choose not to pay up. But we pay for HBO, and the Disney Channel. Who would begrudge a dollar or two, freely given, to sustain the greatest show on earth?

SEEING IS BELIEVING

April makes anarchists of us all. We should feel good about rendering large chunks of our income unto Caesar on the 15th, but we don't. A nasty, petty, complaining mood poisons the spring air. What has Caesar ever done for us?

This is the time for some positive thinking. Just consider some of the things that our tax dollars bought last year. A mere $15 billion poured into schools produced a marginal decrease in performance, thus proving once and for all that money can't buy intelligence. The $270 billion Pentagon budget guarantees that we will be defended against those hordes of wicked communists in North Korea.

But the trouble with most federal government spending is that it's invisible. This set me thinking about a small animal charity in England I have supported for years. It's called St. Tiggywinkles, which (if you grew up on the dramatic animal stories of Beatrix Potter) will immediately tell you that hedgehogs are important in this organization. St. Tiggywinkles is an animal hospital that began by rescuing and rehabilitating sick and injured hedgehogs, and later broadened its scope to include ferrets, rabbits, ducks, deer and just about any wild animal that inhabits those islands.

There are thousands of suckers like me who "adopt" a prickly patient and support the creature until it is well again. Here's what I like about it. When you send money to adopt an animal, they send you news of the patient, a name and a photograph. Sometimes they send progress reports: "Prickles is much better now, and gets around very well on three legs." When I get this information, I feel entirely vindicated and happy that my money is being well spent.

Why can't we apply this same simple public relations device to the federal government? As it is now, when we pay our taxes, we get absolutely no acknowledgement, not even a simple thank you note from the President. The money just vanishes, into the vast bureaucratic hive of Washington, and we hear nothing more from our esteemed leaders until next April.

I'd like a picture of what they buy with my taxes. It won't be very impressive, I know, but if my few dollars contribute a little towards a bolt on a cruise missile, an oxygen cylinder for the unfinished space station, or a Congressman's $1,000 suit, I'd like to have a picture as a souvenir. Federal pensions are very generous: it would be heartwarming to have some snapshots of the federal retirees enjoying themselves expensively in Florida or the Bahamas. If I'm helping to support a poor family, or a hospitalized veteran, or a Peace Corps Volunteer, I'd like to have a picture of them too, and an update on their progress. If my money goes to education, I want a report card.

I calculate that my taxes this year will cover about three days of the President's salary. What is he going to do with it? A snapshot from the golf course would reassure me that my money is being well spent.

If we don't like the picture we get, we should have the right to complain. Like any good department store, the IRS should have a generous returns or exchange policy. If the $1,000 suit is a poor fit, if the missile misses its mark, or if the expensively educated child remains as dumb as before, I want my money back.

No more taxation without visual representation. Please Mr. President, just put me in the picture.

MILITARY INTELLIGENCE

Memorial Day is one of the most elusive of all American national holidays. Nobody really knows how or where it began. Some historians find its origins in the ancient Japanese Festival of Lanterns, or the Zuni Indian All Soul's Day. Others claim that it began in the south after the Civil War, as a day when the graves of fallen soldiers were decorated. But everyone agrees that the symbolic purpose of Memorial Day is to honor and remember the glorious dead of past wars.

I'm happy to say that I am not yet numbered among the glorious dead of past wars, although I suppose I'm still in with a chance. But Memorial Day always sets me thinking, about my own inglorious military experience. Many years ago, I was drafted into the British Army. I wanted to drive tanks, so they put me in the Royal Artillery, for which I was perfectly qualified by being very short-sighted, disliking loud noises, and being bad at trigonometry.

I still like to think that I was the world's worst soldier. That was my ambition. In so far as I had a military model, he was the Good Soldier Schweik, hero of the famous novel by Czech writer Jaroslav Hasek. As an unwilling draftee in the First World War, Schweik discovered a genius for pretending to obey, while subtly undermining and ridiculing the military hierarchy. I made it my business to do the same. Any rational military organization would have put me back into civilian clothes within a week. But that's not how the military mind works.

Having half-trained us, and promoted the least talented into the officer class, the army sent our regiment to Cyprus, where the Turks and Greeks were continuing their thousand-year argument over territory. Our job was to police the conflict. We were hopeless, partly because most of us were unwilling conscripts, partly because we liked both the Turks and the Greeks, but mainly because we had no desire to join the glorious dead of past wars. A good soldier must be willing to lay down his life for the cause, whatever it is. We were not good soldiers, in this or any other sense.

Looking back, I think we were the first wave of a new kind of army - perhaps the first wave of the last army. Consider how military tactics have evolved over the past few hundred years.

In the good old days, the king or general would lead his army into battle. Alexander the Great or King Richard III would be right up there on the sharp end of the conflict, inspiring the troops with their own courage. They started the fight, and they felt honor bound to finish it in person.

Then, sometime in the late nineteenth century, as war became more mechanized and less glorious, princes and generals very wisely decided that their lives were too valuable to risk in mere brute combat, and started leading from the rear. For the first half of the twentieth century, ordinary soldiers and sailors were cannon fodder. Their job was to be killed without making too much of a fuss.

But since Vietnam, we have this whole new language of military engagement. The troops must be protected. Every casualty is a political as well as a personal disaster. No risks must be taken. Our boys and girls must come home safe. This revolutionary idea was anticipated in the 1970s by Danish pacifists, who proposed that the armed forces of that nation should be completely disbanded, and replaced by a tape-recorded broadcast saying: "We surrender."

This bloodless concept of war would have puzzled Alexander the Great or Napoleon. But, never mind, it's a great idea. If we all agree that nobody's life should be needlessly sacrificed, then we are well on the way to a truly non-violent military.

The next and last step towards peace on earth would be to recognize the undesirability of weapons. As I learned in the army, guns are nasty, dangerous things that can go off at any time and cause a painful injury. Bombs and missiles are even worse. The military can keep their nice uniforms, their ranks and the insignia, their ceremonies and martial rhetoric, and even their inflated pensions. But the weapons have to go. That would be progress, that would be evolution. That would be something to celebrate, on some future Memorial Day.

FORCE OF NUMBERS
The proposal floated by two army generals that women should be required to register for selective service is a step in the right direction, but only a step. If we follow through on the logic of this idea it would solve at least one of our global problems.

We have scarcely heard the word "draft" whispered since 2007 at the height of the war in Iraq, when Representative Charles Rangel spoke it out loud, and attracted some Congressional support. Cynical commentators suggested that talking about a draft was just a sneaky way of turning people against the war, but surely no politician could be *that* devious. No, the draft is a way to democratize war, to allow all of us to get involved. The Founders of this nation had no enthusiasm for a professional military. If you have a large standing army, as James Madison pointed out, the temptation to use it, or for it to use you, is almost irresistible. Instead the Founding Fathers planned for a mass mobilization of the population as and when necessary. It is necessary now, or soon will be.

But it has to be the right kind of draft, not a cherry-picking operation that selects all the healthy eighteen-year-olds without rich parents. That was the bad old draft. The bright new equal opportunity draft would include absolutely everybody: pacifists and warmongers, Democrats and Republicans, believers and atheists, all ages, races, colors, and socio-economic profiles, and naturally both sexes: no exemptions, no deferments.

Everyone agrees that in the current regional conflicts we need more boots on the ground, even if they are orthopedic shoes or high heels. The British had 15,000 soldiers in Afghanistan in 1842 and they were wiped out. The United States has about 10,000 troops there right now. President Johnson, in the days of Vietnam, would have laughed at such a half-hearted measures. He threw in 365,000 new troops between 1965 and 1968. But President Johnson had the advantage of the draft.

A universal draft would indeed have many advantages. It would guarantee eventual victory by sheer weight of numbers, or perhaps by sheer weight. It would add interest to the lives of millions of bored housewives and idle senior citizens like me who are reasonably fit, and could carry a gun if it wasn't too heavy and shoot straight if we had our glasses. It would educate women into the world of boy's games that they now find so mystifying (while incidentally scaring the enemy half to death – our particular enemy is terrified of women), and it would introduce many young people to discipline, and allow them to use the skills they have learned by playing violent video games.

Most important, a universal draft would share the pain of war, and the pride that comes from sacrificing oneself in a noble cause. When I was drafted into the army sixty years ago, my comrades and I took much comfort from the thought that we might be sacrificed in a noble cause. We talked about it all the time, although we managed to avoid making the actual sacrifice.

If we must have a war, let's make it a genuine people's war. If we're going to bring democracy to the Middle East, let's set an example with a truly democratic and equalitarian military.

It's a drastic proposal I know, and it would be intolerable to impose such a huge burden on an unwilling public. We'll have to vote on it.

ALL AMERICAN

Virtually everybody on the planet, except the French, wants to be American. This is the only superpower nation, and the dollar is already the effective global currency. We can see where all this is headed in the long run, so why not let's just go ahead and do it right now. We could never in a million years persuade Americans to become Canadians or Cambodians. So, let's do the logical thing and declare that every single person in the world will be an American citizen, as of Memorial Day in the year 2025.

This will be a huge project, rather like the Marshall Plan that set Europe on its feet after World War Two. Great airlifts of burgers and fries, lawyers and golf clubs and lawn sprinklers will bring the new civilization, even to the remotest villages of Asia, Africa, Europe and South America. Everybody will have larger cars, larger houses, larger refrigerators, and they will become larger themselves.

It may sound radical, but there is an historical precedent. At the height of the Roman Empire, Saxons, Gauls, Turks, and dozens of other nationalities were all enrolled as Roman Citizens under a single government, with a single language. The Pax Romana lasted for two centuries. It would have lasted longer, if Latin hadn't been such a wretchedly hard language to learn.

English, by contrast, is easy. When everybody is American, students can throw away their language tapes and textbooks, and we will all communicate in English, as nature and Hollywood intended.

That's the least of the benefits. All this whining about globalization and cultural imperialism will have to stop at once. The English or the Saudi Arabians will scarcely be able to complain about "Americanization" when they are Americans themselves.

With no hordes of foreigners to defend us against, the Immigration and Naturalization Service will be able to shut up shop, as will the State Department and the Pentagon, freeing up tens of thousands of much-needed employees for the fast food industry.

But by far the biggest benefit will be the universal application of the American system of law and government. All of the many schisms in the world will be settled according to the rule of law and the Constitution. Ethnic conflicts will become civil rights matters. Economic and religious arguments will end up in court instead of on the battlefield. The bonanza for lawyers will surpass even the Clinton impeachment fiasco. Meanwhile the United Nations and NATO will become redundant, and go out of business.

What a history-making gesture this will be, two thousand years after the Romans blew it! No more patriotic wars, no more casualties: a true *Pax Americana*. What a memorial it would be to all the people who died because they happened to belong to the wrong nationality, and be in the wrong place at the wrong time. I'm not predicting absolute peace overnight. For one thing, as American citizens, all six billion human beings on the planet will acquire the right to bear arms, a right now strictly forbidden to most of them. This will be a bonanza for under-employed homicide departments everywhere. But in this new global society, we will be sure of one thing: whenever and wherever we meet the enemy, he will always be us.

WARS OF INDEPENDENCE

The campaign for Scottish independence that ended in failure in 2014 aroused intense interest because it posed the most basic of all political questions, namely "What is a nation?" There are almost two hundred recognized nations in the world, but there could easily be two thousand if every independence movement succeeded. Nationalism is back with a vengeance: Uigars in China, Russians in Ukraine, French speakers in Quebec, Flemish speakers in Belgium. The list of restive minorities who want independence is enormous. Even a large, mostly English-speaking nation like the United States is really a patchwork of smaller nations pulling in different directions. What does California have in common with Kansas, except the same fast food chains? Would someone born and bred in Vermont feel at home in Texas? And we won't even mention the Civil War.

The driving force of all independence movements is simply that we like our own territory and way of life, and we tend not to like strangers. It's natural to prefer to live in a familiar place with people like us, and to be governed by people like us who speak the same language. It's the same with a family or a sports team or any group of people who have important things in common. The impulse to divide the world into "Us" and "Them" may not be a noble one, but it most certainly is reassuring. How else can we know who we are?

The pressure to conform to the prejudices of your own group is enormous. I'm sure that a lot of voters in the "no" camp in the Scottish independence referendum were keeping a low profile because they felt they were on the wrong side of the "Us and Them" divide. This it brings us right up against the question of individual freedom, which we value so highly. How can you "do your own thing" if it is different from everyone else's thing? How can you be a team player if you have your own ideas about how to play? The answer is, you can't, and nor can I. We are the prisoners of our culture.

In a traditional society, every tribe and village has a different culture, meaning a set of rules and traditions about how to live. Many of the people of Scotland felt and still feel strongly that they have their own distinctive culture, sharply different from what passes for culture in England where kilts and bagpipes are rarely seen. Every distinction becomes a source of conflict.

Yet at some level we love this cultural diversity. What a dull world it would be if France was the same as Alabama or Japan the same as Mexico. Cultures are rich, fascinating, inspiring, and they remind us every day that there are other ways to live and other ways to think. It's a question of drawing the line somewhere. Once you start calling every whim, habit, sectarian difference, and local prejudice a "national culture" there's no end to it. Some people won't be satisfied until they have their own personal country and the world is divided into seven billion independent fragments.

This is not one of those paradoxes that can be resolved in four minutes, or perhaps ever. But, personally, I'm glad I don't need my passport to get into Scotland. It's a lovely country, and of course it *is* a country whatever the politicians may say.

POLITICS AND LANGUAGE

It is always a waste of time to suggest that: "Everybody should see this" or "Everybody should read that," because "Everybody" pays absolutely no attention. But I'll make an exception in this case. In this perpetual election season, everybody should read or re-read George Orwell's essay "Politics and the English Language." It doesn't take long, perhaps ten minutes to absorb the whole thing, and it works like a kind of linguistic flu shot. Next time a toxic cloud of political rhetoric comes your way you will find to your surprise and relief that you are completely immune.

Orwell's essay is more than half a century old, but it is as on target now as it was then. His subject is political language which, in his words, "Is designed to make lies sound truthful, and to give an appearance of solidity to pure wind." He attacks the clichés that political candidates have always loved, and still do: *our children's future, the healing process, to reach out, time for change, vision, diversity, this great state, this great nation* – and of course the ever popular *at this point in time* and *going forward* – all designed to allow the candidate to keep talking while saying nothing. Such clichés are a sure sign that the speaker is not thinking, probably cannot think, and doesn't expect his audience to think either.

Then there are what Orwell calls "Verbal false limbs" - empty phrases whose only purpose is to avoid direct and unambiguous verbs and nouns: *to render inoperative; to militate against; to have the effect of,* instead of simple words like stop, prevent, cause. And pretentious words for simple things: expedite and clandestine instead of speed up and secret, amelio-rate and liquidate, instead of improve and kill.

Above all political language is full of code words and phrases that are essentially meaningless: *family values, natural resources, human rights, the melting pot, the American dream, fair trade, global leadership, national security* and so on. These all sound splendid, but they are impossible to define. We are all in favor of *human rights*, for example. But what does it mean? No two dictators can agree.

To be fair it's not easy being a politician in an age of total exposure, at least not at election time. Candidates must talk continuously, unhesitatingly, and with apparent authority about all the wonderful things they will accomplish if elected. Any sign of a pause for thought will be penalized by the electorate and the media as a sign of indecision. No thoughts are allowed, let alone second thoughts. At the same time candidates must keep the words flowing without ever saying anything clear or definite that can be held against them later.

Speechwriters have made this kind of non-language into an art form. A strike of political speechwriters would be revealing. Perhaps we would hear the candidates' real voices at last, or simply silence. Or perhaps, in case of such a strike, TV comedy writers might be persuaded to cross the political picket line and bring their satirical skills to the campaign trail. Then at least we would get some entertainment out of the democratic process.

When we can't make much sense of what candidates say, it all comes down to how they look, and how we feel about them. This may be a good way to choose a piece of fish or a new hat, but it's an insane way to choose political leaders. We need to know whether they think, how they think, and what they would say if they could only find the words.

Theme V

Perpetual Motion

Travel is fatal to prejudice, bigotry, and narrow-mindedness, and many of our people need it sorely on these accounts. Broad, wholesome, charitable views of men and things cannot be acquired by vegetating in one little corner of the earth all one's lifetime.

MARK TWAIN

Travel broadens the mind; but first you must have the mind.

G.K.CHESTERTON

To understand Europe, you have to be a genius, or French.

MADELEINE ALBRIGHT

ESCAPE ATTEMPTS

The trajectory of life as a short trip between two dead ends pretty much guarantees that smart creatures like us will never stop looking for an exit. We are forever trying to find the magic doorway from black and white Kansas into the Technicolor Land of Oz.

The verb "to escape" was once reserved for prisoners. Now it has taken on a much grander meaning. Escape is a breakout to freedom and happiness, a liberation from the open prison of everyday life. The the gigantic size of the modern travel industry (2.3 trillion dollars a year by one estimate) testifies to the fact that we are never happy where we are, and always want to be somewhere else. The all-too-true cliché that "Wherever you go, there you are" does absolutely nothing to dissuade most of us from travelling hopefully, and expecting to leave ourselves behind. Escape is movement. Escape is theater. We know we have escaped when the view out the window is different, and our daily routine has little moments of drama in it.

It is rather ironic, although scarcely surprising, that in the richest country in the world with the highest standard of living, so many of us long to take a break from it all. A survey a few years ago suggested that seven out of ten Americans feel that their lives lack novelty, change, and excitement. Security breeds boredom, the way stagnant water breeds mosquitoes. That's why men love wars and NASCAR racing. They are a break from regular work and lawn care. I suspect that boredom even explains why so many people get married, or divorced, or have children. At least it might be the start of something different. We try to tunnel out of our prison, but always come up short of the perimeter fence.

People who have rich inner lives will tell you that the only true escape is the kind that can be achieved through meditation, or listening to fine music, or reading a good book. This makes some sense to me, even though I never stop looking for escape through travel. Reading is another of my favorite and most reliable ways of sidestepping reality. Not even a book is necessary if you have a vivid imagination. Fantasy can take you very far. Most of have season tickets to an inner theater of the mind that can seem more vivid than reality itself. The only problem with an inner fantasy is that it vanishes in a puff of disappointment as soon as you bring it down to earth. Sex is perhaps the best example of this. One person's fantasy can be another person's dreary reality. For the employees of the Disney Corporation Disneyland is anything but a magic kingdom, and for workers in the sex industry their encounters are anything but romantic. The attempt to turn dreams into reality – a frequent promise of the travel industry – often slams up against this unhappy fact. The closer you get, the tackier the dream looks.

On a more intellectual plane there are the high arts, either as a personal passion or as a secret world in which to hide from the crass world outside. For those with the right mental equipment, simple solitude, or even quiet, ironic observation, can be a very satisfactory refuge. We can jump down the rabbit hole of total narcissism by embracing one of the many spiritual or psychological therapies that offer to lead us to our "true selves" although, if your true self proves to be dull, stupid, or disappointing it must be hard to decide what to do next.

Sometimes it seems that escape is the main and most romantic of all human activities. Many lives are illuminated by a passionate interest such as collecting or sport. Bumper stickers, which I take to be a sociological window into the collective unconscious, may be public announcements of such a passion: "I'd rather be...." (playing golf, fishing, sailing, and so on). These are truly cries from the heart, and perhaps confessions of despair.

We have mass entertainment on a scale never dreamt of by the Roman emperors, and now we have the internet where millions live their alternative lives. Secondhand emotions can be consumed wholesale, from fake sentimentality to fake violence. This highlights the difference between *escape* and *escapism*. We have more and better forms of escapism available to us than any previous generation in history. The entertainment industry is so vast and so sophisticated that it threatens to replace ordinary life entirely. If we need distraction we can find it in a million electronic forms, any one of which will blot out the real world for a few minutes or hours. But these are mere distractions and we must to return to earth eventually, if only to pay the electric and internet bills.

Escapism in the non-electronic world is necessarily more active, and seems to have reached a point of desperation. Nothing is new or exciting enough, and so we find young people embracing the near-suicidal thrills of extreme sports. These often involve getting off the surface of the earth upwards (mountaineering, parachuting) or downwards (caving, diving). Then of course there is suicide itself which promises the same result with less expensive equipment, and designer drugs that offer a brief encounter with joy followed by an eternity of nothing.

There are plenty of more mundane possibilities on offer, including commercial courses that promise to turn you into an artist or a writer, plus a whole world of products that promise a new and improved life through the purchase of clothes, cars, or other image-making possessions. At the end of the line we have the sex change, and perhaps the Federal Witness Protection program. It's all a little sad.

So, escapism is fun but it is only a short break from reality. Escape is more serious and profound. An escape takes us beyond ourselves to a new place or a new life, and by far the simplest and most available form of escape is simply to keep moving. Restlessness seems to be part of the human condition. That is how we spread from Africa over the entire globe, and how we would spread through the universe if we could figure out how to do it.

I suffer from the restless disease in a chronic form, never quite happy unless have plans to be somewhere else, and preferably an airline ticket already in my pocket. This makes no sense because I am very happy with my life as it is. But still I want to get away from it. The "to" is often less important than the "from." A few hours in a plane flying in any direction at five hundred miles per hour gives a powerful impression of escaping. I always hope that things will be different at my destination, and of course they are for a while, until I contrive to make them the same.

The great thing about travel is that it puts us firmly in the role of outsider. Once we leave our familiar territory (and perhaps our familiar language) it seems that the people around us – the "foreigners" although of course we are the foreigners – are living in a kind of fiction. We can't share their world or their script, and we have a choice whether to study them actively like ethnographers or watch them passively like spectators. This emotional detachment no doubt explains why some people behaves so badly when abroad. They imagine themselves in a kind of Disney World where nothing is real.

If language and culture are a single package, which they are, then language itself is the ultimate trap. The more you understand and participate in language/culture, the more thoroughly you are locked in by it. Conversely, language allows a form of escape if you are in a context where others are speaking and knowing differently. Teenagers develop their own languages to disconnect from the adult world.

This may be why many creative people live abroad, because it gives them a way of life they find congenial to their own disconnectedness, their need to have a perspective on everyone else's perspective. I feel pleasantly disconnected in this way, when we are living in France. Stepping out in the morning into the beautiful but alien landscape of the village, seeing everything but understanding very little, is strangely liberating. A French conversation in the market, or a short drive on the narrow local roads provides all the excitement I need or can stand these days. Small escapes are sometimes the best.

At the opposite end of the scale of restlessness are people so attached to one place that they never want to leave. They cling to remote villages in the Chinese hinterland, or dull houses in dreary British towns, as though their lives depended on it. How often have you heard or read: "I was born here, and I want to die here"? Such people may be afraid of change, and skeptical that the larger world has anything better to offer than the security of home. They are happy with who and where they are, and who can argue with that as a definition of the good life?

Once I lived in an English village where some of the older inhabitants had never even been to the nearest big town five miles away, let alone to London. Now, in our French village, most of the locals can trace their ancestors back for generations, and live in the same houses as did their parents and grandparents. Meanwhile we jump in and out of village life like migrant birds, or stray cats. They think we must be mad, and they are probably right.

ON THE BEACH

In high summer, it seems as if the whole world is at the beach, and I am the only one with my clothes on and my feet dry. This is entirely my own choice, but it creates an irrational feeling of guilt. On Long Island, we are lucky enough to have the ocean all around us. It seems eccentric and curmudgeonly to avoid the beaches, but I do avoid them with almost religious zeal.

I blame my parents. They took me to the beach regularly, and indeed relentlessly when I was a child. This doesn't sound so bad until you realize that the beaches were in England. The ocean was gray and always cold, with clinging seaweed and stinging jellyfish, our sandcastles were beaten down by the rain as often as not, and our seaside picnics were an ordeal, with sand in the sandwiches and wasps in the jam. In adult life, I have found warmer and more welcoming beach resorts, but I have never discovered the secret of getting comfortable on sand. You can't sit up straight for long because there is nowhere to rest your back, and if you lie down you discover that the softest sand turns to stone after a few minutes. The only way to be comfortable on a beach is to bring furniture, which must be carried miles from the car park, and back again. I won't even mention the effects of the deadly ultra violet rays, although my dermatologist would be happy to fill in the details.

The beach is a false promise. If we look to literature we see that it often has a dark meaning, symbolic of desolation and loss. In Neville Shute's post-apocalyptic novel *On the Beach*, and J.G. Ballard's *The Terminal Beach.* it represents the end of everything. To be "on the beach" is to be washed up, finished. In H.G.Wells's classic *The Time Machine* the hero travels thirty million years into the future to arrive at the last moment of time, on a lifeless beach of dark red sand.

Yet this narrow strip of pulverized rock along the edge of the ocean clearly has a magnetic attraction. Seventy-five percent of Americans live within fifty miles of the sea, and most of them choose to take their vacations at the shore. Almost five hundred million people crowd around the rim of the Mediterranean, and so many vacationers come to join them in July and August that you almost expect the continent to tilt down at the southern edge and sink, like Atlantis. The annual invasion of sun-and-sand seekers brings huge problems of water supply, power supply and garbage disposal to resorts of the sunny south, but nobody seems to care. Everyone is drawn to the beach.

Psychologists have speculated that the close packed crowds on the sand may be recreating a lost sense of community, or even re-enacting some ancient communion with the ocean itself, which is where we all came from four hundred million years ago. Or the attraction may be as simple as being able to take you shoes off, or take practically everything off, and feel the primitive pleasure that comes when your private skin meets the public air.

But I have a more profound, more philosophical theory. Whether we are beach people or not, we all love to *look* at the sea, and perhaps that is what we really want. On the shore, we have the sensation of being on the brink of new things, of having our troubles literally behind us. The beach is the very edge of escape because the sea can take us anywhere in the world. So, a beach is a liminal space, a launching pad, a place for dreams and infinite fantasy. A vacation in the middle of Kansas just isn't the same.

VACATION DREAMS
Early Spring is a busy time for the travel industry. The vacations of last summer have faded from memory, and months of cold and darkness still lie ahead. Magazines and television glow with advertisements for the golden weeks of next summer and how we can enjoy them, at a price. Right now, when we so much want to get away, almost any price seems worth paying.

Vacations are as much a matter of personal taste as food or music. One person's perfect getaway is another's worst nightmare. So, the huge vacation market is roughly divided between packages that offer comfortable and familiar experiences, and those that promote getaways that are new and challenging – between relaxation on the one hand and stimulation on the other. There is also a large intermediate category of trips like European river cruises, that promise travel on calm waters, with a boat full of people just like ourselves, familiar food and comfortable surroundings, gliding at a safe distance through an exotic landscape full of foreigners, some of whom may be persuaded to pose for souvenir photographs. This is obviously the best of both worlds.

I would rather like to take one of those river cruises, they sound so relaxing. But they also seem a bit tame. There are so many parts of the world I haven't seen, and the travel industry has been there ahead of me, preparing for me as it were. Every exotic locale has been exploited to the maximum. No island is too isolated, no culture is too peculiar, no activity is too bizarre to be promoted by the tourist industry as a unique travel experience. There is not a remote tribe or an endangered species that doesn't have its own group of tourists, cameras poised to record each moment. The exotic has become the mundane – bungee jumping in the Sahara, surfing in Antarctica. When everyone it seems has walked on the Great Wall of China or herded wild guinea pigs in Peru, it is very hard to find something different on a small planet.

Vacations are escape attempts. Their purpose is to convince us at all costs – and the costs are often huge – that we really have left our small, crowded planet, and that this is not just more of the same. Hence the market for so-called adventure holidays keeps on growing, although it's nothing new. Forty years ago, when I had a lot of hair and an enviable suntan I worked for an adventure holiday outfit based in London. My job was to be a driver and guide for small groups of intrepid, and sometimes marginally insane tourists who wanted to see the real Greece, the real Turkey, the real Russia or the real Morocco. If "real" means dirty, desolate, and totally lacking in amenities we certainly delivered on that promise. The "adventures" consisted mainly in surviving or even recognizing the food, trying to sleep in our cheap collapsing tents, and being driven by a guide – namely myself – who had no sense of direction and bad eyesight. Nobody ever booked a second trip with that company.

But there's no true escape without a little effort. A vacation *should* include excitement, discomfort, uncertainty and risk. It's exactly what we need to take us out of our mundane everyday worlds. Or, perhaps more precisely, it's what *you* need. I've already been there, and done that.

BON VOYAGE

Nobody chooses to have a flying habit, any more than they choose to have cats or arthritis. It's just one of those things that happens to us, part of the eternally restless pattern of modern life.

My occasional flights are nothing compared to those of a celebrity, an international businessman or a Secretary of State. But I suspect that such privileged passengers somehow avoid the long lines at check in and pass-port control, as well as the increasingly humiliating "security" procedures, and have an altogether less stressful travel experience.

At least the airlines have given up trying to pretend that flying is a pleasure. Forty years ago, they tempted us with seductive advertisements promising delicious meals, luxurious seats and smiling flight attendants. Now all we get is a paper e-ticket with about five pages of warnings, admonitions and instructions that remind me of daily orders in the army – all threats and no promises.

A particularly nasty threat comes from one major European airline, which encourages passengers to choose their seat partners according to their profiles on Facebook or Linked In, thus eliminating just about the only pleasure of a long flight – a few hours of quiet and solitary time. Another promotes its service to France with the slogan "I Care" which, as my wife pointed out, is French for Icarus, the man who flew too close to the sun and crashed to earth. There's not much thinking going on here, and perhaps none. I suspect that airlines have simply dismissed all their advertising and public relations people and replaced them with hard-hearted drill sergeants whose main job is to keep the paying customers in line and obedient to discipline.

Geography is the fundamental problem. Geologists tell us that a billion years ago Europe and America were a single land mass. You could go to the eastern end of Long Island and just step over into the west of

England, thus saving an enormous amount of trouble and expense. But the appearance of some thousands of miles of ocean between created a problem, at least until the invention of the luxury liner.

An aunt of mine had a job that involved a lot of international travel and, in those days, flights were expensive, unreliable, and rather dangerous. Instead she floated around the world on a series of great ships – the Queen Mary, the Normandie, the Mauretania, although fortunately not the Titanic. Each new assignment began and ended with a week or two of vacation at sea when my aunt, who was unmarried, was likely to be one of the few unattached females on the ship. She loved her job.

We can stay at home of course, and we will have to do that anyway when the jet fuel runs out. But much better would be to bring back those old luxury liners. There are hundreds of huge cruise ships drifting pointlessly around the world, and sinking from time to time. If they could be pressed into service as real passenger ships to transport the world's restless millions it would slow us all down, help the environment, and make every trip truly a *bon voyage*.

TAKING CHANCES

When my wife and I travel we organize everything in a thorough and sensible way. We know where we're going and what we are planning to do in some detail before we ever reach the airport. We don't like surprises. But travel didn't used to be like this. Before it became an industry, travel was often an adventure. Surprises came thick and fast, and even a short journey was never guaranteed to end where and when you had planned, or indeed to end without some kind of catastrophe. That's why most people stayed close to home.

This naturally brings us to Christopher Columbus, whose careless sailing trips in the Atlantic have caused so much trouble ever since. He found it hard to plan his voyages because he didn't know where he was going. He didn't even know where he arrived. His assignment was to find a westward passage to India, a semi-mythical land of fabulous wealth. In this he totally failed. The map makers of his time forgot to show that there was a whopping great continent blocking the way between Europe and Asia, and Columbus ran right into it. On his various voyages, he landed in Watling Island, Cuba, Haiti, Honduras, and Panama, but never on the North American mainland or even on Long Island. To his dying day he believed that he had in fact discovered a passage to India, although how he could have mistaken the Bahamas for India, given their very different tastes in food and music, remains a mystery.

The great explorers of the past like Captain Cook, David Livingstone, Marco Polo, Lewis and Clarke, ventured into the unknown. As modern tourists, we venture only into the known. That doesn't mean there are no surprises at all, even in well-discovered countries like Italy or France. Foreign food is a surprise if you have only tasted American cuisine. Foreign driving is always a surprise, not to say a trauma. But, in general, today's traveler knows what to expect anywhere in the world, or can easily find out. Our local library has shelves of guidebooks on France, Spain and Italy, but also guides to Lithuania, Estonia, Latvia, Iceland, the Himalayas, Nepal, Sri Lanka, Namibia and Zimbabwe. Guides to Baghdad, Kabul, and Somalia are readily available, in case you feel the urge to go there for your next vacation.

Not so long ago the interior of Namibia was *terra incognita* for white westerners. Now it has its own glossy tourist guide in our ultra-white suburban library. What this means is that the history of exploration on this planet is, literally, history. There may be scientific discoveries to be made in the depths of jungles or oceans but, essentially, we have the complete map. Ancient charts had great blank spaces labeled "Here be monsters." Now there are no scary blanks, apart from some odd corners of Brooklyn and the Bronx.

This lack of unknowns in the geographical world is strangely deflating. No wonder we look for artificial excitement simulated 'mysteries,' and no wonder we still stand in awe of the great explorers of the past, like Señor Columbus who dreamed of new worlds, and went looking for them regardless of the risks. We may also wonder, as the future stretches infinitely ahead on the same old familiar planet with no place left to discover, where on earth we are going to find the next big adventure.

THE SECRET LIFE OF JUST ABOUT EVERYBODY

It was only a matter of time before yet another version of *The Secret Life of Walter Mitty* made it on to the big screen. I haven't seen the movie with Ben Stiller, but I don't need to. Walter Mitty has entered the realm of mythology, and his biography is as universal as a love story. Everybody knows it, and everybody lives it.

Walter Mitty was an invention of the great humorist James Thurber. He first appeared in a short story in *The New Yorker* just one week after I was born. Can this be coincidence? Walter instantly became an American hero, a mild-mannered man apparently living a boring life in suburban Connecticut. But his real life was all in his daydreams. While doing the family shopping, Walter imagined that he was a famous surgeon, a fighter pilot, even a killer. His imaginary life was infinitely richer and more exciting than anything the suburbs had to offer.

There's no mystery about why this short story became so popular, and has been reprinted and filmed so many times. Walter is all of us - apart from the tiny percentage of people who really do live exciting and important lives. What do *you* dream about when you are at the supermarket? Probably you dream about being somebody else, and doing something much more interesting than bagging groceries.

It is sad but true that everyday life is dull most of the time, and we spend a lot of energy trying to escape from ordinariness. That's why most dramas and soap operas focus on the extraordinary moments – the illnesses, accidents, love affairs, crimes and disasters that rarely come crashing in to disturb our real-life routines. It's hard to make entertainment out of the quiet bits in between, when nothing much happens. As novelist, John Barth, commented: "Realty is a nice place to visit, but you wouldn't want to live there."

So, we are very good at planning escapes, and we need them. Some researchers have suggested that in fact a large proportion of all our mental activity is just that – an attempt to get away from reality. We may daydream about grand adventures, like Walter Mitty, or simply about travel to some exotic place, or a new house, or a better job. Some unfortunate dreamers find their escapes in in drugs, or madness.

Others leave reality behind by immersing themselves in hobbies, or the tribal comforts of sports or politics, special interest groups, or esoteric beliefs, or fantasies of wealth and power. They're all alternatives to everyday life, and it's not necessary to *do* anything to enjoy them. In a former age people read books for an effortless escape, and a few antiquarians still do. But electronic escapes are now readily available on a billion screens. Just about everybody has a secret life. If you don't have one, it's just a few clicks away.

Our secret lives tend to stay secret, because they are embarrassing. If you really want to be a NASCAR driver or a fashion model or a vampire, it's probably best not to mention it to anybody. Fantasies, like vampires, tend to evaporate as soon as they are exposed to the light of day, and the more extreme fantasies may get you locked up. Yet how much more we would understand about each other if we knew the landscapes those secret lives.

Naturally, I have a secret life too, but you will have to wait for the movie. Sylvester Stallone is fully booked.

WHERE AM I?

When I need to find my way around in this complicated world my navigation system, which has always served me well, consists of a collection of tattered maps and street guides, some of them dating back to the 1960s, and a small pocket compass that points randomly in all directions.

The opportunity to move into a new age of technology came one summer with a car rental that included a free portable global positioning system. This turned out to be a little gadget, half the size of a folded road map, with an even smaller set of instructions printed in smudged ink on a scrap of paper, and apparently translated from the Chinese by somebody whose first language was Peruvian.

However, this was a brand new, state of the art, twenty first century GPS, and I couldn't wait to try it. But I didn't throw away my maps quite yet, which was just as well. A paper map shows you the way and takes you right there. The makers of GPS systems have decided that this is much too easy. First you need to persuade the machine to recognize where you want to go, even though you yourself know this already. Your GPS also knows the one and only right way to get there, and will not change its tiny electronic mind, so forget about any creative diversions. If you prefer to use an unconventional route to avoid traffic, for example, or to view some attractive scenery, you are out of luck.

When I plugged in the GPS it thought it was in Wisconsin and had to be convinced that it was currently in France. Then, as a test, I asked to be guided to the nearest town a few miles away, on a road I knew well. It demanded a street name and number, which I didn't have, then offered half a dozen towns with similar names that I might perhaps prefer to visit. Finally, grudgingly, it allowed me to move off, speaking in a flat, authoritarian voice that sounded like a Midwestern school teacher. She had not studied the language of the country she was in, and pronounced the names phonetically which made them funny, but incomprehensible.

She got me on to the right road, after a great deal of what she called "re-calibrating." It was good that I already knew the way because my electronic guide had little sympathy for human foibles, or even for geographical reality. When I took a small detour into a village she ordered: "Stop, turn around." This was in a village street eight feet wide where I had no more prospect of turning than of flying, and that was a one-way street in any case.

The GPS lit up with enthusiasm whenever we approached a gas station, in spite of the appalling prices, but she did not warn me of really important things like speed limits, lurking gendarmes, mad teenagers, or sheep on the road. She was far from infallible. On the return journey, which she did not seem to enjoy, she ordered me to turn right into the front window of a pharmacy instead of left into the main street.

The car and its navigation system went back to the rental agency, and I went back to my collection of moth-eaten maps. Maps worked for Columbus, more or less, and for all the great explorers down to recent times. I may soon be the last person in the world to use a paper map, but I may also be the last to know where on earth I really am.

POOL PARTY

Lots of people like to lounge by the pool on a holiday weekend. But we have no pool and very little experience of lounging. So, we were pleased to get an invitation from friends to come and lounge by their pool. The weather was warm, although perhaps not quite warm enough for such an outdoor extravagance. This, I thought, would be a challenge. The last time I had lounged by a pool, as far as I could remember, was in 1966 at a cheap motel outside Phoenix, Arizona. I was stuck there for a week with car trouble, and the temperature was close to a hundred. The pool was the only alternative to sitting in front of a feeble air conditioner in my motel room. I positioned myself on the concrete rim of the pool close to the water, and did my best to lounge. There is a faded photograph of me doing this, looking bored and discontented.

The trouble with lounging by a pool is that it offers very few distractions. There is nothing to look at except a few thousand gallons of blue water that might be of more use to a farmer in California. If there are bathing beauties it's different, but these visions of bodily perfection rarely appear outside movies and magazines. Mostly what we see at the pool are just regular people, inadequately dressed. The ultra-violent ray hammers down on our vulnerable bodies, and I hear the phantom voice of my dermatologist saying: "Remember what happened last time."

Before you can even start lounging you must learn to ignore all these discomforts, plus swarms of more or less hostile insects that want to feast on your naked body. But there's more to learn. The physical business of lounging proves to be an acquired skill. Normally I am either sitting up or lying down, and if the latter I am asleep. Lounging is a kind of intermediate state, like limbo. The lounge chair forces an awkward posture, half sitting and half lying like a semi-resurrected corpse. If you rest your head back the sun hurts your eyes. If you force your head forward to read you get a pain in the neck.

However, on this occasion, the surroundings were beautiful: intense blues and greens, bird song, cicadas, the hum of subterranean pumps – a soporific combination. Time passed. The temperature climbed and I fell asleep, only to be woken by the siren song of all pool enthusiasts: "Come on in, the water's fine."

You believe this only once in your life. I might have believed it when I was five years old, but years of icy pools and freezing bathing beaches have taught me wisdom. The water is never fine. At school, we were taken for weekly swimming lessons at a pool that was so cold and so heavily chlorinated that it is amazing we weren't bleached and killed by hypothermia at the same time. It was the period of the polio scare and the sensible thing would have been to keep kids out of pools altogether. But no, we all had to learn swim, and even to dive. I would prefer this to be a repressed memory, but the smell of chlorine brings it back every time.

I never complain, so I sat by the pool, lounging as best I could, until it was time to go indoors and sit on proper chairs for much-needed refreshment. As we sipped our drinks I reflected, but refrained from saying, that it's a good thing we're all different. If we all enjoyed the same kinds of pleasures the sunny swimming pools of the world would be impossibly overcrowded, while the all the comfortable chairs in all the air-conditioned rooms would be empty.

LIFE IS NOT A CABARET

We spent a few days in Berlin. It was not long enough to get to know the place well, but I have seldom been in a city that produced such contradictory emotions. On the one hand, we had to admire the sweeping boulevards, the grand architecture from the past, the green spaces, and the splendid public transportation system. On the other hand, at least for people of my generation, Berlin evokes dark images. Seeing the Brandenburg Gate, *Unter den Linden* and the site of Hitler's Reichstag, it was hard to forget that this was the capital of the Third Reich in all its baroque horror. In 1945 Berlin was more or less flattened by allied bombers. Vast areas of the city were rebuilt in the bleak modernist style, and there are still building sites everywhere. There is also plenty of evidence of the paranoid years after the war when the city was divided. You can visit the preserved remnants of the famous Berlin Wall, now a tourist attraction, and the tour buses cross from East to West as easily as they cross from East Side to West Side in New York. On reflection, they cross much more easily, and in a fraction of the time.

Historical memories are short, but it is incredible that so much has been swept away and smoothed over so quickly. Now Berlin is a magnet for young people from all over Europe and, judging by accents, from America too. It has, so I'm told, the kind of night club scene that makes the movie Cabaret look like an entertainment for toddlers. If the whole purpose of cabaret is to forget reality, then Berlin is the capital of amnesia. If New York is the city that never sleeps, Berlin is the place where sleep is never even considered as an option, at least by the young. It is just too exciting.

Perhaps I should never try to judge a city, even though I was born in one. I grew up on the story of the town mouse and country mouse. In the original fable by Aesop, now about two and a half thousand years old but still as relevant as it ever was, a sophisticated town mouse visited his cousin in the country, who offered the city mouse a meal of simple country food. The town mouse was not impressed and invited the country mouse back to the city for a taste of the good life. So, the two mouse cousins ate like kings, and it is true that we ate well in Berlin, and enjoyed wonderful hospitality. But the murine feast was interrupted by dogs that chased the mice away so they had to abandon their gourmet meal to save their lives. After this trauma the country mouse decided to return home, choosing security over luxury. This became a vastly popular moral tale with the message: city bad, country good. Having lived in both I have never found any reason to doubt the truth of this.

A city is full of decadent temptations and dangerous creatures, even in sophisticated Berlin. As a dedicated country mouse, I was glad scurry off home, which right now is a small village in the middle of nowhere. We have no night life, I'm happy to say, but don't lack for fine cheeses here, or interesting society, or even for culture. And down in the basement we have a few real country mice, innocently dancing in the dark, enjoying the good life.

ALIEN POST OFFICE

If you go strolling in the Avalon Nature Preserve in Stony Brook on Long Island you may be surprised by the sight of a large silver sphere, almost hidden in the long grass. The first time I saw it I imagined that the aliens really had landed at last. These visitors from outer space have populated our imaginations ever since H.G.Wells introduced us to the inhabitants of Mars and the moon more than a hundred years ago. Now they have come roaring and beeping back in the latest Star Wars movies, and a hundred others. I am interested in aliens, I am one myself in a way, so I paused in my walk to wonder how I might communicate with them. If they were traditional cartoon aliens they would ask: "Take me to your leader." But who might that be? The manager of the nature reserve? President Trump? Tom Cruise? If they were untraditional or comical aliens they might ask almost anything, like: "Where did you get those shoes?" Or "Can your species recite the value of Ω to the 100th decimal?" Or "What makes you think you have a leader, anyway?"

But when I got close to the five-foot silver sphere, which is surrounded by rocks like a miniature Stonehenge I discovered that it was not a space ship but a very special mail box – a rather beautiful work of art by Spanish artist Alicia Framis, named *Cartas Al Cielo* or letters to the sky. The sphere has a slot, like a mailbox, and note cards and pencils are provided for visitors to write messages to "People who have no earthbound address." This concern for the homeless pleased me at first, but perhaps it was not quite what the creator of the sculpture had intended. Astronauts on the International Space Station are definitely in the sky, and have no earthbound address right now, but they don't need any messages from us. However, the word *cielo* also implies heaven or paradise, so perhaps we are being invited to write to those who have relocated beyond the orbit of the United States Post Office, or even e-mail.

There are many people and cats in my life who have moved on, leaving no forwarding address. I would love to send them a message, although it's hard to know what to say on a 5" x 7" card. In any case such a modernistic, high tech object as this polished silver sphere seems to point us towards the future not the past. In the future, our messages may find readers.

The inhabitants of the future have no earthbound address yet, because they are not in the real estate market yet. But they might profit from our words of wisdom, just as in the Renaissance the wisdom of ancient Greece and Rome helped to put Europe on the right track. I stood by the sphere for a while pondering, while people came and went, none of them leaving a message. What could I tell the future? Once upon a time we felt a heavy responsibility to those future generations. Once we called them our "posterity." Now we just feel anxious and guilty about them.

But will they really need our advice, any more than the astronauts on the space station? Surely, in the future, everything will be better understood, better organized, and fully computerized? They will be superior beings, living in a virtual reality with all the knowledge and wisdom of the world at their fingertips. Surely, they won't make the dumb mistakes we have made?

I took a card, wrote *"Good luck"* on it, and popped it in the box.

DISAPPEARING ACT

When winter approaches, our neighborhood seems to empty out as the climate refugees head south for the sunshine. Costa Rica seems to be popular, and the Bahamas, and even good old Florida. Whatever fresh horrors winter has in store for us in the northeast a lot of our neighbors prefer not to share the experience.

Who can blame them? I can for one. Those of us who are left behind, keeping an eye on empty houses and feeding abandoned cats, can't help feeling a certain resentment as we check our generators, stock up with salt and shovels and anticipate the discomforts and disruptions of the coming weeks. Why can't we all go south? If a notorious Mexican bandit can escape from a maximum-security prison twice, surely, we can escape from a wide-open, frozen suburb? The grass must be greener on the other side, especially if it's not buried in snow.

The desire to run away is particularly strong in January, but it persists at a low level all year. Escape, that's what we all dream about. We want to vanish from here and re-appear somewhere else, painlessly, without explanations or apologies. About three quarters of a million people go missing every year, and many of them are never found. They are probably all down in Costa Rica, soaking up the sunshine. But wherever they are, some of them have certainly gone missing by choice. They walked away from their lives, felt the sunshine, purchased some lime green Bermuda shorts, changed their names, and vanished.

It is the plot of a thousand novels. I was just reading one by the French writer Simenon, called *The Flight of Monsieur Monde*. The main character is a successful businessman with a family who, one wet, cold day in Paris, walks to his office and just keeps walking. He takes a train, to the south of course. I've never heard of anyone escaping to the north apart from a small sub-category of extreme masochists who go to Vermont in January. Down by the Mediterranean Monsieur Monde works in a casino and lives a completely different life for a few months before astonishing everybody by returning calmly to his home and office. He needed to escape for a while to preserve his sanity, and he did.

The sudden overwhelming desire to just go, to disappear, leave everything and start again sometimes hits people in the middle years of life when they look back, look ahead, and see more of the same. For me it's more a matter of the weather forecast. When the forecast says snow, it's time to go, when the forecast says ice, even Florida sounds nice.

In the long run, Global Warming may save us from this annual meteorological torture, but it's hard to be patient. I want to join the great exodus and go south right now, and stay there. Within hours I could become a lounging, sun loving climate exile with not a care in the world. Unfortunately, this kind of escape, like a dramatic prison break, has a rather large price tag attached and, in any case, I fear I may have left it too late. Costa Rica seems to be full.

MYSTERY CRUISE

When I was a kid we took summer vacations on an island off the British coast. There was always some battered old boat on the beach with a battered old captain in a sailor's cap offering a "Mystery Cruise." The boats smelt of dead fish, they always seemed on the point of sinking, and the mystery destination was always the same: a pub on the other side of the island. Since then cruising has become a much larger industry, but there's no more mystery to it than there ever was.

My cousin phoned me the other day from the middle of the ocean. She was returning from a cruise to the Amazon and was being tossed around by giant waves in the Bay of Biscay, somewhere off the coast of Spain. What was the cruise like? It was awful, she said, although she used stronger language. There were storms all the way, her fellow passengers had done nothing but eat and drink from morning till night, and the Amazon had been hot, flat, and dull.

This was not a good advertisement for cruising. But nobody seems to care about negative reports. Storms, food poisoning, legionnaire's disease, fires, shipwrecks and even attacks by Somali Pirates barely make an impression on this buoyant industry. Who remembers the Costa Concordia or Carnival Triumph, let alone the Titanic? The image of glamor, freedom and luxury is stronger than the reality. A cruise seems to offer a complete escape from the responsibilities and pressures of life on land. An extraordinary thirteen million vacationers from the USA took cruises last year alone. It is the fastest-growing sector of the travel industry, and about two hundred ships are sailing the ocean blue at any given moment.

Boredom is not a problem, even in the middle of an empty ocean. Every kind of amusement and entertainment is provided right there on the ship. A few steps will bring you to a bar, a restaurant, a casino, a pool, a cabaret, or just about anything your nautical heart desires. The cruise companies spare no effort to provide perpetual distraction as well as unlimited food. The mega-ship "Anthem of the Seas," in addition to all the usual diversions, offers something called a bionic bar, a zero-gravity experience, a surfing simulator, a rock climbing wall, and eighty-inch floor to ceiling televisions in some staterooms. There's not much chance of getting bored, unless you switch the giant TV on.

These vast ships are like small cities, and they cushion the anxiety of being far from dry land on an unstable element. They take you straight to the things you must see. All you have to do is step off the ship in the Galapagos or Bora Bora or Venice, and explore the undiscovered treasures of place with five thousand other people from the same boat.

The sea used to be a harsher and more uncertain element. Columbus didn't have a swimming pool or a rock climbing wall aboard the Santa Maria, nor did his voyages take him where he expected to go. Every landfall was a complete surprise. He didn't even know which continent he was on, or what souvenirs to buy.

River cruises seem to be getting more popular. There's no danger of rough seas or shipwrecks. You can't be lost on a river, but then you can't be surprised either because it goes where it goes. Even Captain Ahab couldn't get into much trouble on a river. Perhaps that's why my parents loved those mystery cruises round the island that always went to the same place, and returned to the same place. That's what a vacation ought to be: no thrills, no surprises, and a predictable lunch at a nice pub.

TAKE ME HOME

My parents never sent me to summer camp. They believed that families should go on vacation together, no matter how painful the experience was for all concerned. But a lot of things have changed since my childhood. Dr. Benjamin Spock dreamed up the idea that children should not be repressed by arbitrary discipline, and must be allowed to express themselves. Since then, the family vacation has declined, and the summer camp industry has boomed.

American parents send more kids to more summer camps than parents anywhere else in the world. Eleven million children will go to twelve thousand residential camps this season. A web search for a Summer Camp" turns up thousands of advertisements for camps in faraway places with strange-sounding names, often vaguely Native American, like Wampum, Totem, Pemmican, Blackjack, or Roulette.

"Faraway" is important. An essential part of the summer camp mystique is to encourage your offspring to see remote and exotic places without strip malls. The Poconos and the Catskills seem especially popular with East Coast parents, although some choose to send their little ones all the way to California, or even Hawaii, for the full faraway experience.

The word "camp," like the words "limousine" and "salad," has largely lost its original meaning. There won't be much crude tent camping in California or anywhere else, except in a few euphemistically named "adventure camps." Today's young campers don't sleep in fragile tents that collapse in the rain in the middle of the night. They don't suffer voracious bugs, rock-hard camp beds, or horrible messes of food cooked in filthy cans on kerosene stoves. These so-called camps are more like country hotels, with solid walls and roofs, hot and cold running water, real food, and real bathrooms: in short, they are havens of decadence and luxury. There is a distinct danger that kids might actually enjoy themselves in these places, instead of learning the old camping virtues of stoicism and endurance.

Most summer camps are promoted as pure fun, a kind of secular childhood paradise, with baseball, canoeing, horse riding, gymnastics, tennis, and even singing. There are camps where boys can be boys, others where girls can be girls, and there are coed camps where nature can take its course. But, reading between the lines, it seems that many young campers are also threatened with weight loss regimes, remedial math, SAT score enhancement, and other kinds of compulsory self-improvement. Self-improvement is never fun.

The summer camp phenomenon is explained or justified with an eclectic mixture of ideas from Emerson, Thoreau, Nathanial Hawthorne, and of course Lord Baden-Powell the father of scouting. The basic assumption seems to be that nature is good, and that a child exposed to nature will somehow become a better person. So, a beautiful natural site is obligatory. Freezing cold lakes are very popular, and mountains are advertised just about everywhere except on Long Island.

Yes, the kids may suffer, But the parents are the true heroes and heroines of the summer camp industry. Parents pay the whopping bills, parents must grit their teeth and send their precious offspring alone into the wilderness, armed only with a truckload of sports equipment, electronic devices, and designer resort wear. Parents must sit and wait for the phone to ring in an empty house, bravely listening to the sounds of silence while they study the advertisements for next year's summer camp.

OTHER PEOPLE'S LIVES

When we bought our first home on Long Island it was advertised as being in "Move in Condition," but it wasn't. There were no cats: we had to bring our own. The refrigerator was empty, and there was no junk in the base-ment. We had to bring that too. How can a place be in move in condition without cats, food, or junk?

It is very strange when you think about it that most of us physical-ly move the more-or-less identical contents of our homes from place to place at enormous trouble and expense. Some of our expatriate neigh-bors in France have imported every last stick of furniture and décor from their former homes in other countries, no matter what the cost. When the Russian composer Sergei Rachmaninov settled in Hollywood his house was an exact reproduction of the one he had left in Moscow. It tells us something about the power of familiar things over our lives

Wealthy people have so much stuff that they prefer to avoid the expense of moving it, and simply multiply their possessions with each new property. They buy their homes complete: furniture, decoration, appliances, servants, and possibly children too, all included. Collect the keys and you're good to go. That's why you don't see billionaires wandering around in furniture stores testing the beds, or worrying about their precious glassware getting broken during the move. They back up their homes the way other people back up their hard drives. They can always walk into another place and start again, with no fuss and no packing cases.

The rest of us are like refugees dragging our old and worn posses-sions from house to house, when it would be easier and more interesting to settle into a home that truly was in move in condition, and adapt to what we found there. Adaptation is good. It's the first principle of survival and evolution, and we all need to evolve. There is a thriving industry of home exchanges, swaps and rentals that allow us to travel anywhere in the world without paying hotel bills or giving up the comforts of domesticity. These home exchanges are mainly used for vacations, temporary work assignments and so on, but they could and should become the only way to move.

Over the years we have lived in a lot of borrowed, rented and exchanged homes in several countries, each one filled with other people's stuff. There are some personal things we always take of course: books, music, and a toothbrush. But it is always a challenge to come to terms with *their* furniture, *their* kitchen, *their* peculiar TV channels – a whole world of unfamiliar things in unfamiliar places, plus little traps like self-triggering smoke alarms and aggressive automated cleaning devices patrolling the swimming pool.

One cold winter, for reasons now forgotten, we rented a rather grand old house in Barbizon, near Paris. In the nineteenth century Barbizon was famous as the home of landscape painters like Rousseau, Corot and Millet, and it still has some of its bohemian charm. The house we rented had stayed firmly in the nineteenth century, including its plumbing and utterly inadequate heating system. The beds and chairs were as uncomfortable as any Victorian could wish, and the whole house was like a huge, cluttered antique shop. Faded family photographs looked out at us from every flat surface, drawers were still full of personal possessions, and the billiard room was set for a game. We guessed, but could not confirm, that the original owners of the house had died at a great age, after changing nothing since 1880, and the place was being rented while the sale was being arranged. Meanwhile we lived their lives as best we could, shivering and grumbling and reading nineteenth century French novels in lieu of television.

By renting other people's homes we move into their lives, and some proprietors leave such detailed instructions that we virtually have to live their lives for them. Do we really need to feed the garden birds twice a day, or scrub the shower curtain every time we use it? But even without instructions you can infer a lot about the lifestyle you have inherited. A huge TV screen and no books, or half a dozen restaurant guides and no cooking utensils, give you all the information you need.

Our last house was in something very close to move in condition: it had a full complement of furniture, everything you could possibly need in the kitchen, and even a cat sitting on the roof and a bottle of wine in the refrigerator. We had nothing to do but sit on the terrace and drink the wine, corkscrew also provided. This was obviously how the previous owners lived. But it's our life now, and we intend to enjoy it.

HEAD FOR THE HILLS

Back in the 1960s and 1970s, when we were all anticipating nuclear war with varying degrees of eagerness, a few exceptionally prudent or nervous people became what were called "survivalists." They headed out to some unimaginably remote part of the country – Montana seems to have been a favorite – found a suitably inaccessible location, and built houses with *en suite* nuclear bunkers, stocked with generators, food, board games, and videotaped episodes of The Survivors TV series. They were hoping, presumably, to emerge from their rural bunkers when the rest of us were dead, when they could enjoy the ultimate sensation of *schadenfreude*. No doubt they looked forward to saying "We told you so," if they could find anyone alive to say it to. How they hoped to get along in a post-nuclear wasteland without strip malls is a mystery to me, but obviously they thought that any kind of survival would be better than the alternative.

I assumed that this whole survivalist fad had died out long ago, after the collapse of the Soviet Union in 1989 and the arrival of a kinder, gentler, less testosterone-driven politics. But I was wrong. The survivalist movement is still out there, stronger and better-organized than ever. There are real estate agents who specialize in what are called sustainable homes, with food storage, an independent power source, and defensible barriers like a medieval castle. By their own account the people who invest in these homes are anxious about a lot of things, including but not limited to war, global warming, financial collapse, comet strikes, a second Trump Presidency, and terrorism – although how ISIS could even find Montana, let alone any infidels out there in the hills, I don't know. Inside their fortress-like homes the survivalists hope to be secure against just about everything, unless they step outside.

I have always observed that a certain proportion of people are born worriers. Every person has a more or less fixed Anxiety Quotient (or A.Q. for short). We each worry all the time at our personal level. Events in the outside world may re-arrange our worries, but the intensity of anxiety stays constant, high or low as the case may be. A first-class worrier will maintain a state of high anxiety 24/7, regardless of any real cause. When the daily news doesn't provide enough material, he or she will resort to old standbys like electromagnetic fields, Radon gas, hurricanes, asbestos, asteroid strikes, global warming, and of course *The Unknown*. With the unknown, you never know. Amateur or inadequate worriers drift through life ignoring all these terrible threats, and fretting only occasionally about small matters like how to pay the bills or how often to change the cat litter.

Clearly, these survivalists are world-class professional worriers and, in the past, I found it rather amusing to read about them and think how much money they were wasting on their flimsy defenses against fate. But the grotesque election season of 2016 has made me think again. Every kind of madness was suddenly back on the political agenda, up to and including nuclear war. So perhaps the survivalists were right all along, although for the wrong reasons, and they may indeed have the last laugh from their mountain retreats, feasting on their baked beans and boiled water as everything falls apart.

Is it too late to find a nice bunker and move into it? Montana, wherever it is, seems a long way off, and I would prefer something local. If anyone knows of an old nuclear shelter to rent, preferably with a small wine cellar and a well-stocked library, I think I'm ready to say goodbye to the world for a while.

MURDER WITH A SMILE

When the evenings draw in and the temperature falls with the leaves, there's nothing so comforting as a nice murder. Every night millions of respectable, non-violent Americans double-lock their doors and settle down to an evening of mayhem and homicide. The murder rate has been going down for a long time, but on television it has gone the opposite way. By the age of eighteen, according to Mr. Google, the average citizen has watched forty thousand murders on the small screen

The good news is that some TV producers have discovered ways to make murder amusing, if not for the victim then at least for the viewers. Most of these good-humored murder stories come from Britain, Australia or Canada, perhaps because the chance of really being murdered in those countries is very low indeed, so that the stories can be enjoyed without anxiety. These lighthearted foreign murders are typically set in a reassuringly stylish and civilized past, and in delightfully picturesque places. Those are the settings for popular and endlessly repeated Public Television series like Midsomer Murders, Miss Fisher's Mysteries, Father Brown, Poirot, Miss Marple, and a dozen others. Every charming English village is a war zone, with a murder once a week.

What makes them funny and not gruesome, like the nightly celebrations of violence on commercial television, is the invariable formula that, as it were, sanitizes the murder or murders (there are usually several) and provides a satisfying ending. The formula calls for a detective, professional or amateur, with a comical or incompetent sidekick, a disagreeable police chief, and a medical examiner who, unlike most real medical examiners, is often female and beautiful. There is a love interest, and a plot that almost always involves a vast inheritance, romantic jealousy or some betrayal in the distant past. Nobody seems to have a regular job, so they can devote their time entirely to constructing plots that are so ludicrously complicated that Mr. Holmes himself would be baffled.

The amusing murder mystery has been on the decline in recent years, and this is a symptom of the decline of murder in general - not the *quantity* of murders, which is more than adequate, but the *quality*. They have no elaborate plots, no false clues, no subtlety at all. How often do we hear (for example) of a notorious criminal being murdered on a train, which is stuck in a snowdrift, by a conspiracy of all his past victims, each of whom strikes one blow with the knife, and the mystery is solved by a Belgian detective who just happens to be on the train at the time? This sort of thing almost never happens these days, even on the Long Island Rail Road, but it happened in Agatha Christie's *Murder on the Orient Express*. Most modern murders are committed over trivial amounts of money or drugs, and a third of them are never solved. Who wants to watch a TV show about such sordid disputes, without as much as a happy ending?

Have today's young thugs never heard of the Public Broadcasting Network? If they can't do better than this they should get with the program, or just give up homicide altogether and, like the rest of us, get their guilty pleasures from television.

YOUR VACATION THERAPIST

Three thousand years ago, the Delphic Oracle revealed the secret of successful vacation planning: know thyself. Never mind about the rest of the family, they must make their own mistakes. But your personality is the key to the success or failure of your vacation. There is no need to consult an expensive psychiatrist. Just take this simple test.

Imagine that, in the middle of a busy working day, you suddenly have an unexpected hour of free time. Would you:

(a) Take a brisk, healthy walk, regardless of the weather, perhaps taking in a museum exhibit along the way?

(b) Grab the phone, get on the Web, and try to make the time as profitable as possible?

(c) Collapse on to the nearest couch, and take a nap?

If you answered (a), your psychology is "Puritan." If you answered (b), you qualify as "Paranoid." If (as I hope) you answered (c), then you fall into the category that, in psychological jargon, is called "Decadent," and is more popularly known as "Normal." Now, you can plan your perfect summer vacation based on your personality. A Decadent person should not even think about a hiking holiday in Iceland, any more than a Puritan should contemplate a Mediterranean cruise.

The Puritan Vacation is a throwback to the harsh early days of American life, when the best time out you could hope for was a short nap in church. The hallmark of the Puritan vacation is the pursuit of virtue through suffering. Most people spend money on vacations, but Puritans save it. They camp miles outside town in mosquito-infested swamps (very reasonable site fees), and dine off dried packaged foods bought at a quantity discount before the holiday. They have nothing but contempt for tourists who stay in comfortable motels, eat at good restaurants and drink fine wines, as if vacations were about pleasure.

Puritan vacationers also have very firm rules about holiday activities. They must be cheap or free, physically uncomfortable, and as boring as possible. The Puritan holiday activity must also have an element of serious self-improvement, so that the trip can be seen to justify its miniscule cost. So, Puritan vacations tend to be heavy on culture: painting adobe churches in the noonday sun, toiling through endless museums, hiking down remote gorges to view Indian rock carvings, making long detours to worship at historic sites (Buffalo Bill slept here), and so on. The ultimate Puritan vacation would a camping and bicycling tour around North Dakota in March.

The payoff of the Puritan Vacation is not relaxation or amusement, but virtuous achievement. "It was a lovely four weeks. We saw every museum in New England, and it only cost a hundred and fifty dollars."

The second vacation style, which I call the Paranoid, is very different, being entirely focused on maximizing pleasure time. The characteristic concern of the Paranoid vacationer is the terrible fear that a moment of leisure value might be wasted. The Paranoid holiday vehicle can easily be spotted on any highway, sagging under the weight of recreational equipment. Skis, surf boards, bikes, canoes and inflatable rafts are piled high on the roof, and all-terrain vehicles are towed behind.

In spirit, the Paranoid vacationer - who is usually male - has never left the office. His laptop and cellphone are never switched off. He has projects to complete, resources to mobilize, and personnel to manage. The personnel consists of his unfortunate family, whose assigned task it is to use all that recreational equipment, even if it kills them. Any spare moments are scheduled for swimming, climbing local mountains, and visiting National Parks.

The United States is too small for the seriously Paranoid traveler. He is the ideal candidate for those whirlwind six-countries-in-six-days tours promoted by travel agents, or for any vacation packages that combine intense activities with an exhausting schedule ("Hang glide in Hawaii, walk the length of the Great Wall of China, safari in Africa and cross-country ski in Antarctica, all in five action-packed days...")

The essence of the Paranoid Vacation is not virtue, but productivity. One can imagine the exhausted family on the homeward journey, tallying up all the miles driven, paddled, rafted, cycled, skied, climbed, swum, scuba-dived, surfed and hiked, as well as games played, theme parks visited, fairground rides taken, and jogging assignments completed, to say nothing of photographs snapped, burgers eaten, sodas drunk, states and nations ticked off the list. "Well," says dad, entering the details into the family vacation database as they head home, "We made a 6.4% improvement on last year. That's what I *call* a vacation!"

Those of us who are fortunate enough to enjoy the type of personality that (implying no value judgement) I call "Decadent," regard both Puritan and Paranoid vacations with horror. Fortunately, there is a whole industry devoted to our needs.

The Decadent vacation requires no strenuous activities or compulsory sights. It is located outside of time and space, at a resort, or a fine old hotel, or a rented cottage in the south of France. Resorts are the fastest-growing part of the US leisure industry. Chains of them reach across the country and across the world, advertising their product with slogans like "The Pursuit of Happiness" and "Relaxation is our Business."

The true purpose of the Decadent vacation is to have nowhere to go, nothing to do, and nothing to remind you of things you ought to be doing in other places. This type of vacation paradise sets sharp boundaries between itself and the outside world, and tries to be all the things that the outside world is not - totally calm, utterly safe, perfectly beautiful, and ineffably convenient. Everything is laid on, from decorously slow-moving sports, to soothing and respectable entertainments. Entirely satisfactory meals arrive at regular hours, and the sun almost never goes behind a cloud. It's like being dead, except that you continue to eat.

The great American utopians of the last century believed that perfect happiness would come from collective work. They were Puritans in disguise. The twenty-first century has straightened this out, like so many other historical mistakes, and revealed to us that perfect happiness comes from perfect idleness. The Decadent vacation, unlike any other, is the one you wish could go on forever.

MEMORIES ARE MADE OF THIS?

Even the happiest vacation has a dark cloud of anxiety hanging over it.

What should we get for Aunt Ethel, who looked after the cats? What about the cats themselves? We *must* take something back for mother. And we daren't forget the lawn care person, the chiropractor, and all the people we love to hate at the office.

The moment the word "souvenir" raises its ugly head, all the pleasure goes out of a vacation. "Souvenir" is a French word, meaning "to remember." When we visit a new and beautiful place we want to bring home a keepsake. That's why most of the ancient monuments in the world are getting smaller every year. So, the last precious days and hours of every vacation must be spent in a quest that is doomed to failure, because souvenir shops are always and everywhere identical. From Bridgehampton to Bombay, from Newport to Naples, they all sell the same awful stuff.

This is because all the souvenir shops in the world get their stock from one central source, the giant "Tourotat" warehouse in Outer Mongolia, stuffed with billions of mugs and T shirts with dumb messages like "Whatever," and ancient jokes about age and sex. The rest of the global stock of souvenirs consists of stuffed animals, enough china fairies and shepherdesses to populate a season of baroque opera, a lot of very peculiar "shell creations," CDs of New Age music that sounds like whales with toothache, twee little birdhouses that no self-respecting bird would ever inhabit, wind chimes, British bath products with names like "Sweet Almond" and "Gardenia", and so many candles that anyone would think Thomas Edison forgot to invent the light bulb in 1879.

The stock of souvenir shops has scarcely changed since my childhood, when we always returned from vacation with nasty teapots shaped like thatched cottages, glass tubes full of colored sand, and painted ashtrays of incredible ugliness inscribed with the words "A Present from Abu

Dhabi." These embarrassing objects would sit around on the mantelpiece for a while, gathering dust. Then, usually around Christmas, they would be consigned to the oblivion reserved for all holiday souvenirs. From there, they would mysteriously make their way back to Tourotat Central in Outer Mongolia to be recycled. Next summer they would reappear in the same souvenir shops, dusted and re-labelled, and looking as repulsive as ever.

In the classier destinations, such as expensive villages in the south of France or Tuscany, different souvenir choices do appear, although perhaps it would be better if they didn't. Local artists and craftspeople have seized on the tourist trade as a source of income. Their short-lived boutiques offer a selection of local food products (usually in tiny pots at extravagant prices), pottery creations, carvings, paintings, scarves, and a well-nigh incredible variety of what can only be called baubles. These souvenirs are designed to be tasteful, but only the recipient will know for sure.

History tells us that first souvenirs were brought back by the Crusaders of the eleventh century. They went to the Holy Land with the intention of making it more holy by killing everyone in sight. The Crusaders liked to bring back a piece of the true cross, or a Saracen's head, just for the memories. By 1291, the modern souvenir industry had started up in Venice, making exquisite glass objects for tourists. Seven hundred years later, Venice is literally sinking into the ocean under the accumulated weight of cute glass souvenirs. Despite the invention of plastic in 1907, glass is still the favorite souvenir material in Venice. But it doesn't travel well in an overcrowded family car, or in the overhead luggage compartment of a plane, where the next passenger is waiting to pulverize it with a carry-on bag the size of a Volkswagen.

The whole souvenir industry obviously needs to be rationalized and brought up to date. Instead of wasting good vacation time sweating in and out of tiny shops smelling of potpourri and hot candle wax, we should be able to order your souvenirs ahead of time on the internet, in the comfort of our own home. Enter the vacation destination under "search," browse through the local offerings, and choose exactly the right souvenirs, all localized and personalized. Just think, authentic and identical gifts from Montauk, Madagascar or Milan would be delivered painlessly to our home address just in time for your return. The best part is, we wouldn't even have to go there.

Theme VI

I HAVE A COMPLAINT

We need to work on mastering the art of complaint.

JULIAN BAGGINI

I will not listen to reason…Reason always means what somebody else has got to say.

ELIZABETH GASKELL

THE NICEST GUY IN TOWN

People have been known to call me a nice guy, because I never complain. It's true. Nobody loves a complainer. Complaint seems like a whiny, weak, ineffective thing, not likely to produce any result except irritation.

The modern world seems to demand something more than a simple complaint. A grievance must be inflated until it reaches the level of outrage, at which point it becomes worthy of media attention. Residents' complaints over (say) broken elevators in a public housing project is not worth any attention. Anger, outrage, and perhaps violence over class, race, disability and sex discrimination that leaves poor people to struggle up many flights of stairs in summer heat quickly attracts the cameras and the commentators, already pumped up with fury on their behalf – an emotion that is about as synthetic as the rage of King Lear.

The news media are far more emotional and less rational than they were even twenty years ago. They too have discovered that outrage gets attention. A leading exponent of this style is a British TV commentator called John Snow, who rages against some injustice or other every day on the evening news. In his normal life he is probably a perfectly reasonable person, but on TV he is the very incarnation of public indignation about injustices that the public, including Mr. Snow, have no intention of doing anything about, and cannot possibly do anything about. Like Howard Beale in the movie *Network* they cry: "We're mad as hell, and we're not going to take it anymore." But they do take "it," whatever it is, because outrage is a fire that must never be allowed to go out.

This public catharsis makes viewers feel good. Not only does it tell them what they should be angry about today, but gives them the reassuring feeling that something has been accomplished. How could so much

195

public anger *not* accomplish something. They feel morally improved and self-righteous just because they heard about it, and shared the indignation.

Evangelical preachers and politicians use the same trick. Synthetic indignation gets people on their side. The (un)reason seems to be that if some blowhard is almost exploding onscreen with righteous anger there must be a good reason for it. There isn't. The man is out of control, or putting on an act that is too-well controlled. The trouble with outrage is that it is blind, like loyalty or faith. People full of outrage don't want to conciliate or negotiate, they want to fight. In the end, they often do.

This leaves the more liberals and rational part of the population – the vast majority - at a serious disadvantage. We can't very well be outraged about not being outraged. We can't build a winning argument on the basis that things aren't as bad as they seem, or that some modest improvements might be made. Any such approach will be drowned out by the growls and shrieks of the outraged. It's not healthy.

So, I would like to put in a word for the simple complaint: the mild annoyance, the gentle irony, the helpful effort to put problems into focus when they are blurred by too many undisciplined feelings. I am a calm and civilized person, and outrage is not my style. But I do have a few modest complaints, and here they are.

HOW YOU PLAYED THE GAME

I missed the Super bowl this year, because I miss it every year. Games are harmless, but professional sports have gone too far for me. They're too much like show business, too much about money and celebrity and, yes, too violent.

There's nothing wrong with games as amusements for an idle hour. Restless, worrying creatures that we are, we need amusements. Children play games naturally, because they are simply fun, and to learn physical and social skills just as young animals do. Play is free, and play is freedom. It keeps us young.

Games are organized play. They should be joyful, liberating activities. But even children's' play isn't allowed to be spontaneous for long. Before they know it, their innocent games have become children's' sports, requiring complicated bureaucratic rules that are treated with almost religious reverence, coaches to impose the rules, training sessions, and expensive equipment. Kids are assigned to imaginary teams, based on some random fact like their school district, and taught to compete against other imaginary teams, teaching them a lesson that they may never forget.

The team is an extension of the ego. If we feel rather frail and vulnerable as individuals, we can feel strong as a member of a team, or even as a supporter. Team spirit appeals to some of the oldest survival instincts in human nature and, in one form or another, is the source of all the wars and pogroms and crusades in human history, including those going on now.

The infamous sentiment that "winning is the only thing," attributed to football coach Red Sanders, has infected American culture far beyond the perverse world of sports. In politics, it has almost obliterated intelligent debate between the parties, and President Trump's crude "I'm a winner" rhetoric has for the moment replaced any other governing strategy. The passion to win has invaded every human leisure activity. Even in fishing, that most tranquil of hobbies, you can attend seminars on 'how to be a winner.' Even flower arrangers compete to win. Grantland Rice, a famous sportswriter from another age, once daringly suggested that how you played the game was more important than whether you won or lost. Try telling that to the losing team and their multi-millionaire coach. Winning really *is* the only thing: that's what we get when we pay other people to be athletic for us, especially when we pay them such ridiculous amounts of money.

Sports are taken with great seriousness all over the world. Tune a short-wave radio, and you will hear sports reports coming from everywhere: India, China, Scotland, or Argentina. The energy that men - mostly men - put into sports must be the equivalent of the power of the atom. If only we could harness it, and avoid the fallout, the world's energy problems would be solved.

Only professional wrestling seems immune, since it is more like play than sport. Wrestling, as the French intellectual Roland Barthes remarked, is a dramatic performance of good and evil, suffering, defeat, and justice. It doesn't matter who wins. In wrestling, as in life, the injuries are mostly faked, and the final result is meaningless. The more I see of other sports, the more I like the open, unapologetic joke of wrestling.

THINGS ARE AGAINST US

Do you ever get the impression that your life is a perpetual struggle against inanimate objects? The French have a phrase for it: *"Les choses sont contre nous,"* meaning that things are against us.

Consider a typical day of persecution by things. It begins with the alarm clock, one of the nastiest things ever invented, then continues with coffee that is always too hot or too cold, a healthy cereal that tastes like cardboard and probably *is* cardboard, a morning newspaper that is too big and awkward to read at the table, and in which every interesting story on the front page is continued on page ninety-four. You know the routine. Things have the upper hand over us even before we get out of the front door, where we probably discover that the car battery is dead, and the garbage can has been ransacked by raccoons. When and if we get to work after battling against the hydra-headed monster called traffic, we sit down in front of a computer which, after the alarm clock, is just about the most hostile mechanism ever conceived by the human mind. Nobody is to blame for all this. Like Frankenstein, we create our own monsters.

When I got my first computer in the eighties I started off on the wrong foot, thinking that it was nothing but a useful tool. It took me a while to realize that I had become the tool of the machine, and the computer, like a jealous god, was using *me*. It is astonishing how much of my day, and probably yours too, is spent serving the whims and needs of one or several computers.

We are in dark territory here. The living world and the world of things are closer together than we like to think. Deep in our superstitious minds we know this. One of the most ancient forms of religion is animism, in which familiar objects, plants and creatures are inhabited by spirits of their own - the spirit of the tree, the spirit of the rock, and so on. People living close to nature made no rigorous distinctions between animal and human, living and dead. The whole world seemed alive and meaningful to them. They worshipped significant places or living things, or avoided them as taboo. They crept terrified through the forest, where every plant and creature might be actively hostile, just as we creep through the jungle of our gadgets, machines and devices, worrying what they might do to us next.

We know, at some level of consciousness, that things have a life of their own. We get angry at our dysfunctional possessions, as if they cared. What is so curious and paradoxical is that we love those things too. Some people seem to worship their portable electronic devices, as if their smartphones are inhabited by some benevolent spirit. I am sorry to tell them that this is not the case.

I blame evolution. Like all the other creatures on earth we must confront the physical world, and tame it if we can. This intimate struggle between people and things is a personal and dangerous relationship, with winners and losers. The first humanoids to stand upright banged their heads against the roof of the cave. Five million years later we have suburban homes with cathedral ceilings. That was a victory, that was progress, but we daren't relax for a second. Sooner or later the things we create will take over our lives. The French, for once, are right: things *are* against us.

DÉJA VU ALL OVER AGAIN

It may be simply because of my age, but the literary world seems to be running out of ideas. Searching the library, the TV schedule, and the latest movie offerings gives me an overwhelming feeling of *Déja Vu* all over again. Nobody seems to have a new idea.

In the world of novels, we have seemingly endless pastiches and iterations of the literature of the past. Everyone has tried Jane Austen, including P.D.James. Sebastian Faulkes has re-done P.G.Wodehouse (very well) as well as James Bond. Joanna Trollope has updated Anthony Trollope, Jean Rhys has had a shot at Charlotte Brontë, and so it goes on. For a bit of originality, we must go back to the eighteenth century, and read Laurence Sterne or Tobias Smollett.

On television Sherlock Holmes has been reincarnated as a teenager, Agatha Christie's Miss Marple gets younger and younger, and country house soap operas, each one apparently the same as the last, have become a plague on the Public Television channels. We are supposed to be enchanted by the new young stars, but they are never as good as the old old ones. A fine performance fixes a character in the mind: Jeremy Brett as Sherlock Holmes for example or David Suchet as Hercule Poirot. Unlike the legendary stage actors, we can view their classic performances again and again, and make comparisons.

At the movies, the list of remakes runs into hundreds, including many that should never have been made even once, let alone twice. Everything from *The Invasion of the Body Snatchers* to *The Wizard of*

Oz has been re-packaged and re-sold. It might be better to issue the remake on the same day as the original so we could see them both together and save time.

The problem is that in fiction there is only one basic plot – conflict, struggle, resolution – and therefore a limited number of stories that can be built around it. We have the drama of love of course, the coming of age saga, the quest, the flight and pursuit story, crime and punishment, family feud and inheritance, calamity and salvation, but they are all variations on the same primordial plot, which was spectacularly written up in The Bible. Some writers introduce space aliens or magic, or elaborate symbolic games with words, but it always comes out remarkably like the universal soap opera that hasn't changed much in the three thousand years since Homer wrote the *Iliad* and the *Odyssey*. Why mess with a good story line?

Perhaps that's the answer. We love a familiar story. Old tales and old characters, even old TV series and movies, induce warm feelings of nostalgia. From the point of view of writers and producers a copy of a popular story is a sure thing with a guaranteed audience. I must admit that I am part of that audience: I enjoy these pastiches as much as anybody, if they're well done.

But surely, writers can create *something* fresh, something never seen or imagined? As a writer myself it seems that I have some responsibility here, and I spent a painful ten minutes trying to think up an original story line, with absolutely no result. My most promising inspiration, as I soon realized, was nothing but a pale shadow of Jonathan Swift's four-hundred-year-old satire *The Battle of the Books*, which in turn was copied from an even older French source.

If even I can't come up with a new idea, it must be because there *are* no new ideas. We have used up all the dramatic possibilities offered by various combinations of two sexes, greed, and violence, and must just keep recycling them until doomsday. Fortunately, if we can believe the stream of identical apocalyptic movies coming out of Hollywood, dooms-day is not too far away.

SPORT FOR ALL

One of the most encouraging news stories I have read for years reported a bold suggestion that the rules of golf should be changed – specifically that the hole should be made larger. This is an idea whose time has assur-edly come. The problem with golf, as with so many other sports, is that it is too hard, too annoying, and it takes too much time.

Full disclosure: I have never actually *played* golf, although I have seen it on TV, and once we visited St. Andrews and saw the famous course in the distance. However, I enjoyed miniature golf as a child, and once I visited a driving range on Long Island. But I could scarcely hit the tiny white balls at all, and it was obvious to me that trying to get them into a four-inch-wide hole about half a mile away would be a complete waste of time.

Who invented these rules anyway? Obviously, they were not written by or for people who are awkward, short-sighted, unsteady on their feet, or simply old. But now, all of a sudden, we have this brilliant proposal to tear up the rule book in the cause of equal opportunity.

Once we begin to think about equal opportunity in sports dozens of possibilities come to mind. Why should basketball belong to guys who are eight feet tall? Short guys can jump too, but just not so high. The standard basket height is ten feet above the court. I can reach ten feet with a small stepladder, but it would hardly be practical to have each player carry-ing one of those. Here's where technology might be useful. A telescopic adjustable basket could be rigged to move up or down according to the height of the player attempting the shot. It could be controlled by a neu-tral referee or by a computer linked to a laser measuring device. Either way the game would instantly become playable by everyone, and not just those who have the luck to be very tall.

The same principle of equalization can be applied to any game or sport. Anyone who has tried to play tennis knows all too well that the net is the problem. Get rid of the net, and the peculiar scoring system, and anyone would have a chance at tennis. Baseball could be made more player-friendly by the introduction of softer balls for the nervous and wider bats for those with poor hand to eye coordination. There should also be less running around, and to this end I would suggest a simple linear pitch, rather like a cricket pitch, instead of a diamond.

Football is in a class by itself. The existing game would be hard to adapt for the fragile and the elderly. The same goes for boxing, wrestling and martial arts which are not very appealing to those of us who prefer to avoid personal injury. The only possible answer would be a no contact rule, so these sports would become more like ballet or Tai-Chi, spectacles of beauty in movement rather than violence.

Speaking of rules there are too many of them, and so complicated that ever the referees often get into arguments about them. In the words of Henry David Thoreau we should simplify, simplify, until everybody can understand what's going on.

So, the proposal for larger holes in golf courses sparks off any number of creative ideas. Once we have accepted that all rules are arbitrary and can be changed, sports really could be open to all.

EMPLOYMENT OPPORTUNITY

In the distant past when I was looking for work instead of trying to avoid it, the main problem was one of choice. The unemployment rate was around two per-cent, and employers were almost desperate to find workers. My contemporaries and I bounced heedlessly from one occupation to another in search of something interesting. We had no notion that the jobs would ever run out. The classified advertisement sections were always full of new ones. I could have walked into almost any kind of employment that did not demand good eyesight or serious qualifications.

Fast forward fifty years, and I found myself looking at the section called "Employment Opportunities" in the local weekly paper. Although I was not in the market for a job, idle curiosity made me leaf through the four pages of small ads. The unemployment rate is six to ten per-cent now, depending on who you believe, and much higher for young people. What choices are left for someone who wants to find paid work?

Based on admittedly rather sketchy research, here is my career advice in two words: medical billing. That's where the opportunities are. Half a century ago most employment on Long Island was in agriculture, engineering or fishing. Now our main industry is medicine. Instead of fields and factories we have medical parks. On a recent drive, I started counting. In seventeen miles, I passed twenty-two medical office complexes and professional parks, encompassing every "ology" you could possibly imagine and some you would rather not, plus seven chiropractors, and two large hospitals. Also scattered along the highway for emergencies were several establishments for the walking wounded, advertising "Instant Medical Care," plus four funeral homes and eight attorneys to deal with the failures of all the rest. The local Yellow Pages confirm that this is no illusion. Physicians occupy twenty pages, the largest single category after auto repair.

So, it makes sense that the employment ads are dominated by medical billing, because that's the most important thing. You may not be cured, but you will most certainly be billed. The second most common category of employment advertised in the local paper was for medical secretaries, and after that for legal secretaries, which again makes perfect logical sense, because one thing leads to another.

Then came food service jobs – there is obviously a symbiotic relationship here that I don't need to spell out - and a surprising number of openings for counsellors of one kind or another. We seem to need a lot of counselling. The remaining ads were for miscellaneous occupations like school bus drivers and dancing instructors. I also saw several ads for town planners, which was surprising because Long Island where I live shows no signs whatever of any planning of any kind at any time. Perhaps they are just starting now, in which case it is too late.

My generation was lucky to have so many employment choices and so little pressure to compromise. I would find it hard to choose something from the job offerings in today's local newspaper, and I doubt whether any of the employers would have me. It's a sad thought that, without even trying, I have become completely unemployable and that my only way back into the labor force would be to learn the secret art of medical billing.

WHAT'S IN A NAME?

In the year I was born David must have been the most popular given name in Britain, and possibly in the western world. As a result, most of my male schoolmates were called David. When those of us without influential parents were drafted at the age of eighteen we entered an army of Davids. For a couple of years I had to use my middle name, so I could remember who I was.

David was a distinguished name in history. There was the Biblical King David of course who defeated Goliath and had eight wives. It is hard to decide which was the more astonishing feat of bravery. I can claim a nominal kinship with the French revolutionary painter David, David Livingstone the explorer, David Foster Wallace the novelist, David Niven the actor, David Attenborough the naturalist, and many other distinguished namesakes. On the other hand, I'm rather embarrassed by the murderer David Berkowitz, the entertainers David Bowie and David Beckham, and the former British Prime Minister, David Cameron.

We don't choose our names, and it must be hard for parents to make the right decision at a stressful time. The father in Lawrence Sterne's novel Tristram Shandy, an autodidact and amateur philosopher, was obsessive on the subject of names and believed that they were the key to a person's fortune and destiny. He divided up the world of boy's names into those that were dull and neutral, like Jack, Steve, or David, those that were lucky, like William or Andrew, and those that were absolutely catastrophic, like Tristram. By a comical series of accidents his own son was named Tristram, and spent the rest of his life complaining about it.

This just goes to show how careful parents need to be. But an awful lot of them fail in this duty, and give their children ludicrous and inappropriate names that, like Tristram, can only be a lifelong handicap. Today this is a problem that mainly affects young people, because their parents grew up in an age of liberation when all the old rules were abandoned. Teenagers with solid names like Tom, Dick or Harry can still be found, but too many parents want to be more creative and burden their unsuspecting babies with the names of ephemeral celebrities, cartoon characters on TV, favorite sports teams, or what sometimes seem like random combinations of syllables.

It shouldn't matter, but it does. The poet T.S.Eliot declared that even the naming of cats is a difficult matter, which it is. But cats don't have to go to school or college, or have a social life or, most important, get a job. A bizarre name is like a clown's hat. It's distracting, and makes it hard to take the owner seriously.

Take any random selection of great Americans and you will find a parade of the classic Anglo-Saxon names: John, Martin, Susan, William, Andrew, George, Alice, Eleanor, and even the occasional David. The Presidential hopefuls for 2016 showed much the same pattern: John, Jan, Jim, Hillary. There was not an exotic name among them except Rand Paul whose name managed to evoke both Ayn Rand and Paul of Tarsus at the same time. But it was Donald who won, a candidate named after the eponymous cartoon duck.

The President has not been able to rise above a name that evokes a dizzy Disney character. But anything is possible. We may even have a President called Tristram one of these days. How could anyone fail to vote for a President called Tristram?

LOSING THE LANGUAGE

The English language is always in decline. People have been complaining about it for five hundred years, ever since the translators of the King James Bible finished their masterpiece, and Shakespeare put down his quill and went into retirement. But the decline has speeded up. We seem to be losing our ancient language in several different ways.

Perhaps the least important danger is the collapse of grammar. There have been too many pedantic, scolding books about grammar and punctuation in the last few years. Frankly, most of these rules are trivial. If I hesitate over "I" and "me" or "him" and "he" I can check the grammar book which says: "Any pronouns that appear in an appositive are assumed to have the same function as the word the appositive refers to." Fine, I can live with that, whatever it means. But who really cares about fine distinctions between "less" and "fewer," "that" and "which," "may" and "might"? Who can figure out "who" and "whom" in the proper case? Who can get excited about the floating apostrophe? Not I (or me).

My education was grammar-free. We had a splendid English teacher, Mr. Thomas. He taught us to appreciate fine literature, which was no easy task in a school for uncultured and unruly boys. But he didn't teach grammar at all. He believed that grammar was learned by reading good writers and imitating them, not by following a set of rules. We never parsed a sentence, or discussed the difference between adverbs and adjectives, and we never even suspected the existence of the subjunctive tense, even though it may have been the case that we used it all the time. As a consequence, I am not qualified or willing to correct the English grammar of anyone else, as long as I can clearly understand what they are trying to say.

There's the rub as Shakespeare himself might have pointed out. It's not grammar but *meaning* that worries me. Whatever the secret of good writing or speaking, it is certainly not grammatical pedantry. It is all about words. The best writers use simple, direct language, the exact opposite of the foggy, euphemistic stuff designed to avoid hard truths and painful feelings. But plain old words are losing their meanings faster than we can reinvent them. Many of our best insults and negative expressions like "old" or "crazy" have vanished into the fog of political correctness and flabby sentimentality, and words referring to things that make us uncomfortable, like "posterity" and "modesty" have simply faded away. It's a process of simplification and impoverishment, the Twitification of the language.

Alongside this blurring of exact meanings comes the plague of wild adjectival inflation which aims to substitute emotion for content. The advertising industry has debased just about every superlative in the language. What words are left once every tacky mass-produced product is described as magnificent, perfect, great, wonderful, a masterpiece, exceptionally unique, or even incredible, for things that are sadly all too credible? Advertising and politics are the enemies of language, because nothing in them can be expressed plainly, least of all the plain truth.

George Orwell had a lot to say on this subject and I can't compete with a writer who was so incredibly unique.

There's nothing to be done about this. We can't get back to the language of Shakespeare, or even the stately and supple prose of the eighteenth and nineteenth centuries. But it is worth remembering and regretting the awesome language we once had before we, like, totally lost it.

HOW AM I DOING?

The plumber came to our house to make a small repair, and almost as soon as he got back in his truck we received an e-mail from the company asking us to rate our satisfaction with his promptness, his work, and his attitude (but not, we noticed, his bill). The house was not knee deep in water, and what more can you ask of a plumber? We gave him an A.

But these things make me uneasy. More and more purchases arrive with a questionnaire, on paper or by e-mail, asking: How did you like our product or our service? This seems harmless enough on the face of it, and may even be a good thing. Anonymous feedback is easier than a personal confrontation, and may produce more and better answers. But the appetite for customer evaluations seems to be growing out of control, so we are filling in little questionnaires all the time. Some of them are not so little. I got one from a computer company that was more like an interrogation by the CIA and demanded a whole lot of personal information as well as true confessions about my experience with the product. Fortunately, it was one of those questionnaires with a box at the bottom for comments. After having spent two days on the customer helpline with the experts in Bombay before I could get the product to work, I had plenty to say in the comments box.

If you buy a book online or stay in a hotel you will probably be asked for a review. In restaurants, it happens twice: once in person when your waitperson demands "How is everything?" before you have swallowed the first mouthful, and a second time on the internet before you have even digested the meal. Doctors and auto repair shops are anonymously reviewed on Angie's list or Yelp. Contractors, stores, real estate agents, handymen, and even boarding kennels suffer the same fate. College students can rate their professors, and see their own ratings too, which is the end of all polite dishonesty in that relationship. Now I hear that Uber taxis allow drivers to rate their passengers, as well as the other way around. Think of that next time you take a cab, and behave yourself.

Are we overdoing it? Along with the thefts of private data from the internet, the CCTV cameras everywhere, and all these mutual evaluations, we are turning into a nation of people who spy and are spied upon.

There is no oversight in most cases. Anybody can say anything about any place, person or product. What are such evaluations really worth? We've all had the experience of (for example) visiting a hotel described on some travel web site in ecstatic terms, and discovering that it is just one step up from the black hole of Calcutta.

Also, I have noticed that those who least want our feedback somehow forget to ask for it - airlines, emergency rooms, DMV offices, the IRS, prisons. They never ask: "Did you enjoy your experience with us." It is almost as if they don't want to know.

THE REAL WORKING CLASS
I enjoy watching other people at work, especially if they know what they are doing and I don't, which is usually the case. There is something fascinating about the interior mechanism of a dishwasher, or the mysterious web of wires inside an electrical junction box. We depend on these devices and we ought to understand them, but usually we must call in a technician of some kind when things go wrong. Competent technicians are hard to find and expensive to hire. We are overloaded with computer geniuses

and brain surgeons, but there are not enough people who can reliably fix a leaky toilet or a broken garage door. They are simply not being trained.

The reason they are not being trained is that slippery thing called status. Status is what other people think of us, and has nothing at all to do with our actual skills or qualities. In our upside-down system, many essential jobs that might involve the worker wearing an overall and getting his or her hands dirty are low status, while totally non-essential jobs that involve nothing more than wearing a suit and tapping a keyboard are high status. So, naturally enough, young people fix their sights on white collar work and the so-called professions, and despise vocational training that might teach them something useful. Not everybody can be in Wall Street or Silicon Valley although every new graduate seems to be trying.

The truly skilled workers of the world deserve to be better recognized and valued. Which of us would want to be struggling with a dangerous downed power line on a freezing night, or driving a 5 am commuter train to the city, or cooking in a busy restaurant kitchen for eight or ten hours a day? Which workers could we most easily do without: plumbers or telephone salesmen? The answer is obvious, and has ever since a French thinker called Saint-Simon spelled it out early in the nineteenth century. His radical theory that absolutely everybody should do useful and productive work, and there should be no parasites. This went the way of all such uncomfortable theories, but it may be time to bring it back.

One thing that might restore some sanity to our job hierarchy is a revival of the old apprenticeship system. This allowed young people to begin work at the most basic tasks and rise step by step, according to their skills, perhaps to a very high level. Michelangelo and Rembrandt started out as boy apprentices, mixing paint. But they improved over time.

What destroyed the apprenticeship system was the paper credentials system. A young person must gain the right degree, and often an MA or MBA or PhD or MD or LLD or BLT to move on to the next level, which is a huge investment in every sense. It's not an apprenticeship, it's an obstacle course. All the useful learning comes later, after certification, which may be too late.

What is considered an important or prestigious job changes over time. Entertainers were once despised, but now they are celebrities, and virtually gods. In medieval times bankers were considered not much better than robbers, and surgeons also worked as barbers, and sometimes as butchers. Politicians and lawyers were denounced as scoundrels from Aristotle to Mark Twain.

Thank goodness time has corrected those unfortunate mistakes. But irony is not enough. We need to give a lot more credit to the *real* workers of the world, before the world falls apart around us.

PROFIT AND LOSS

Our taxes are filed weeks ahead of time every year, and I feel smug about that. In truth, it is easy if you are self-employed - just a matter of adding up the losses from the year and then not paying tax on them. Profit would complicate matters, but I have no talent for it.

I have tried my hand at business from time to time, and I have never been able to figure out how entrepreneurs like Donald Trump and Bill Gates make so much money out of such very chancy enterprises. If I understand the rules of the game correctly, the object is to buy or manufacture something, say a skyscraper or a piece of software, and then sell it for more than it cost. The margin is called profit or, if you are one of the last half dozen followers of Karl Marx, surplus value. If there's no profit everyone involved feels that they are wasting their time, and the whole enterprise collapses.

There are complications of course, such as shareholders, stock markets and so on, but the essential business principle is as I have described it. My lifelong problem is I can never persuade anyone to buy anything from me for more than it cost. They argue, they bargain, and they just walk away. I don't even do well with garage sales, when I'm trying to sell stuff for *less* than it cost. I have whatever is the opposite of the Midas Touch; everything I touch turns to debit.

Years ago, I ran a small retail book business, and then a larger one. Later I was sales manager for a specialist publishing firm. All three companies went bankrupt almost as soon as I got my hands on them. After this, I decided that I wasn't cut out for business enterprise, and looked around for an occupation where profit would never be a problem. Naturally I became a writer. Some people have suggested that a writer is a businessman of a sort. This is true only in a very notional way - the way that Kim Kardashian is an entertainer.

To supplement my negative cash flow as a writer I have worked in non-profit organizations. In fact I can say that I have worked for many years in two of the most spectacularly non-profit making organizations in the known universe: education and public radio.

The world seems to be divided into people who can make a profit and those who can't. Non-profit sector workers, and there are about twenty millions of us, regard successful businesspeople with a mixture of awe and envy. Sometimes we are tempted to feel a bit superior, as if teaching or charitable work or public broadcasting is a higher calling.

But perhaps we aren't as different as we seem. Reports in *The Wall Street Journal* suggest that plenty of people with my talent for negative profits have found their way into the business sector by mistake. My financial losses were always modest, but some of these high-powered CEOs can lose billions of dollars in a year, and are very well paid for doing so. It seems that my way of doing business is beginning to catch on. Some large American corporations don't seem to believe in profit any more than Karl

Marx did. They seem almost proud to announce multi-million-dollar losses year after year. I was looking at the summary of earnings reports in *The Wall Street Journal* and it all looked very impressive until I saw the note saying, "Figures in parentheses are losses." Then I realized that I was looking at a corporate culture in which well-known companies like Amazon, Bank of America, and IBM are obviously packed with closet communists. How can *anyone* lose fifty-eight million dollars accidentally?

If this is not a conspiracy then it must be a sign that business culture has profoundly changed. The profit motive is yesterday's news, and we are moving into a new evolutionary stage in which *everything* will be a non-profit enterprise for the benefit of the public. I just hope that Donald Trump, Bill Gates, Warren Buffet and their friends will find a way to fit in.

PERILOUS PLANET

What should we do on Earth Day? Back in the 1970s, when this celebration began, the answer was simple: plant a tree, raise consciousness, promote cleaner air and water. It was a ritual of purification and celebration, a feel-good day.

Now it is more complicated. Global warming is a mega problem. A few hybrids and windmills won't solve it, let alone devious evasions like carbon credits. We need to change completely how we live: no more long-distance flying, no more pointless short car trips, no more thermostats set to our perfect comfort zone three hundred and sixty-five days a year. The penalty for failing to change these habits, so we're told, will be a new and more comprehensive version of Noah's flood, with the low-lying east coast one of the first places to go under.

But the habits of a lifetime don't change so easily. As the water rises I guarantee that we'll see the first amphibious SUV's splashing down the street towards the Mall, gulping gas at fifty dollars a gallon. Global warming must take its place in the hierarchy of human anxieties and, given a choice of problems, we will always prefer the ones that cause the least personal inconvenience. Why worry about global warming when the cosmos itself is such a dangerous place? Here we are, zipping through infinite space on a ball of dirt so small that even the most intelligent aliens have never noticed it. Killer comets and asteroids are coming at us like paint balls from all directions at about twenty-six thousand miles an hour. We are threatened by giant cosmic clouds of poison dust, and black holes that could gobble up the earth faster than Washington gobbles up our tax dollars.

This is disturbing, but at least it puts our anxiety about global warming in proper perspective, somewhere between cholesterol and the Islamic State. There is nothing to be done about vast cosmic threats like exploding galaxies, so we can worry about them, as it were, free of charge. There's no need to revolutionize the way we live.

But global warming and climate change are closer to home. They seem to demand action, and I thought a partial solution might be in sight when the drought-stricken state of California announced plans to build giant desalination plants to draw unlimited water from the ocean. As the sea level threatens to rise, Californians will suck up zillions of gallons to water their green lawns, fill their swimming pools, irrigate their vineyards, make their ice cubes, fill their plastic bottles, and wash their lovely hair. The sea level will stay where it is, and the globe can go on warming without causing anyone the slightest inconvenience. Problem solved.

Unfortunately, it won't work. Even Californians can't consume the whole ocean. A general migration to high ground in Alaska would be more practical. That leaves us exactly where we were when the environmental movement started almost fifty years ago: thinking globally, and doing small things locally. It's not exactly a rousing slogan, but it's probably all that most of us individually can do on Earth day: plant a tree, or maybe some rice, buy a recyclable shopping bag, get the old bicycle out - just do what little we can.

HONEST DAVE

There never was a time in history when it was safe to have a naïve and trusting nature. Look at what happened to Voltaire's *Candide*. And I am beginning to wonder whether the last remaining naïve and trusting personalities have been selected out by evolution – not so much biological as commercial and political evolution. Only the tricksters and scammers seem to flourish.

In my respectable bourgeois family every stranger was assumed to be honest and trustworthy unless they showed some obvious contrary evidence, such as a prison uniform or a knife dripping with blood. So, I was brought up to take people at face value. It is hard to hold on to this benign view of humanity for a whole lifetime, and in any case things have changed. Now, like Hercule Poirot, we must suspect everyone of everything.

Until a few years ago my trusting nature had remained more or less intact. Obviously, there was plenty of dishonesty around, and I suffered from it occasionally like everybody else. But, on the whole, I assumed that I could trust those I dealt with, with certain obvious exceptions like used car dealers, tabloid newspapers, and politicians. My credulous generation had its eyes opened by the internet, when we became the victims of a deluge of lies, heartless tricks, cheats, impostures, and deceptions such as we had never imagined. It was as if a veil had been lifted, allowing the non-criminal majority to see that we might not be a majority after all, or like discovering a hornets' nest hidden in the wall of the living room. They were there all the time, waiting for a chance to sting us, and we never knew.

We recently tried to rent out a small property, which we advertised on a well-established and reputable website. Some of the responses we got were almost (but fortunately not quite) beyond belief. "I would like to rent your property for three honeymoon couples for three months," said one. This is a place with one bedroom. Many enquiries were of this surreal type. There were sub-letting scams, immigration scams, time-share scams, tax scams, identity theft scams: if you can imagine some sleazy form of trickery, then somebody else has thought of it already, and will soon try it on you.

Our naïve presumption of innocence has taken a beating right across the board. For most of our lives we assumed that scientific research must be impeccably honest, and that bankers were sober and trustworthy people. We believed implicitly that school grades, athletic performances, prescription medications and company accounts were, more or less, what they appeared to be. Not anymore. Once suspicion has taken root it spreads in all directions.

It is no fun to be suspicious of everything all the time. But I squeezed tiny glow of virtue out of it. At least *I* was still honest and trustworthy, as I was taught to be. This self-satisfied feeling lasted only as long as it took me to remember that I am a lifetime member of the most untrustworthy tribe on the planet, namely writers. We have our Bernie Madoffs too, authors like Clifford Irving and James Frey who made literary deception into an art form. But all of us make things up, that's our job: stories, fables, fantasies, and especially memoirs. We change reality around to make it more interesting. Does that sound honest?

I was sorry to give up my fleeting moment of moral superiority. But now I can no longer remember if I really felt it, or just made it up.

NICE AND NASTY

Some of us were depressed by the news that the Walt Disney Company is planning to makeover the image of Mickey Mouse, to show his darker side and so increase his profitability. Now I'm not naïve. I kept mice as pets when I was a boy, and I know that even the most agreeable white mice have a dark side. But please, not Mickey. Soon kids will have no place to hide from the media's obsession with violence and nastiness. What next? Will Public Television transform Big Bird into a vulture, to make him more interesting? Will Mrs. Tiggy Winkle the hedgehog be fitted out with poison spines for her next movie?

Nastiness sells, but I don't understand why. Where's the entertainment value in things that are ugly and cruel? It's a curious commentary on human nature that a lot of people have always enjoyed being scared and revolted. This perverse taste for horror goes back much farther than Frankenstein. Pick just about any society from the ancient world, from the Mayans to the Romans, and you will find that depraved and violent myths were at the very heart of their cultures. Humans seem to be the only creatures that take conscious pleasure in the suffering of others. This is nothing to be proud of, or to encourage in young children.

You might hope that as our society becomes kinder and gentler, which it has, and as science and rational thought make steady progress, which they have, we would naturally discard these sick hangovers from the dark ages. But here we are, almost two decades into the twenty-first century, absolutely awash with bizarre twaddle about zombies, vampires and werewolves. New movies and books about them appear all the time, including one called *Pride and Prejudice and Zombies*, which is apparently ultra-violent and very nasty indeed, and even the civilized game of chess has been given a perverse twist by a British impresario who has competitors alternate four-minute rounds of chess with three-minute rounds of boxing. No, I didn't make it up.

Two of the favorite adjectives in today's entertainment world are "gritty" and "edgy." It seems that, as our real lives become safer and more civilized, we need to escape backwards into a darker world, with the aid of edgy cartoons, thuggish chess games, thirsty vampires, and restless zombies. I won't even mention video games, most of which are as maca-bre and nightmarish as anything the ancient Romans could imagine.

What saves us from being overwhelmed by all this profitable nastiness is a sense of humor. Most of the stuff designed to horrify and frighten us is just plain silly - ludicrous plastic vampires, cheap electronic sound effects, and so on. There is, after all, some balance in our universe. The birth an-niversary of Boris Karloff is also the birth anniversary of Harpo Marx, who never spoke in performances, let alone screamed, because he didn't have to. All Harpo needed to prevail against the forces of darkness were his bemused expression, his little horn, boop boop, and of course his harp. When the gritty mice and wicked werewolves come calling, that's all any of us need. One little boop, and the laughter blows them all away.

A STEP UP

Everything moves outdoors in summer, including music. We often stay in a French village where a lot of outdoor performances happen in summer. It's a common sight to see temporary stages being put up in parks or open spaces, ready for the next show. The stages are sim-ple structures, made from scaffolding covered with boards, and about three feet high. From Carnegie Hall to the village square, every per-former needs a stage.

The young musicians who perform there are mostly amateurs or semi-professionals who subscribe to the belief that real music began in the nineteen sixties. They don't have many instruments but they do have pow-erful amplifiers, and speakers so huge that they often dwarf the band members themselves. This tells us that the purpose of the stage is not to allow the band can be heard. They could be heard two miles away even if they were playing in a deep hole in the ground. It can't be that the audi-ence wants to see them because, to put it politely, and with rare excep-tions, they are not much to look at. It must be because that little step up, three feet above the ground, makes them feel good.

Everyone loves to be on stage. Kids absolutely adore it. Like grown-ups they will clamber on to anything that gives them a bit of extra height, and height is what it's all about, elevation, superiority. In any public event, there are several possible arrangements of seating, some of which put the audience in the superior position and others that elevate the performers. In the theaters of the ancient world, the seats rose high above the performers who looked up towards the audience like mice caught in the bird seed bin. Entertainers in those days were considered the lowest form of life. In Shakespeare's Globe, as in most modern theaters, people in the cheap area (the groundlings) are on a level with the stage, while the wealthier members of the audience look down on the players. You can't have a much clearer metaphor than that. Then, finally and most seductively, there is the stage or podium that puts the performer clearly above the whole audience. This is the authoritarian listen-to-me-because-I-know-best arrangement, favored by old-fashioned teachers, radical preachers, and all politicians.

How true it is that all the world's a stage, and all the men and women merely players. I have strutted my brief hour upon a few stages, and plenty of lecture platforms, and I must confess that I am not immune to the pleasure of elevation. It's not hard to understand. No psychoanalysis is necessary. As children, we were all controlled for years by persons taller than ourselves, so we spend the rest of our lives trying to compensate. Competition over height starts early with young boys. Tall men have a distinct advantage on the basketball court of life, and we build ludicrously high and ugly buildings presumably because they seem powerful and important. A President who lives at the top of a tower turns the metaphor into a reality. Any lofty mountain presents a challenge. Every year several hundred otherwise sane people try to climb Mount Everest, for no reason except to turn around and come down again. Moses went up the mountain to get The Word, not down into the basement. Money experts speak of the commanding heights of the economy. In war, everyone wants to seize the commanding heights, so they can rain destruction on their enemies. But even the highest military position can be dominated by a fighter plane, or a drone. The ultimate masculine height dream is to put weapons out in space. Nobody could beat that, either militarily or psychologically.

Compared to these dangerous fantasies a temporary wooden stage is nothing. I can't begrudge the musicians their harmless three feet of elevation, or their few minutes of psychological superiority. If I could play the electric guitar I'd probably be up there with them.

THE PEDAGOGIC CREDIT CARD

The bills for the Holidays arrive with the New Year. All those happy credit card purchases that seemed so effortless at the time now, suddenly, have a real price tag attached. We often hear how much simpler and less expensive the holidays were "in the old days," and it's true, I was there in the old days, and I remember that Christmas gifts were annoyingly small and cheap. Children naturally prefer flashy and expensive, and I can't help feeling some envy for the kids of today. A six-year-old across the street got a real electric go-cart, and almost every child over the age of three seems to have been gifted with a state of the art smartphone. My cell phone is far older than most of these kids, not at all smart, and cost about ten dollars.

I can't complain because I know that my parents weren't mean. They just didn't have credit cards, so when they bought something they paid in real, tangible cash. There's something very sobering about handing over cash. It's almost physically painful, and credit cards act as a powerful painkiller, one of those dangerous painkillers that takes away the pain and makes you feel good at the same time.

Credit is delightful, but risky, as we discovered in 2008 and will no doubt discover again in the near future. The banks that issue credit cards should take some responsibility for this, and it occurs to me that, with today's technology, a sense of responsibility could be built into the cards themselves.

You must have seen those electronic speed limit signs that signal your speed as you pass by, with a warning if you are going too fast, which almost everybody is. These are very common in Europe and the French call them *panneaux pédagogique* or educational signs. So why not an educational credit card that would teach us to pay some attention to how much we are spending, and why?

Perhaps in some more economical future age we will be issued with cards that simply get hotter and hotter as we spend more and more, until it they get too hot to hold and eventually melt into little puddles of plastic. That would work. But, right now, a less technically sophisticated solution would be a monthly card statement with added commentary on our purchases. Was it wise to go to that expensive restaurant in Berlin, by taxi? Did you really *need* that new tablet computer?

A truly helpful credit card statement could even nudge our whole lifestyle in the right direction. Why so many restaurant meals and so few museum or concert tickets? Why so many DVD rentals and no gym membership? Each statement would be like a scolding message from an all-seeing mother.

The good advice would come too late, but it might have a cumulative effect. Psychologists call it the conditioned reflex. In time, the very sight of the educational credit card would remind us of all the criticisms we have endured from it in the past. Every tempting web site, expensive restaurant, jewelry store, or up-market car dealership would set off mental alarm bells. STOP, THINK, DON'T DO IT! What would the credit card say?

After a few such reminders of extravagance there would be a rush back to cash transactions, consumer debt would go down, and we would all live economically ever after. But the banks wouldn't like it, and I don't think we would like it. Who wants to listen to the infuriating voice of reason?

PLUMBING THE DEPTHS

There is no emergency like a water emergency. When the plumbing fails, we panic. It brings out our most primitive fears. We inevitably think about Noah's flood and the final deluge. When water runs out of control indoors we have the worst kind of domestic crisis.

The typical suburban house provides plenty of opportunities to panic. Basements flood, cesspools collapse, valves, pipes and faucets disintegrate without warning, and drains block up for no reason at all. For those accustomed to French plumbing, this is business as usual. But, in America, our whole lives depend on the assumption that plumbing should be perfect. In Manhattan, people who suffer from bad plumbing simply call the janitor and go straight to their therapist. Here in the suburbs, we must take responsibility for our own plumbing disasters.

Plumbers are a suburban aristocracy, like firefighters. They are heroic, almost mythical figures, with their elusive habits and their vast estates in the Hamptons. People whisper the names of favored plumbers like those of elite cosmetic surgeons or particularly successful brokers.

We used to have an excellent plumber called Joe, which is the perfect name for a plumber. Joe always arrived promptly in his ancient truck, which leaked oil all over the driveway. We assumed that the Mercedes stayed discreetly in his garage at home. He tackled the latest catastrophe with a skeptical air of one who had seen it all before, and indeed had waded in it all before. According to Joe, there were only two kinds of plumbing emergencies: water that appears in the wrong place at the wrong time, or water that refuses to go away. Water is the plumber's enemy - nasty, slippery stuff with that alarming tendency to find its own level that we learned about in science class at school.

I never quite understood how water knows what its level should be. But, in our house, it is always about three inches above the floor of the basement.

Joe's diagnostic skills were reassuring. Like a physician, he began with a standard catechism of questions:

"When did the trouble start?"
"Did you notice any symptoms before that?"
"Have you heard any gurgling sounds right here?"
"Have your bathroom habits changed lately?"

Being slightly deaf, he ignored the answers and headed straight for the basement carrying what seemed to be his only tool - a huge wrench which also served as a hammer, a crowbar, and a kind of conducting baton to accompany his lectures on hydraulics, pressure, gravity, and the inadvisability of flushing major household appliances down the toilet. When the job was done he would invariably apologize profusely for the bill

Joe retired and went to his reward in Florida or on the French Riviera, and it has been hard to replace him. Big companies have overwhelmed the independent plumber, much as they have the swept independent family doctors into health care corporations. The plumbing companies are efficient. They send a big shiny truck full of equipment, and what is now called a "technician" with an iPad full of instructions and a cell phone to call the chief plumber back at headquarters if things go wrong. These technicians speak more politely than Joe ever did, but they seem to have a kind of script to follow. "I am Sebastian, and I will be your plumber today." They have an annoying tendency to recommend new repairs, new spare parts, and new equipment. Joe would always fix the old worn out stuff somehow, like the traditional family doctor. Instead of a heart bypass a few rubber washers or an aspirin would do the job. And there's another thing. I've noticed that the brave new water management technicians of the brave new twenty-first century never, ever, apologize for the bill.

VANITY FAIR

Vanity lives on long after the excuse for it has gone. We had an important wedding anniversary recently and, in a moment of romantic excess, we called in a professional photographer to record the moment, and I must say she did a splendid job. It's amazing what can be done with a carefully arranged pose, a good background and a clever photographer with a very expensive camera. We are delighted with the results. If we really looked like that we would be even happier.

"The camera cannot lie" is one of those empty clichés, like "Every child has a special gift." Nobody believes it, but we find it convenient to pretend because we all love the things that a good photograph can do for our self-esteem.

In John Bunyan's inspirational story "The Pilgrim's Progress," which first hit the best-seller lists in 1678, he tells of a town called Vanity in which self-esteem was the major industry. In Vanity, every kind of honor, title, position, pleasure and flattering self-image could be bought at a great market, run by Beelzebub. The place was a bigger success than the Mall of America. Everybody went to Vanity.

In the 1840's, William Makepeace Thackeray used Bunyan's fantasy to satirize the narcissism of the human race in a wonderfully entertaining novel called *Vanity Fair*. And you won't be surprised to hear that human nature hasn't changed since then. In the spirit of twenty-first century there is even a magazine called *Vanity Fair*, a slick and glossy production that offers three hundred pages of pure narcissism and self-delusion every month.

On Long Island, the nearest thing we have to a real Vanity Fair is the local mall, which may also be run by Beelzebub. The mall exists entirely to sell flattering self-images -- fashions, hairstyles, life styles, fingernails and all the other devices we need to live up to our own illusions.

Last time I went to the mall, I noticed a proliferation of photographic studios. At every turn in the labyrinth there was another glossy portrait emporium, hung with pictures of amazingly attractive people. I practice a simple kind of photography myself: point and shoot and hope for the best. But seeing the products of these professional studios, I began to suspect that this is not exactly how they do it. The contrast between the photographs displayed on the walls and the customers walking in and out is just too great.

I was reminded of the art of the portrait painter in the days before photography. The portrait painter was hired, inevitably by someone wealthy, to create an impressive and flattering image of that person. Too much realism meant no fee. It's a revelation to go to the museum and look at portraits by Gainsborough, for example. When he was painting aristocrats for money, their portraits came out entirely beautiful. When he painted poor people for the love of art, the people came out looking horribly real.

Hogarth was the only great portrait painter who could cross this tricky boundary. Somehow, his portraits of the rich and famous always managed to hint at the (sometimes very nasty) character just behind the handsome image. But it was so subtle that Hogarth usually got paid anyway.

The modern portrait photographer doesn't have to be an artistic genius. He or she can take fifty or a hundred shots to get one that looks just right. Last time I had to have a picture taken for a book jacket, the photographer had to use half a dozen rolls of film to get one image that looked halfway human. If not even one shot comes out right, digital technology can improve our image in any way we like. Hair can be added or removed. Pouches under the eyes can vanish. Skin blemishes can magically fade away. Digital photography can make a handsome bridegroom out of Frankenstein's monster.

This explains why still photography has not yet been swept away by the craze for video cameras. The video image is less forgiving, and far less easy to manipulate. In unskilled hands, the video camera is an all-too-true recorder of life, and offers the awful possibility of seeing and hearing ourselves exactly as others see us. Awkward gestures, incoherent speech, undisciplined hair and a bad attitude are just impossible to conceal on video. You might have observed, in political campaigns, how splendid the candidates look in their formal portraits, and how much less than splendid they appear on the television screen. Reality hurts, and the virtue of the old-fashioned still camera is that it can and does lie, if only you use it right.

Our obsession with our self-image is probably as old as the first primate who caught a glimpse of herself in a pool of water and realized that it was a bad fur day. It is reassuring to know that, even if we've made no progress in modesty, we have made great strides toward the democratization of vanity. We may not all be created exactly equal in our exterior beauty. But Photoshop can take care of that.

SPARE TIME

Hobby shops are small and vanishing part of the suburban landscape, and the word 'hobby' has a strangely old-fashioned ring. Hobbies, according to my dictionary, are "spare time" activities. Nobody admits to having spare time these days.

Judging by the contents of the hobby shops, the answer is: over-imaginative boys and frustrated men. These stores are crammed to the roof with model trains, boats, rockets, radio controlled racing cars and off-track vehicles, military vehicles and weapons, historical fantasy simulations. Hobbies seem to be mostly a masculine vice, although there is a mysterious subtext of dollhouses, which sit uneasily beside the various devices of speed and destruction.

Hobbies tend to be a secret vice, perhaps because they are often somewhat embarrassing. They must be done at home alone, in the basement. That's why most suburban homes *have* basements, despite all the problems of damp and drainage. A man must have a place to hide, a "man cave" in which to pursue his hobby.

Most hobbies demand no physical effort. When it does require more than minimal exertion a hobby becomes a sport which you can't easily do in the basement. In fact, when any hobby takes you out of the basement (shopping, golf, ballet) it contradicts the whole hobby idea, which is to stay in a small safe world. An outdoor hobby is more like a psychosis.

On the face of it, hobbies are an enormous waste of time and effort. As a child, I can remember spending endless tedious hours with my father in the basement, making model planes that would never fly, and model boats that would sink the moment they touched the water. The only hobby I really enjoyed was a primitive model train, propelled by clockwork. It went racketing along noisily at unpredictable speeds, and would come to a complete stop for no reason. When I first rode on the Long Island Rail Road, I realized where the designer must have found his inspiration.

Some hobbies are relatively painless. Bird watching, although annoying for the birds, is entirely relaxing, especially if you do it in the basement with a picture book. But most hobbies produce high levels of anxiety and frustration. Have you ever tried to construct one of those models that come in about a thousand parts, with a single page of smudged instructions in Japanese, or built a cathedral out of matchsticks? Other diversions like violin playing or watercolor painting produce high levels of performance anxiety and depression, because they are so difficult to do well. And some hobbies are just so painful that it's hard to believe the frail human psyche can tolerate them at all. Watching ballet springs to mind. I sometimes wonder whether some human beings can even tell the difference between pleasure and pain, let alone make rational choices between them.

Psychologists have tried to explain hobbies by suggesting that they reflect the deep and ancient hunting urge in humankind. It's true that we do talk about "pursuing a hobby," and many hobbies involve tracking down and collecting things - like antique steam engines or duck decoys - just the way our ancestors tracked and collected the weekly protein supply on the African savannah.

But this hunting explanation isn't very convincing. Our ancestors hunted for survival, not as a hobby. They didn't pile up dead mammoths in the back of the cave as collector's items: they ate them. The hunting instinct hardly explains dollhouses, or for that matter toy railways as hobbies.

Many hobbies involve collecting stuff. I collect dust balls under my desk, but this is not considered by connoisseurs to be a serious hobby. Collecting must focus on things that are obscure, difficult to get, and totally useless. In fact, the very definition of a collectible is its uselessness. Almost every week special offers arrive in my mailbox for once-in-a-life-time collectible opportunities: a 1953 Chevy Pickup Truck 11" long; rare coins of the 20th century; exotic stamps of Bolivia. Dedicated collectors must keep extending their basements, until they undermine the whole neighborhood.

It may be simply that hobbies originated in the pre-TV dark ages, as a way of occupying the long winter evenings in the back of the cave. That's why we feel the primordial urge to do them in the basement. But my own belief is that hobbies are about power. The world often seems to be an out-of-control place, and life itself is more like roulette than chess. A hobby offers the chance to control one small corner of the great chaos out there. Many hobbies involve the literal miniaturization of the world, and it makes sense to carve out a tiny slice of reality, just big enough to manage. While you are down there in the basement, you can be in full control of your little universe. Your trains will run on time, and even your dolls house can be a neat and tidy place, without dust balls or family feuds. The hobbyist bestrides his little universe like Gulliver among the Lilliputians. Models of all kinds are popular; dolls and dollhouses; train sets; decorative figurines. Even a garden is a tiny world unto itself. All sports and games have this quality of miniaturization, reducing the drama of life to the dimensions of a playing field. The hobbyist can make his trains run on time, send his racing cars around the track at well over the fifty-five miles an hour limit, and fly without a license. Better that men should crash their toy trains and cars, and exterminate the forces of evil with their toy weapons, than get involved in the real thing.

When we ask: "What do you do?" we expect to hear a description of work, not of a hobby. Yet consider the employment ads in your newspaper. Take a Magic Marker and highlight all those that offer control and self-expression and creativity and meaning. I bet your paper stays unmarked. We have elevated the most trivial bureaucratic pursuits to the status of "real work," while degrading all the unique things we really care about down to the status of hobbies. Observe the hobbyist in the throes of his or her obsession -- energized, enthusiastic, intent, even when things aren't going right. Observe the same person doing their regular job, their *real work* -- listless, bored, and distracted. Quentin Crisp, who knew how to live, once said that "Hobbies are instead of life." But perhaps the truth is the other way around. The passionate, free-spirited, difficult stuff of hobbies should be the stuff of real life, and the workaday routines of life should be put in in their proper perspective, as a distraction for our spare time: a hobby.

MY SECRET KNOWLEDGE

Everybody loves a secret. We love to keep them, we love to learn them, and we love telling other people about them, especially if we promised not to. Every profession is a conspiracy of secrets, like the Guild of

Magicians. Once non-professionals know how the tricks are done, there goes the profit margin.

Most secrets are harmless. Clubs, lodges and religious cults have secrets that are, for the most part, simply archaic and amusing, although they can take a sinister turn. The traditional church kept its secrets safe by wrapping them in Latin, until translators like John Wycliffe came along and ruined the mystery with versions of the Bible that anybody could understand.

Then there is the kind of knowledge that is not exactly secret, but is so arcane and restricted to a tiny group of people that it is quite as satisfying as a secret. Enthusiasts on any subject treasure this kind of knowledge. For example, there is a group of hobbyists in Britain who dedicate their lives to knowing everything about the long-obsolete World War II bomber, the Avro Lancaster. Well, why not? We know from the Antiques Roadshow that there are avid collectors for every historical relic, however obscure, and anyone who has been around a university knows that there is nothing too insignificant to be the object of serious and expensive research. Having special knowledge allows us not to feel too bad about all the other things we don't know. I may be completely ignorant of (for example) Portuguese irregular verbs, but suppose I know all the baseball scores from Japan since 1956: isn't that something?

The main thing is that nobody else knows your knowledge, whether it's a juicy piece of scandal or the fact that the engines on the Avro Lancaster bomber had floating gudgeon pins. If knowledge is power, then secret knowledge *feels like* power.

There are false secrets, purely imaginary and designed for entertainment. Cooks and gardeners often claim they have secret knowledge, tricks and recipes passed down for generations, which they then proceed to reveal in books and on TV shows. Every detective story depends on keeping and then revealing secrets. Dan Brown's book *The Da Vinci Code* and its sequels succeeded, I'm sure, because they reveal nonexistent secrets about events that never happened. Television is full of documentaries that pretend to uncover the "secret" of this or the "mystery" of that.

I am perpetually embarrassed by my lack of secret knowledge. As Will Rogers used to say, all I know is what I read in the papers. But then last week I had to dispose of a bunch of old computers that had accumulated in the basement, and I was inundated with warnings that the hard drives of those things are packed with secret knowledge – not really interesting things like the location of the Holy Grail or the exact ingredients of Coca Cola, but the dull and tedious secrets of our electronic age: passwords, account numbers, and so on. Other secrets could be prized out of these old computers, I'm told: things like my e-mail and web browsing habits. If anyone wants to read thousands of my old e-mails, or learn that I spend my time on the web searching for cheap bird seed or funny anecdotes about nineteenth century composers, they are very welcome.

But, in the end, I bowed to the universal paranoia and pulled out the drives before taking the computers to the recycle center. Now, apparently, I must smash up the hard drives with a hammer. But I don't want to do this. Somewhere, hidden on those blank, shiny surfaces, is the only secret knowledge I have.

THE ENTHUSIASTS

The world in general seems too excited about too many things. Not only is there a perpetual ferment in the Middle East – which at least has several thousand years of tortured history to explain its madness – but even out here in the peaceful suburbs of the (mostly) peaceful United States we are constantly teased and tempted to "share the excitement," especially when there isn't any.

A lot of e-mails come from organizations that claim to be excited about some product or service or charity they are promoting. "We are really excited about our new customer service web site," said one company. This is strange. Not only is "customer service web site" a kind of triple oxymoron – that is three mutually contradictory terms in one - but even if it described a genuine customer service there would be no reason to get excited about it. That's what a service web site is supposed to do, just the way a gas pump is expected to pump gas, and we don't get excited about that. I would be more inclined to believe the claim that "Our new customer service web site is not half as bad as some of the others."

Another variation on the same theme is the unlikely claim that an organization or company is "passionate about" something or other. "We are passionate about quality," or "Share our passion for excellence in rabbit food." But organizations don't have feelings of any kind, let alone excitement or passion, so it's just possible that they may be hoping to gain attention by claiming feelings they cannot possibly have. If a real, known individual wrote to me personally declaring their excitement and passion I would have to take it seriously, and maybe change my address as a precaution. But I can't get my mind around the idea of a huge corporation with thousands of employees all moved and motivated by the same emotion.

It is nonsense, of course, they know that as well as you do. But it is such a universal nonsense that sometimes it seems almost normal. We are completely accustomed and even conditioned to absorb emotional overstatement, hyperbole, wildly exaggerated claims, and plain lies: the "biggest" burger, the "most effective" antacid. It's as if nobody feels they can sell any product or any idea without turning it into a caricature of itself.

Our local impresario P.T.Barnum started it all back in the nineteenth century, with his circus, billed as "The Greatest Show on Earth" - an outrageous claim when you remember that the Franco-Prussian War was going on at the time. Barnum believed that the only way to sell something was to oversell it, and we are still living with his legacy of wildly inflated promotional claims. Every product or experience must be superior, amazing, perfect, great, incredible, and every emotion must be extreme. Nothing must be ordinary.

This mindless exaggeration is a silly and dangerous habit, especially when it infects our politics, as it has done. Exaggeration promotes excitement and passion and, in the end, enthusiasm. And there is a very thin dividing line between enthusiasm and mania, as you may observe every day on the evening news.

As an antidote to all this I offer you my own law of idiotic enthusiasms, which is infallible like the law of gravity. It states that the more people who become excited about an idea, product or person, and the more comprehensive, satisfying and superior that idea, product or person is imagined to be, the more likely it is to be complete rubbish. This is absolutely the best and truest law ever discovered in the whole history of the universe, and I'm quite passionate about it.

234

Theme VII

THE HUMAN COMEDY

What keeps a reflective and skeptical man alive? Mainly it is his sense of humor.

H.L.MENCKEN

Life is a jest and all things show it, I thought so once and now I know it.

JOHN GAY

The great philosophers are very serious. Sometimes it is hard to understand everything they say. Humor, on the other hand, is what makes people laugh, and that gives a lot of envy to philosophers.

MEXICAN CARTOONIST EDUARDO DEL RIO

WHAT'S SO FUNNY?

My father and uncles all loved a good joke, or even a bad one. But I can't tell jokes, or even remember them, which has been a lifelong source of frustration. A friend of mine was a born raconteur who could keep a whole dinner table in an uproar of laughter for hours with his stories, and I would sit there thinking: "I must remember that one, I must remember that one." Now I can't remember any of them, except for a few that are too obscene or politically incorrect to repeat.

My favorite childhood reading included a lot of funny writers like Lewis Carroll, W.W.Jacobs and P.G.Wodehouse. What I learned from them was that humor is an infinitely moveable feast. Jokes are not necessary, once you have realized that practically everything has a funny side.

But I wasted the second-best years of my life trying to be a serious writer. How else could I communicate my deep insight into the meaning of things, the sadness of the human condition, the fragility of love and the pain of a sensitive soul doomed to live in a crass materialistic world? After writing thousands of tedious pages on these tedious themes, it dawned on me that they were already old news in William Shakespeare's time, that I had nothing to add, and that it was time to lighten up.

Being exiled to America helped. Living on Long Island provided me with such a rich new world of absurdity and strangeness that I immediately started writing newspaper columns about my life there. The columns found a regular home for ten years in the Sunday edition of *The New York Times,* and led to a weekly spot on the local National Public Radio station. There was and is never any shortage of funny material in the Long Island suburbs, or in any other suburbs I have ever lived in including the London suburb where I grew up. Suburbia may be the goal to which all human life has tended – no surprises, and unlimited shopping opportunities. In the suburbs, all dreams and self-delusions can find a comfortable home. They are the heartland of the great American illusion that anybody can do anything, the subdivisions of opportunity within the land of opportunity. Properly understood and lived in, suburbs make the business of getting from birth to death virtually painless.

But after some thirty years of writing more-or-less humorous columns and essays, I can tell you that, even in the suburbs, it is not as easy as it sounds. Not only is the whole gloomy world working against you, but any writer or performer who is expected to be funny on schedule knows that it doesn't work that way. Humor is almost completely spontaneous, like a sneeze. You can't just sit at your desk and think it up.

Some time ago, I tried to teach humor writing at several writers' conferences. It was not a great success. It was easy enough to explain the mechanics of humor – techniques like exaggeration, understatement, reversal, anachronism, absurdity, parody and so on that anyone can learn. But what I discovered through teaching was the old truism that, when you take humor seriously, you kill it stone dead. As E.B.White so elegantly put it: "Analyzing humor is like dissecting a frog. Few people are interested, and the frog dies."

Another thing I discovered through sheer dogged persistence was something I should have known from primary school: that not everyone has a sense of humor. There are many things in the world that I find funny, including religion, cheerleading, opera, golf, and the education system. Not everybody feels the same way, although the evidence is there for all to see. Popular humor is strangely childish, at least on television. It revolves around idiotic gags about celebrities, movies, family disasters, and political scandals. There's not much room here for subtlety. Irony and satire tend to sink like proverbial lead balloons in America, a nation notoriously serious about itself. But I refuse to give them up.

Some of the people who came to my classes seemed to expect that I would somehow cure their humor deficit. Others were disappointed that

I was not more amusing myself. More than once I was told, half-seriously: "You don't *look* funny." They wanted a clown with a string of jokes, and I was not it. Other students complained that irony and satire were cruel, which left me wondering what they were doing in a class dedicated to writing those things.

Leading these classes and by publishing my regular work also taught me that even a little humor convinces your readers or listeners that you are not a serious person and do not have an intelligent thought in your head. This also I have learned to live with. It may be true.

Even a little foreign travel reveals that every national sense of humor is different. Some nations have none at all, and are proud of it; some adore slapstick; others appreciate nothing but satire; and some enjoy only extremely long and complicated jokes that nobody else can understand. Telling what you imagine is a funny story to a group of mixed nationalities is almost certain to get a response of blank incomprehension. North Korea has not been able to see the funny side of the movie "The Interview," any more than Hitler and Mussolini were amused by Charlie Chaplin's film "The Great Dictator."

All of which makes me wonder whether the misunderstandings that divide us might have as much to do with humor, or the lack of it, as with anything else. If we could all laugh at the same things we might get along better. You may say, and you would be right, that there's not much in today's world to laugh at. The news comes at us like a serial Greek tragedy, new horrors every day. But, as we should have learned from Shakespeare, tragedy must be balanced with comedy. After every sad scene, he brings in the clowns.

So, what *is* funny? I can only speak for myself, and I find the best humor in the spectacle of human beings, myself included, playing or failing to play our fragile roles – in other words, the daily struggle of pretending to be who and what we would like to be. Writing without irony is flat, like a painting without perspective. Irony exposes the incongruities of everyday life—the half-truths, deceptions and self-deceptions that help us all get through the day. Things are never what they seem, and the essence of ironic humor is the lack of fit between life as it is and life as we imagine it should be. We think the world should make sense: it doesn't. We think life should be dignified: it never is. We think life should have a serious purpose, like football or lawn care. But the purpose always turns out to be very silly in the end. This fundamental irony is the humor writer's richest and most inexhaustible resource.

Life may not be a good joke, but it is certainly a joke of some kind, and the one joke we all share is ourselves: our customs, habits and prejudices, our crazy institutions, and our bizarre cultures. The joke is not just *on* us, it *is* us. We are not, as a species, even trying to be serious, but we think we are. If that's not funny I don't know what is.

REHEARSING FOR LIFE

I spotted my first bride of the season, in full white regalia, in the lobby of the local Best Western Hotel, along with a whole wedding party. A large sign at the back of the lobby announced: "Glen and Cindy's Wedding Rehearsal."

The men looked uncomfortable in their uniforms, like farmers press-ganged into the British navy during the war of 1812. Some still showed the circular dint of a ghostly baseball cap in their newly-trimmed hair.

Glen and Cindy, arm in arm and glowing with energy like characters in a TV sitcom, were taking the whole thing very seriously. The cliché is: bad rehearsal, good wedding. This rehearsal was going so well that a catastrophic wedding day seemed inevitable.

We love weddings in America, which is why we have so many. Our ancestors thought that one was enough, but two is the average now, some enterprising folks manage three or four, and in Hollywood the sky's the limit. There are two and a half million weddings every year, and the wedding industry is enormous. It's a big investment for the family, and rehearsals help to guarantee that every player knows his or her part, and doesn't laugh in the wrong places. It gets easier after the first time.

We don't rehearse nearly enough. Most of life is a ragged performance with missed cues and half-remembered lines. When we do rehearse, we practice only the easy bits: the wedding, for example, and not the honeymoon. Any expert on marriage will tell you that more things can go wrong on a honeymoon than could ever go wrong at a dozen weddings. Glen and Cindy would be well advised to rehearse being stranded for hours or days in remote airports, being struck down by seafood gumbo in alien restaurants, losing luggage, and spending long nights in a stiflingly hot hotel room with no air conditioning or television.

They should certainly rehearse having children, one of the least well-planned of all human activities. A full-scale rehearsal would involve borrowing a baby and learning to do without sleep for a year or two; borrowing an eight-year-old and learning to yell at a brick wall; and borrowing a teenager so as to get accustomed to diabolical music shaking the foundations of the house twenty-four hours a day. Then they would be perfectly prepared for the experience of parenthood, assuming they decided to go ahead.

It may seem cynical to suggest that Glen and Cindy should rehearse divorce. But they have a fifty-fifty chance, which is much better than the odds of winning the state lottery. Divorce is always a shock if you haven't trained for it. A few more yelling exercises, several volumes of mutual accusations, and a hundred simulated hours in a lawyer's office, should make the whole process comfortably familiar.

Everything predictable can and should be rehearsed. I wish now that I had put some time into rehearsing old age, experimenting with bifocals, arthritis, memory loss, and unwelcome senior citizens discounts in hardware stores. Perhaps I could tolerate the whole process more gracefully.

Optimists could have fun rehearsing for their future success. What a shock it must be to become rich and famous overnight, with no preparation. Rehearsing for success would involve some tough assignments, like trying to make intelligent conversation with other members of the country club, opening tons of mail appealing for money, and no longer knowing who your real friends are.

Pessimists should rehearse for failure, by lowering their self-esteem, putting on the traditional sackcloth and ashes, and residing in the traditional cardboard box for a while. Really dedicated pessimists might enjoy training for a whole range of predicable disasters, like the stock market collapse, the next hurricane, the first east coast earthquake, universal terminal gridlock, and a second Trump Presidency leading to a Trump dynasty.

Rehearsal takes the fear out of the unknown. In 1950s, kids used to rehearse for nuclear war. "Duck and Cover" became a sort of macabre game. Today, you can see young people energetically rehearsing for the end of their own lives, lying totally immobile and watching TV all day. When they finally get to the nursing home, they will be perfectly prepared. When they die, they will scarcely notice the difference.

All life, like all art, is experimental. There is no post-experimental stage when we have it exactly right. So, in life, as in the theater, rehearsal is always more fun than the actual performance. Glen and Cindy are on the right track. One day they will sit down with their grandchildren and share the memories: their wedding rehearsal, their first baby rehearsal, their vacation rehearsals, their daughter's wedding rehearsal, and so on to their retirement rehearsal, and their funeral rehearsal. After all, you only live twice.

EQUALITY AT LAST, I THINK

Young men today take sexual equality for granted. They think it was always ok for men to express their feelings, change diapers, and go all the way on a first date. Nobody remembers the casualties, the men who went to the wall for equality when the wall was a million miles high.

We male veterans of the sex war are well past middle age now, and still suffer twinges of guilt and regret. National Women's Equality Day, August 26, brings on a sad, reflective mood. It's a time to look back and repent of our past sins and present failures. Raised in chauvinism, indicted by feminism, and bypassed by the sexual revolution, some of us have spent half our lives coming to terms with the complicated demands of sexual equality.

It began with a paradox. The militant feminist movement appeared first and spoke most forcefully in America in the late sixties. In America, of all places, where women's power and freedom were internationally legendary. Most men of my generation were stunned. It had never occurred to us that women were oppressed. They seemed to do extraordinarily well out of the games we all played. After all, who was setting the rules? The rules of courtship, for example: the chaste dates, the first kiss, the gifts, the first meeting with her parents. These were things young men had to learn the way rats learn their way through laboratory mazes. The game made no sense to us, but we ran the maze out of training and habit.

Having played the game, we collected the prize: marriage and suburban life. About three days later, or so it seemed, along came feminism and the sexual revolution.

Sexual intercourse began
In nineteen sixty-three
(Which was rather late for me) -

243

*Between the end of the Chatterley ban
And the Beatles' first LP.*

lamented the English poet Phillip Larkin. All the rules were changed. Women were declared the equals of men, and no longer to be treated as passive wives and sex objects. The New Woman would be sexually and economically free, just like a man. "I wouldn't mind being a sex object for just one day," muttered a confused male friend of mine, almost weeping into his beer. The great liberation had arrived, and we had missed it.

But there was something intriguing about the prospect of sexual equality at last. Some men decided that the liberation of women and the liberation of men were part of the same problem. We came to see sexual liberation as a total, revolutionary thing, that would abolish male responsibility for women and children, and equalize (finally) the sexual game. We gritted our teeth, and set out on the road to equality.

The process was full of surprises. Number one was the discovery that sexual equality was a terrible bore. Women had always complained that housework and child care were tedious and exhausting. Now we knew the truth of it. The men who took on an equal share of domestic work discovered that they had bought into a zero-sum proposition. One less boring job for her was one more boring job for him. Large chunks of our free time vanished into domestic tedium, and we got little in exchange but the cold comfort of self-righteousness.

Things weren't much better at work. The flood of highly qualified women into every business and profession simply made life tougher for men, as more people competed for the same number of good jobs and promotions. The war between the sexes expanded out of the home and into the office.

And, of course, the family changed. The new, two career equalitarian family felt different, more businesslike, less homelike than the families we grew up in. Clearly, we had to change our dreams. Exit those nostalgic family stories of grandma the apple pie wizard and grandpa the successful entrepreneur. Welcome to the new post-feminist nostalgia: how grandma became a midlevel IBM executive with the support of grandpa, the busy househusband. It was all a bit deflating.

But the abolition of the traditional family was nothing compared to the abolition of sex. We early male enthusiasts for feminism misunderstood the sexual consequences of equality. Sex was never about equality but about difference, and sexual equality seemed to imply the phasing out of male/female differences in the jargon of the times, androgyny. Yet the appearance of women as different and beautiful and sexually exciting turned out to be more fundamental than we had imagined. Women who looked and acted like men baffled the impulse to desire and to love. Superwoman, with her business suit and busy schedule and stuffed briefcase, was too much like the guy at the next desk. And Superwomen soon began to say out loud that the domesticated, emotional male was unattractive too: the term "wimp" was freely used.

But we didn't give up. We learned a lot about ourselves as men, most of it bad; and the struggle with the Old Adam continues. Male chauvinists, like recovering alcoholics, are never completely cured. But I've been trying to make myself over into an equalitarian male for almost a quarter century. On good days, I can persuade myself that the feminist revolution is over, and that both sexes won.

Yet most of my friends have slipped or crawled back into traditional marriages, and the younger generation looks strangely familiar. Teaching and talking to teenagers, I get a dizzying sense of *déja vu*, as though peering down a long funnel into the fifties. Forget about androgyny. There they are, lined up in the college classroom, row after row of Barbies and Kens. The gulf of misunderstanding between these young women and men seems as great as it was thirty years ago, and they still play the games I remember so well. Sometimes, the post-feminist relationships of the twenty-first century look like reruns of old Doris Day movies. Were we missing something? Could biology possibly have something to do with this?

This is the thought that keeps me awake the night before National Women's Equality Day. Suppose I have finally changed, and the rest of the human race has remained the same?

THE BUSINESS OF AMERICA

Calvin Coolidge once famously remarked that the business of America is business. But an unbiased visitor from another galaxy, observing what most employed people really do with their time, might conclude that the real business of America is holding meetings.

Meetings are as old as civilization. Great leaders like Alexander the Great and Queen Elizabeth the First held "Councils," which worked just like modern meetings: that is, the less powerful people would try to guess what the more powerful people wanted to hear, and say that.

But in modern times, meetings have become a whole way of life. Almost everybody I try to call these days is either in a meeting, or pretending to be in a meeting. Those of us who work alone are at a permanent disadvantage here. We can never take refuge in meetings, because we have nobody to meet with. This is one of the many subtle forms of discrimination not dealt with in the existing civil rights laws. Important people can enjoy meetings from morning till night, while unimportant people just have to get on and do the work.

I suppose I shouldn't complain. I have been to meetings in my time, thousands of them. Educators spend as much time as possible in meetings, the alternative being too awful to contemplate. So I have studied the psychology, the sociology and what I might call the *theology* of meetings quite exhaustively. Here are some of my conclusions.

About twenty-five per-cent of all meetings are almost completely pointless. They are called because somebody in the organization must make a difficult decision, and wants to spread the blame around. This type of meeting can have one of four results: 1. New guidelines are issued, so that they can be ignored like the old guidelines; 2. A working party is set up to look into the matter further, by holding more meetings; 3. Recommendations are issued, to be considered by another committee at another meeting; or 4. Most cunning of all, a "mission statement" is concocted, which has the result of confusing the issue so thoroughly that dozens more meetings will be needed to straighten things out.

All these outcomes, separately or together, add up to doing nothing at all, which is exactly why they are so popular.

The seventy-five per-cent of meetings that are not almost completely useless are, in fact, *completely* useless, with no reason to exist at all, and have no results whatsoever. These are routine meetings scheduled on a regular basis - weekly, monthly or whatever. Since the meeting has no purpose, the agenda is a piece of creative fiction dreamed up by the chair. The function of these pro-forma meetings is not so much to avoid hard decisions as simply to avoid work, and to allow members of the organization to vent their emotions.

Regular meetings are said to build team spirit. But you don't have to be a psychologist to know that team spirit, like patriotism, flourishes best with a lot of imagination, and not too many facts. In bureaucracy, as in war, distance lends enchantment to the view.

Conferences are inflated meetings, where more time can be wasted more efficiently at much greater expense. Every group in America, from dog groomers to dentists, has an annual conference. There are three hundred giant convention centers nationwide, and you can hold conferences anywhere from Disneyland to the QE2. Conferences today are what vacations used to be in an earlier age, marvelous excuses for taking time away from home and work, while indulging in naughty behavior. Since most conference goers, except at Baptist Conventions, are permanently drunk or hung over, conferences are even less practical use than ordinary meetings.

None of this implies a criticism. Committees, meetings, and conferences are essential to the smooth running of society. They keep people occupied who might otherwise cause endless trouble by actually doing things which would usually be stupid and counter-productive. In my view, a large part of the turmoil in the inner cities is caused by people who have too few committee assignments.

So, let's add this new category to the growing list of victims of this and that - the meeting-deprived. And let's not stop there, with empty sympathy. I suggest setting up a national organization for people who don't have meetings or conferences to go to, an organization that would fill this sad gap in our lives. Of course, we will need to call a planning meeting, draw up a mission statement, set up a working party, issue recommendations and guidelines. Come to think of it, that may be all we need to do.

THE RIGHT TO ARM BEARS

There's lot of outdoor activity on the east end of Long Island in November. Cars and pickups are parked near every small patch of woods or open land. It would be nice to think that the drivers are out walking, enjoying the bracing autumn air and the last of the fall colors, perhaps even doing a little photography or watercolor painting.

But these aren't nature lovers. They are hunters, searching the woods for beautiful animals in order to kill them. Out on the far fringes of suburbia at this time of year it's like a war zone. We are surrounded by snipers with six-packs, and the legal system does not encourage us to shoot back.

Hunting has played a big role in American history. When the frontier was being pushed westwards, there was always a gap between the arrival of the first settlers and the arrival of the first full-service supermarket. In the interval, the settlers had to shift for themselves with guns and traps and fishing lines. But by the time the frontier was officially declared closed in 1893, food distribution was already a big industry and hunting was only necessary in the remotest corners of the emptiest states.

It's a sad comment on human nature that, more than a hundred years later, hunting is still going on in areas packed with people and supermarkets. Mindless violence against humans and property is punishable by law. Mindless violence against animals is dignified with the name of "sport." Tolstoy referred to hunting as "Evil legitimized." Those are strong words. But hunting is certainly evil *sanitized* - made acceptable and normal simply by being so commonplace.

There's an unbridgeable gulf of non-understanding between those who kill living creatures for fun, and those who do not. It's not one of those things you can resolve in a discussion. Hunters aren't monsters. The hunters I've known have all been perfectly nice people. They just enjoy killing things.

The favorite justification for hunting is overpopulation. It's true that the whole metropolitan corridor from Boston to Washington is heavily overpopulated, but with human beings. We have met the overpopulation, and it is us. Wild animals are scarce in our area compared to humans. But can we issue licenses to kill a random sample of suburban dwellers, based on the undeniable fact that there are far too many of them?

Hunters argue that nobody who is not a vegetarian has any right to point the finger at hunting when the commercial meat business is such a horror show. This is fair comment, but hunting is not really about substitute sources of meat, it is about a certain kind of male romance. Hunting is the last gasp of traditional masculinity. There's not much scope for macho behavior these days, or for dressing up in military-style gear and carrying guns in public places.

The hunting magazines blatantly suggest that the equipment and the outfits will turn you into a *real man*. The camouflage suits, the high-tech rifles with scopes, the two-way radios and the four-wheel drives, all promise a pale imitation of frontier-style masculinity in the midst of the suburban wilderness.

Human nature isn't likely to change any time soon. Hunters will hunt. But I would like to even the odds a bit. Hunting is far too safe. Safe, that is, for the hunters. Baseball is two hundred and eighty times more dangerous than hunting, in terms of injuries. The main human victims of hunting seem to be walkers, and suburban householders shot down in their back yards or even in their homes by over-excited men in camouflage suits.

So, I have an idea to even the odds. The animals should get their own defensive weapons. The government has been generous enough to arm every homicidal regime on the planet. How about placing a few simple weapons in the paws of our beleaguered animal friends? Nothing fancy, no nukes.

Let's begin with the right to arm bears. Bears are smart animals, and they can stand up on their hind legs and use their front paws. In the old-time circus, bears were often star performers. With a little training, they could certainly handle a simple firearm. Their aim might be a bit vague, but we could compensate for that by giving them automatic assault rifles, and teaching them to fire off a hundred rounds at any-thing in camouflage pants.

Deer are more of a problem, being fairly stupid and having no manual skills. A lightweight rocket launcher would be the thing for them, pro-grammed to home in on the smell of Jack Daniels. The launcher could be slung under the belly of the largest stag, just to give a boost to *his* masculinity.

Clever raccoons could lay mines; squirrels could toss tiny acorn-size grenades. A day out hunting would become much more exciting, like a day on the front line in the latest Middle East War. I know it sounds aw-fully noisy and violent. But I bet that, if the animals could shoot back, the woods would soon become very quiet.

LOOKING AT PROZAC

If there really was a first Thanksgiving in 1621, we can be pretty sure that the Puritans didn't enjoy it. They had an old-fashioned Calvinistic attitude towards pleasure. Pleasure led to happiness, and happiness led almost inevi-tably to self-indulgence, being late for church, sin, and in the end damnation.

It's a mystery what happened to American culture between 1621 and 1776. It certainly wasn't the British influence. But, by the time the Declaration of Independence came to be drafted, it contained that fa-mous phrase about life, liberty, and the pursuit of happiness.

This was a huge mistake. It sent everyone off on the wrong track, chas-ing after something quite impossible. If the Declaration had recommend-ed the pursuit of property, for example, as it did in Thomas Jefferson's early draft, or the pursuit of knowledge, or even the pursuit of common sense, most people could manage that. But plain, uncomplicated happi-ness is so rare in adult human beings that it deserves to be classified as a disorder.

Since 1776, Americans have invested a lot of energy in the pursuit of happiness. Just about everything has been tried: baseball, war, cars with tail fins, lawn care, love, rock music, and giant hamburgers with pickles and French fries. Nothing seemed quite to do the trick.

In the 1980s, the fashion was to *pretend* to be happy. In 1988, Bobby McFerrin released a song called "Don't Worry, Be Happy," that sold ten million copies. And do you remember all those happy face buttons? They didn't work, either.

In the very same year that we were all being told "Don't Worry, Be Happy" twenty times a day and, I suspect not coincidentally, Prozac arrived on the scene. Now, the name Prozac is as familiar as aspirin. Books have been written about it, for and against. There are hundreds of Prozac jokes, and people tell Prozac stories at social gatherings the way they used to tell stories about their grandchildren.

In case you have been living in a cave for the past several years, Prozac is an anti-depressant drug. It was tested down south, where people are particularly prone to get the blues, and leave their homes in Georgia, and annoy everybody by singing sad songs about it.

There's no doubt that this thing works. People in Georgia, if properly medicated, stay home, and put away their guitars. There are so many testimonials to Prozac, so many tales of recovery and darkness lifted, that we must believe that this particular chemical cocktail has the power. After all, we are chemical creatures. A couple of glasses of Chardonnay can improve our outlook on life quite alarmingly.

This seems to be good news mixed (as always) with bad news. Nobody should have to live with depression, if it can be cured. But that's not the whole story. If what I read is true, this medication is being widely prescribed for much more trivial reasons, to smooth out the ordinary bumps and sadness of everyday life. In other words, to make people happy because they feel they should be happy.

But life never goes quite the way we want. That's why we have Hollywood and, for that matter, Chardonnay. The comparison with Aldous Huxley's novel Brave New World is irresistible. In that book, published in 1932, the author imagined a drug called Soma, that gave perfect happiness without side effects. Whenever the citizens of Brave New World felt some disturbing emotion, like anger or boredom, they would take a Soma pill, and everything would be fine. Huxley was being satirical, of course, but satire has a way of coming true.

The ancient Greeks believed that the purpose of human existence was mainly to entertain the gods. What a cosmic joke it would be on the human race if, after all our agonizing and all our searching for hundreds of years, the pursuit of happiness ended in a small brown pill. What would we do for an encore?

PHILOSOPHY IN THE SLOW LANE
When first I joined the great tidal flow of commuters on the Long Island Expressway, I was impressed by the spiritual quality of the other drivers. They had reached a calm, almost Zen like state of resignation.

I quickly realized how far I had to go, in every sense, before I could aspire to their fatalistic patience. Grinding my teeth and digging my nails into the wheel as we crawled to a halt at Exit 58, I was continually amazed by the stoical faces all around me. They gazed into the distance, expressionless, relaxed. It was as if they had never *intended* to go anywhere. They didn't scream or moan, or leap out and beat their heads on the guard rail. They had all the time in the world.

Lacking their inner serenity, I had to cheat. Instead of going mad, I lost myself in the simple escapism of talking books. I learned to choose my talking books carefully, cunningly, with the Expressway in mind: no fast-moving thrillers or space odysseys to remind me of my real situation. Lengthy and tedious classics proved to be the best, and if you're not sure what a classic is, hear Mark Twain on the subject: "A classic is a book which everybody praises and nobody reads." In this way, I had the illusion of improving my mind, and I was never likely to run out of long books. If I did run out, I could listen to the same books again. That's the beauty of classics.

Mark Twain was one of my first Expressway companions. For three weeks, I listened to his autobiographical *Life on the Mississippi*, and what a balm it was to the tortured soul! Twain tells of his apprenticeship as a river boat pilot, plying the 4,300 miles of the great river down to New Orleans and up beyond Saint Louis in the great days of the paddle wheelers. Rapids, hidden snags, floating logs, whirlpools and cutoffs kept the Mississippi pilot constantly on his toes. Fogs, shallows, floods and wrecks menaced his steamer daily. But never once in all those years, in all those tens of thousands of river miles, did Mark Twain ever report being stuck in a steamboat jam.

Just as the river pilot had to learn every inch of the waters and the banks, every landmark, sign and changing detail, so I began to chart my progress from the great, flowing plains of Exit 68 down to the dark and turbid shallows of the 40s and 30s. Here a dead possum, there a dead Toyota. Switch out of the middle lane before Exit 44 to miss the potholes; brace up for the wicked merge at the Meadowbrook. One anonymous stretch of median is memorable because I once saw two dogs there in pursuit of a rabbit, all oblivious to the traffic on either side. Another point recalls a fist fight between two half naked young men whose car had stalled. The banks are marked with hub caps, milk cartons, old tires (some with wheels), enough mufflers to set up a shop, garbage sacks, and fragments of clothing, a sea wrack of driftwood and old boxes, and the occasional graffiti. At Exit 43, a bridge admonished me daily, "Only you can make a difference," as if I didn't have enough problems already. Every yard of the Expressway had a landmark and a memory for me, once I had listened to Mark Twain.

If Twain encouraged a mental discipline, Thoreau's *Walden* was a moral discipline to me on the Expressway. "Most men lead lives of quiet desperation," intoned the philosopher, as an overhead sign announced: "Long Delays Ahead Exits 49-35."

"Nothing can be more useful to a man than a determination not to be hurried," admonished Thoreau, as I exited from the Expressway to the Northern State Parkway, only to join another four-mile jam. "The cost of a thing is the amount of what I call life which is required to pay for it, immediately and in the long run," Every day was an inspiration.

My best commuting companion was *Moby Dick*, my favorite fishing story. Captain Ahab's good ship Pequod, all her sails set, could cover a thousand miles of blue Pacific while I covered two miles of greasy tarmac. The long cadences of the hunt for the great white whale were soothing. The whale, as it seemed to me, had hypnotized Ahab and drawn him on, much as we were all hypnotized and drawn endlessly along the Expressway in pursuit of some greater purpose. The whale was a symbol of something more magnificent, beyond hope, beyond repentance. Like a decent rail service, for example. I could sit in the traffic and dream about Moby Dick and hope that, in the last cassette, he would get away.

Was everyone on the Expressway listening to Moby Dick? Is that why they looked so peaceful, imagining themselves free, out there in the boundless ocean beyond the Southern State Parkway? Did they share the great calm of Ahab, as he accepted his fate? "All my means are sane, my motive and my object mad."

LET'S HEAR IT FOR THE CHEERLEADERS

Mobs of young men have always been considered a menace, but young women had a much gentler reputation. Now gender equality has arrived, and no man is safe. I was nearly trampled to death on an otherwise peaceful college campus by a horde of very young women wearing very short red skirts and chanting something that sounded like "A fence! A fence!"

A fence might be a very good idea, perhaps with some razor wire and a warning sign saying "Danger: Cheerleaders Ahead." Long Island is host to more than a dozen cheerleader camps. For the educationally gifted, Hofstra and Adelphi Universities even offer cheerleading scholarships ("Give me an A! Give me an A!").

This was a phenomenon that, as a foreigner, I knew nothing about until my alarming encounter with the local team. I took time to learn something about cheerleading, and I think I now understand the basic principles. But I also think that there is some intellectual work to be done here. Cheerleading needs a history, a philosophy and, above all, a more sophisticated theory of communications.

The cheerleading phenomenon is almost unknown in the rest of the world. British soccer fans do their own cheerleading, with a medley of traditional songs, bricks and bottles. In less civilized parts of the world, fans express their enthusiasm by running onto the field and beating up the opposing team. Only in America do we have professional partisans to do the jumping and yelling for us.

Strange as it may seem to foreigners, the cheerleading industry has many ardent supporters. It is said to build self-confidence, positive attitudes and a mysterious quality called "spirit," which seems to involve smiling a lot. Cheerleading also teaches the value of teamwork, something that women have often despised in the past as a male excuse for mindless violence and idiotic loyalties. "Be a hundred percent behind your team a hundred percent of the time" is a sentiment that would be heartily endorsed by the leaders of the Islamic State or North Korea.

Young cheerleaders also acquire valuable practical skills: impossible balancing tricks, back flips and the brass lungs they will need for child raising, or being heard at the departmental meeting. Above all, they learn to *compete*, in hundreds of local and national events. Cheerleaders are clearly the corporate leaders and the political stars of the future.

Cheerleader culture is much broader and shallower than I had imagined. There are glossy magazines and webzines featuring the essential equipment: deodorants, contact lenses, Cheer Gear, makeup, party dresses and miracle diets. Novices can learn how to create a successful cheer routine with hot music, unique moves, fab formations, and multiple levels. They can also learn to make their own pom poms (called just 'Poms'). There are international stars out there you've never heard of, and even a few anonymous muscular cheerleading males, whose job it is to support the base of the feminine pyramid.

Despite cheerleaders' obsession with pyramids, my research suggests that cheerleading began in ancient Greece, rather than in Egypt. The first cheerleaders were called Maenads, female attendants of the god Bacchus. Their task was to encourage the crowds to have a good time, with frenzied rites and extravagant gestures. The opposing squad, the Furies, were merciless goddesses of vengeance who would swing into violent action if their team was losing. The ancient Greeks must get the credit for being the first to give young women these important career opportunities.

So many teams were decimated by the Furies or led astray by the Maenads that cheerleading fell into disrepute for two thousand years, until it was revived in a kinder, gentler form in the United States. But it's still a dangerous activity. In an average year, high school footballers lose 5.6 playing days to injuries, according Harper's Index, a compilation of statistics. Cheerleaders lose 28.8 days. These accidents are blamed on excessive acrobatics and the passion for building taller and taller pyramids.

All enthusiasm is dangerous, especially when it takes a physical form. If cheerleading is part of education, let's use it to educate by focusing on the message. Surely they can do better than waving their poms, doing somersault,s and chanting:

> *Champs take it away*
> *Now Play by Play*
> *Move that ball*
> *Win win win.*

Let's face it, this is not exactly a stellar example of the English language. To reduce the risk of injury, and make the sport more educational and less distracting for the fans, I would propose to substitute verbal skills for physical high jinks. Routines should become more static, and chants should become more grammatical, more literary and more conducive to the kinder, gentler society we all hope for in the next century, or the one after that.

> *Why don't you fellows*
> *Pick up that ball*
> *And move it carefully*
> *To the other end of the field?*

If we really want to teach good social values, let's chant this famous verse from Grantland Rice:

> *For when the one great Scorer comes*
> *To write against your name*
> *He writes not that you won or lost*
> *But how you played the game.*

Now there's a catchy message for the sporting world in the twenty-first century.

Why not bring that youthful spirit and those brilliant visuals out of the stadium and into the workplace? Cheerleaders should be in every office, with a chant for every corporate game. In a lawyer's office, for example, a spirited cry of "Rule of Law! Rule of Law! Sue! Sue! Sue!" accompanied by some eye-popping dance steps, would give courage and purpose to desk-bound drones. On Wall Street, a simple chant of "Free Trade! No Regulation! Never Mind the Small Investors!" would create a positive environment for growth. In this way cheerleaders would share their boundless enthusiasm with the rest of us who, in the game of life, so often find ourselves on the losing team.

PERSONAL SPACE

For a long time, I have been intrigued by the steadily increasing size of suburban houses. During the last four decades, the average family size has decreased by ten per-cent, but the average home size has increased by sixty per-cent. A few years ago, I visited a model home in one of the developments that had sprung up in the potato fields of eastern Long Island, because I was curious to see how such a quantity of domestic space could be used by an ordinary family.

I chose to view one of the more modest houses in the development - only about 5,000 square feet. I didn't have the energy to walk around the largest, which was 8,000 square feet or about the size of a supermarket.

The interior was like stage set waiting for the camera crew and actors to arrive. One space flowed into another, each area copiously furnished with places to sit or lounge, although the couches and armchairs were so copiously scattered with cushions that it was impossible to sit down. Flowers were perfectly arranged. This, I am told, is called "staging," the art of presenting a house so that it looks as if nobody has ever lived in it, and nobody ever could. The sales brochure emphasized the extravagant use of space: "oversized" bedrooms, "huge" kitchen, "gigantic" deck, and "monster" living room. The house lived up to its language. The sales manager assured me that, yes, these houses were purchased by normal sized American families and not by boatloads of refugees, religious cults or expanding hotel chains.

The *pièce de résistance* was the supersized master bedroom featuring a Roman Emperor sized bed, next to a truly enormous bathroom with a whirlpool. Bathrooms seemed to be everywhere in this house. The bill for soap alone must be larger than most people's mortgages. The predictably huge kitchen was equipped like a restaurant with a huge freezer, a professional stove and a double oven. Expensive olive oils and other gastronomic treats were carefully arranged on the immaculate surfaces. The formal dining room featured a table glitteringly set for six. Everything gave the impression that the buyer could step straight into a gourmet paradise. In case of culinary emergencies, the nearest MacDonald's was only two miles away.

The rooms were labelled on the plan, suggesting a relaxed lifestyle of endless leisure, so that the future owners would know what to do with them: exercise room, game room, recreation, entertainment, den, sunroom and club room (a place to keep golf clubs?). Children were banished to a luxuriously appointed basement with a giant TV screen and expensive educational toys scattered carelessly about. These houses are a kind of domestic pornography. They suggest both an ideal family life and an elegant style of living that vanished more than a hundred years ago.

Wealthy Victorians preferred to keep as much space as possible between themselves and their children. They were also notorious for locking up their inconvenient relatives in remote corners of the house, as any reader of Victorian Gothic tales knows. Whole dysfunctional families could live in one of these homes and scarcely ever meet each other.

This house and others like it seemed impressive when I first visited them a dozen years ago, but now they have been reduced to the status of huts or garden sheds. Today's mega-wealthy buyers are looking for something more on the lines of a renaissance palace. I read about one new construction in LA that weighs in at 38,000 square feet and comes complete with a cinema and a bowling alley. In the Hamptons, where only too much is enough, you can still find a cozy little cottage of around 25,000 square feet, but that's not going to impress anybody.

The only other practical use for these monster houses is entertaining on a grand scale, and I hope their construction heralds a new age of sociability. Most of us would like more space for entertaining. When we have a party, our little house bursts at the seams. But we wouldn't want to live in a place the size of a catering hall, just because of the occasional party.

It all sounds rather extravagant, but in historical terms it is quite modest. Highclere Castle in England, the scene of the fictional *Downton Abbey*, has interior space of a hundred and twenty thousand square feet, with eighty bedrooms, and some other great houses are twice as big as that. When it came to bloated self-importance, nobody could beat the Victorian aristocracy. So, although we are clearly moving backwards into the Victorian age of housing extremes, we still have a way to go. Far from being greedy for too much personal space, today's plutocrats are, if anything, rather cramped.

IT'S ALL LUCK

As each new school year begins and ends, we invariably hear a lot of sniveling, whining, ill-informed complaints about the failings of the education system. It's true that test scores are terrible and four out of ten New York students need remedial courses when they get to college, assuming they can find their way to the college. Even the intellectual stars may think that "ad infinitum" is a rock group, or that Ulysses is a kind of foot fungus.

This is a healthy sign. It shows that the sovereign values of consumerism have finally begun to make their mark on our tradition-bound education system. Schools have been teaching and testing all the wrong things, and students are beginning to realize it. Educators simply have not done their market research, with the result that they offer quite the wrong product mix for twenty-first century. They should stop pushing students to acquire knowledge that they don't want, and offer them something that they do want.

For example, who needs grammar and spelling? The computer will take care of that, just as the calculator will handle the math. History and literature are yesterday's news and, as for geography and languages, the less we know about those pesky foreigners the better. What students really want is a break, a bit of luck. Any child who studies the television five hours a day already knows the secret of success. You never see those people on the small screen working, let alone reading hard books or taking exams. They're just lucky, or unlucky. Every day's news confirms that life is a gamble, from Wall Street to Pennsylvania Avenue, and that success and failure are as random as lightning strikes.

Thirty years ago, the distinguished Harvard sociologist Christopher Jencks, in a book called *Who Gets Ahead*, revealed the awful truth that success or failure in life is mostly due to dumb luck. Education has almost nothing to do with it. Successful college dropouts like Bill Gates, Oprah Winfrey and Mark Zuckerberg seem to confirm this disturbing discovery. Educators naturally chose to ignore this book, but I suspect that its essential message has trickled down to today's young students.

It is an old, familiar message. In the rags-to-riches tales of America's golden age, the young hero always makes his fortune by a stroke of luck – he strikes gold, or rescues a millionaire's daughter from drowning, or has a dream that leads him to a brilliant invention. Folklore is full of lucky people who hit the jackpot by investing, getting the votes, or landing the big contract, just at the right moment. The long slog of school and examinations seems hopelessly slow and uncertain by comparison.

How do we teach children to get lucky? We don't want to fill their heads with nonsense about astrology, fortune telling, or lucky numbers. The rational and scientific way to get lucky is to gamble. Children learn at an early age that this is what grownups really believe. Do they see their dear old grandparents upgrading their qualifications for late-life career success? No, they're off to Atlantic City or Foxwoods to play the slots. Are their parents and teachers taking evening classes in voodoo economics to improve their financial prospects? No, they're lining up for lottery tickets. It's clear to the dumbest child that adults don't believe that success lies in knowing the answers to boring exam questions about the main exports of Peru or French irregular verbs. Like all adults back to the beginning of time they believe in luck.

So, let's scrap the obsolete curriculum and deal students a better hand in the game of life. Put a few roulette wheels in the classrooms, hand out playing cards instead of flash cards, and run a twenty-four-hour bingo game in the home room. Students would learn their numbers at least as far as 54, so they can fill in their Lotto cards. Higher math would involve calculating odds, and creative investment strategies based on birth dates and phases of the moon. For light relief, there would be field trips to local casinos, and readings from the wit and wisdom of Donald Trump.

This would get students ready for real life, when a throw of the dice can decide everything one way or another. If there must be tests they should reinforce the same lesson. What are the odds that "jackpot" is a verb? In how many states is gambling legal? How do folks manage to get rich in other states? All tests would be graded randomly by the school janitor, using a roulette wheel.

With such an education, students would be perfectly prepared to seize their chances and take a gamble on the future. In the lottery of life, anybody might win anything. And if, by some fortunate chance, you just happen to be a reality TV star whose father just happened to be a millionaire two hundred times over, you might even get to be President. In fact, you could almost bet on it.